PROGRAMMING SKILLS THROUGH C

Programming Skills Through C

By

B.M. HAVALDAR

ANMOL PUBLICATIONS PVT. LTD.
NEW DELHI - 110 002 (INDIA)

ANMOL PUBLICATIONS PVT. LTD.
4374/4B, Ansari Road, Daryaganj
New Delhi - 110 002
Ph.: 23261597, 23278000
Visit us at: www.anmolpublications.com

First Published, 2004

PRINTED IN INDIA

Published by J.L. Kumar for Anmol Publications Pvt. Ltd., New Delhi and Printed at Mehra Offset Press, Delhi.

Dedicated

to

My Teachers

S.A. Kagawade and N.B. Avarade

Contents

Foreword

Twelve years back I started learning C language. I have taken almost two years to understand the basic fundamentals and master the programming skills. Since then I still continue to experiment various ways I can use this powerful tool. So far I haven't find the end point where I can stop learning and exploring the new features. Till now I have surfed almost 250 editions of C programming and other related information, every edition or every author is coming out with some hidden surprises from the ocean of C.

In this book, my goal is to surf again and see if I am interested in learning again C and look for more surprises. Also I will look for whether it will provide required necessary information from the student's perspective.

First Four chapters provide a decent information and vast number of examples for every syntax, interpretations and command, which I can learn. The introduction and the basic examples in these chapters are quite enjoyable. These chapters cover most of the fundamentals of C including the loops backed by good examples. In the study of the fundamental concepts in programming languages, as opposed to learning a wide range of languages. Languages are easy to learn, it is the concepts behind them that are difficult. The basic features we study in turn including higher-order functions; data structures in the form of records and variants, exceptions, objects and classes, and types are quite nicely explained.

Chapters 5 and 6 will give some serious C programming concepts on strings and structures. In the strings I see some good examples like search a string in another string, counting of number of digits along with characters are good interesting examples to show the strength of the language. Similarly I see some good work in structures, which explain the meaning of structures related topics backed by some good examples. For a beginner the narration of the language to explain seems to be good.

In chapter 7 & 8, second level of C programming fundamentals like pointers and functions has been covered with some good examples. These examples will take the students to get in to the next level of C programming where they can write good mathematical based programmes. Adding two numbers, function to print all primes between m&n, function for swapping of two numbers call by value, number of recursive examples, conversion numbers in to various forms, position of occurrence of each digit in integer, examples on stacks and queues are some of the interesting examples.

Moving to chapter 9 I see lot of inner functions like file structures, illustration of some special functions like getw(), putw(). This chapter also provides lot of small project based examples like student information system, employee information system developed by using C language. These project examples provide good overview knowledge about C programming language to the students.

Students can use this experience to develop more skills and later develop a good hold on the language.

Other interesting and unique aspect about this book is that, the author has given some special unique programmes, which I have not noticed in most of the C language learning editions. He covered a good number of special programmes like generating of series of numbers of various permutations and combinations and some unique programme like phone number problem.

Some of the other interesting things I noticed about this book is that the author has provided a different approach for solving of the example programmes in various methods and arriving at a same result. Which means student can explore the various ways of solving the problem there by better understanding of the C programming language.

Over all the author tries to keep the students' interest in first place and limits himself to that goal. For students this book looks simple and yet delivers what he looks for which makes lot sense in my view.

Now, make sure your seat belts are buckled, sit back, relax, and enjoy the ride...

—D.V. Venkatachalapathy
Chairman & Managing Director
Vikas Global Solutions Ltd.
Bangalore

Preface

Learning the Programming Language and learning to design the logic of the program are two different entities. Many of the available computer programming books explore the syntax of the programming language to the extent but hardly stress upon the programming skills. As we can develop a solution to the particular problem in many different ways we can write program code for a particular task using different logics.

This book intends to develop the programming skills of the reader through C programming language. This book covers the basic syntax of C programming language and stress is given mainly on developing programming skills of the readers. This is accomplished by including a huge number of problems and finding solution to each problem using many different programming logics.

This book is prepared keeping in the mind the current requirements of the students of various courses in undergraduate and postgraduate levels and the current curriculum of different universities. It covers most of the practical and examination programs of various courses like B.Sc. Computer Science, BCA, MCA, M.Sc. Computer Science, Engineering and Diploma Courses of most of the Indian universities and technical boards.

'C' is a general-purpose structured programming language that is very powerful, efficient and compact. In the recent years 'C' has become the language of choice for the beginners and experienced programmers. This book is intended to teach programming skills through C and it is assumed to prior knowledge of programming is necessary for the reader. It is useful for both beginners and experts. It contains more than 330 programs all of which are tested on DOS operating system using TC (Turbo C) compiler. The output of each program is also given along with clear explanation of how each and every program works. The programming parameters like time complexity, memory space utilization and different programming styles are also discussed with the help of these programs.

In one word I can assure to the readers that 'Programming Skills Through C' is the best choice to learn C and Programming.

—B.M. Havaldar

Acknowledgements

Any achievement needs the contribution of many people and this work is also same. It is my privilege to thank all those who supported me directly or indirectly in bringing out this book.

The material is largely derived from the lectures I delivered to my students of undergraduate and post graduate levels and a number of short courses on C progamming. I thank all my students for their positive criticism and feedback, which helped me a lot in gaining expertise in the subject and finally prepare this material.

I specially thank my student-friend ***Keshav S.*** who accompanied me right from deciding the topics, finalizing the method of presentation, documentation and his constant support throughout the completion of this project.

I express my neatest gratitude to the staff of Anmol Publications Pvt. Ltd. in bringing out this book. My special thanks to Mr. Srinivas Murthy of Anmol Publications Pvt. Ltd. for his constant support in publishing this book.

Finally I thank my wife Prathibha for her kind cooperation throughout the completion of this project.

In spite of my best efforts readers may find errors in this material. All suggestions from the readers towards the improvement of this material will be gratefully accepted.

Readers can communicate to my email **havaldar2k@yahoo.co.in** for their valuable suggestions.

— B.M. Havaldar

List of Programs

Chapter 10 special programs.

1

Introduction

C is a structured programming language developed by Richie, at BEL laboratories in 1972. It is a middle level language and more suited for systems applications. It is the language of choice for the programmers to develop Compilers, Interpreters, Assemblers, language editors, operating systems etc.

C is a procedure oriented language, which means that most of the C statements contain functions. C contains number of library functions, which are included in different header files provided with the C compiler. For using any of the library function it is necessary to include the respective header file, through the pre-processor statement(#include<headerfile>).

1.1 Structure of C Program

```
#include<headerfile.h>
Global variable declaration;
Global function declarations;
void main()
  {
     Body of main function;
  }
```

We will discuss all these one by one. Consider the following program that displays the message "Learn C through Programs" on the screen.

```
/* Program name : intro1.c */
/* Program to display message*/
#include<stdio.h>
#include<conio.h>
void main()
{
```

```
        clrscr(); /* for clearing the screen*/
        printf("Learning C through Programs");
        getch();
    }
```

Output:
Learning C through Programs

Now we can look at the statements. The first statement includes the header file "stdio.h" to the program. C language provides number of library/built-in functions, which are kept ready to use by the programmers. These library functions are grouped depending on their purpose and stored in different files. These files are called as header files. There are number of header files in C language which may vary from compiler to compiler and version to version. The purpose of "stdio.h" is to include all standard input and output functions to the program file. In the above program there is only one output function i.e., printf(), which is used to print the message or value on the screen.

The second statement is also preprocessor statement used to include header file "conio.h", which contains library functions related to 'console input and output'. The library functions "clrscr()" and "getch()" used in the above program are consol IO functions. The clrscr() function used to clear the screen and is optional statement in the program. The other statement 'getch()' is also optional and is used to take a character from the keyboard. This function is useful because when we execute the program (by pressing ctrl+F9) the program executes, displays the result and as soon as it completes execution control comes to the C editor, and programmer is unable to see the output. Because the speed of the computer is so high. The getch() function makes the computer to wait until pressing any key, so that it becomes easy for the user to observe the result and then press any key to come back to the editor.

The other important statement in the above program is 'void main()'. This is the function which is to be included in each and every C program and this is the point from where the program execution starts. The keyword 'void' indicates that the function will not return any value. We will discuss about the keyword 'void' in detail in the 'functions' chapter.

The body of each and every function in a program is enclosed within a pair of brackets { } to make it as a compound statement(group of statements). All the simple statements in C program ends with semicolon ';'.

To make the program readable we are free to include comments in the program. Any statements or words or sentences that are included in between the symbols /* and */ are non-executable statements. The compiler ignores these statements while compiling and executing the program. It is a good practice to include comments in the programs, which makes the programs more readable and easily understandable.

Note: C language is case sensitive. Upper and lower case characters are considered to be distinct. All keywords and library function names are written in small letters and variables declared by the programmer should be used in the same case as declared by him.

Let us make slight changes to the above program to get output differently. The character '\n'(new line) can be used in the printf() function to get the cursor to the next line. This character is called as 'escape character'. On execution of \n the program control goes to the beginning of next line automatically. The following program and its output illustrate the function of '\n'.

```
/* Program name : intro2.c */
/* Program to display message*/
#include<stdio.h>
#include<conio.h>
void main()
{
        clrscr(); /* for clearing the screen*/
        printf("Learning\n C \n through\n Programs\n");
        /* for printing in different lines*/
        getch();
}
```

Output:
Learning
C
through
Programs

In the following program we will consider another escape character '\t' (tab gap) which gives one tab gap (usually 8 characters) on its execution. With the help of '\n' and '\t' we can easily make the output to be displayed in different readable formats. The successive tabs (\t\t) give two tab key gaps and (\t\t\t) gives three tab key gaps etc. The following program and its output shows the effect of using '\t' and '\n'.

```
/* Program name : intro3.c */
/* Program to display message*/
#include<stdio.h>
#include<conio.h>
void main()
{
        clrscr(); /* for clearing the screen*/
        printf("Learning\n\t  C  \n\t\t through  \n\t\t\t
                                    Programs\n");
        getch();
}
```

Output:

```
Learning
        C
                through
                        Programs
```

Variables and Constants

1.2 Variables and Constants

After discussing simple program with different display formats, now we will discuss about variables/identifiers. When we need to store a value during program execution, we have to store it in a variable. Variable is the name of memory location where values are stored and are subjected to change. For naming the variables we have to follow some rules that are given below:

1) Variable name must starts with an alphabet.
2) It may contain alphabets, digits and underscore (which if used must not be first or last character in the name).
3) Keywords are not used for naming the variables.
4) The maximum length of the variable name is limited to 31 characters.
5) Case sensitivity. The upper and lower case names are considered to be distinct.

When we need to store the value in a variable, we have to declare that variable by specifying its type. The C language provides number of fundamental and user defined data types. Each fundamental data type has its own format specifier. In printf() or scanf() or any of the formatted IO statements, while inputting or displaying the value, we need to use the corresponding formats for different data types. The different types of data, their size in bytes, their formats and range of values are given below in Table 1.1.

In all these (except unsigned) one bit is used for sign and remaining bits are used for storing data. In the following program, we declare three variables for storing integer values and use them for arithmetic operation.

```
/* Program name: intro4.c */
/* Program to add two integers*/
#include<stdio.h>
#include<conio.h>
void main()
{
        int a, b, c; /* declaring the variables*/
        clrscr();
        a=10;
        b=20; /* assigning the constant values to a and b*/
        c=a+b; /* adding the contents of a & b then storing the
                                          result in c*/
        printf("sum=%d",c);
        getch();
}
```

Output:
sum=30

1.3 Data Types, Ranges and IO Formatting

Table 1.1

Type	*Size in bytes*	*Format in IO*	*Range of values*
[signed] int	2	%d for decimal	-215 to +215 – 1
		%x for hexadecimal	
		%o for octal	
		%b for binary	
[signed] long	4	%ld	-231 to +231 – 1
unsigned int	2	%u	0 to 216 - 1
unsigned long	4	%lu	0 to 232 - 1
float	4	%f for fixed	
		%e for exponential	-231 to +231 - 1
		%g for general	
double	8	%lf for fixed	
		%e for exponential	-263 to +263 - 1
		%g for general	
character	1	%c	Any one character

In above program we have used some of the operators, which are having importance. The different operators used in C programs are given below.

1.4 Arithmetic Operators.

- \+ for addition of numerical values.
- \- for subtraction.
- * for multiplication.
- / for division to get quotient and
- % for getting remainder after division. It works only on integers.

1.5 Assignment Operators

- = assigns right side value to left side variable.
- += add and assign. Eg. A += b; is equal to A=A+b;
- -= subtract and assign. Eg. A -= b; is equal to A=A-b;
- *= multiply and assign. Eg. A *= b; is equal to A=A*b;
- /= divide and assign. Eg. A /= b; is equal to A=A/b;
- %= take modulus and assign. Eg. A %= b; is equal to A=A%b;

The other operators will be discussed whenever we encounter them in the coming chapters.

The main problem in the above program is, it assigns constant values to the variables. We can run that program any number of times we will get the same result. Instead of taking the constant values which leads to static outputs, we can take the values from the keyboard during execution. By taking the values from keyboard, the input becomes dynamic and we are free to input any values from keyboard, during the execution of the program. For inputting the values C language provides number of input functions. scanf() is one of the most commonly used input function for inputting the values from keyboard. The syntax is,

```
scanf("format specifier", &var);
```

Where the 'format specifier' depends on the type of variable (see table 1.1.). The operator '&' is used to specify the address of variable where the value is stored. The following program takes input from keyboard and finds the sum.

```
/* Program name: intro5.c */
/* Program to add two integers */
#include<stdio.h>
#include<conio.h>
void main()
{
        int a,b,c; /* declaring the variables*/
        clrscr();
        printf("enter first number\n");
        scanf("%d",&a);/* inputting the value of a from keyboard*/
        printf("enter second number\n");
        scanf("%d",&b);/* inputting the value of b from keyboard*/
        c=a+b; /* adding the contents of a & b then storing the
                                         result in c*/

        printf("sum=%d",c);
        getch();
}
```

Output:
enter first number
20
enter second number
40
sum=60

The scanf() function can be used to read more than one value at a time. In such a case we have to specify format specifiers for all variables and specify each variable with the address operator (&) and separated by ','. The following program illustrates this.

```
/* Program name: intro6.c */
/* Program to add two integers*/
#include<stdio.h>
#include<conio.h>
void main()
{
        int a,b,c;
        clrscr();
        printf("enter two numbers\n");
        scanf("%d%d",&a,&b);/* inputting the values from
                                         keyboard*/
```

```
        c=a+b; /* adding the contents of a & b then storing the
                                result in c*/
        printf("sum of %d and %d = %d",a,b,c);
        getch();
    }
```

Output:
enter two numbers
30
40
sum of 30 and 40 = 70

1.6 *Operator presidency of arithmetic operators*

()	high presidency
* and /	second from left to right.
+ and -	third from left to right.
%	last presidency.

If we do not consider the operator precedence then the meaning of the expression changes and we will not get the correct result. For example average of three numbers a, b, c can be written as (a+b+c)/3. if we write a+b+c/3 then first c/3 will be calculated according to the operator precedence and then that result is added with a and b. observe the output of the following program.

```
    /* Program name: intro7.c */
    /* program to find average of 3 numbers*/
    #include<stdio.h>
    #include<conio.h>
    void main()
    {
        int a,b,c;
        float avg; /* variable for storing the result, which may
                                be float*/
        clrscr();
        printf("enter three numbers\n");
        scanf("%d%d%d",&a,&b,&c);/* inputting the values from
                                keyboard*/
        avg=(a+b+c)/3; /* gives the average in terms of integer
                                as numerator & denominator are
                                integers*/
        printf("\n average of %d %d and %d is %f\n", a ,b, c,
                                avg);
        avg=(a+b+c)/3.0; /* gives the average in terms of fraction
                                as one of the numerator &
                                denominator is fraction*/
```

```
        printf("\n average of %d %d and %d is %f\n", a, b, c,
                                      avg);
        printf("\n average of %d %d and %d is %.2f\n",a,b,c,avg);
        /*gives the result with 2 decimal places*/
        getch();
}
```

Output:

enter three numbers
8 10 8
average of 8 10 and 8 is 8.000000

average of 8 10 and 8 is 8.666667

average of 8 10 and 8 is 8.67

Note: While making division operations we have to take care of fractions. When we are dividing one integer by another, the result we get is also an integer(truncates the fractional part and considers only integer part). To avoid this and to get the float value we have to make either numerator or denominator or both as float value by proper type casting.

C displays 6 digits of precision by default. If we want to specify the required number of digits of precision, then that can be achieved by specifying number of digits of precision in the format. For example %.2f gives only 2 digits after decimal point(.). %.8f gives 8 digits after '.' and so on. The following program and its output illustrates this concept.

```
/* Program name: intro8.c */
/* program to find area of rectangle*/
#include<stdio.h>
#include<conio.h>
void main()
{
        float a,b,area;/* a,b for 2 sides and area for result*/
        clrscr();
        printf("enter 2 sides of rectangle\n");
        scanf("%f%f",&a,&b);/*  inputting  the  values  from
                                keyboard*/
        area=a*b; /* finding the area by multiplying two sides*/
        printf("\n area of rectangle with sides %.2f & %.2f =
                                %.2f",a,b,area);
        /*gives the result with 2 decimal places*/
        getch();
}
```

Output:

enter 2 sides of rectangle
20
30
area of rectangle with sides 20.00 & 30.00 =600.00

The following program finds the area of a circle.

```
/* Program name: intro9.c */
/* program to find area of circle*/
#include<stdio.h>
#include<conio.h>
void main()
{
        floatr, area;/* r for radius and area for result*/
        clrscr();
        printf("enter radius of circle\n");
        scanf("%f", &r);/* inputting the value from keyboard*/
        area=3.142*r*r; /* finding the area */
        printf("\n area of circle with radius %.2f =
                                    %.4f",r,area);
        /*gives the result with 2 decimal places*/
        getch();
}
```

Output:

enter radius of circle
5.2

area of circle with radius 5.20 = 84.9487

To define the constants and macros we are using the preprocessor statement '#define' (we will discuss 'macros' later in the functions chapter). In the following program we are defining the constant 'pi' whose value is approximately 3.142.

```
/* Program name: intro10.c */
/* Program to find area of circle */
#include<stdio.h>
#include<conio.h>
#define pi 3.142
void main()
{
```

```
        float r, area;/* r for radius and area for result */
        clrscr();
        printf("enter radius of circle \n");
        scanf("%f", &r);/* inputting the value from keyboard */
        /*Finding the area by using the constant value of pi
                                  defined by #define*/
        area=pi*r*r;
        printf("\n area of circle with radius %.2f =
                                  %.4f",r,area);
        /*gives the result with 2 & 4 decimal places*/
        getch();
}
```

Output:

enter radius of circle
6.52

area of circle with radius 6.52 = 133.5504

When we have to do complicated programs that involve mathematical functions, C language provides number of mathematical functions that are grouped in header file called 'math.h'. The following program utilize the mathematical function 'pow(x,y)' which gives the value of x to the power of y. 'math.h' includes number of built-in functions explained in the appendix .

```
/* Program name: introll.c */
/* program to find area of circle*/
#include<stdio.h>
#include<conio.h>
#include<math.h>
#define pi 3.142
void main()
{
        float r, area;/* r for radius and area for result*/
        clrscr();
        printf("enter radius of circle\n");
        scanf("%f", &r);/* inputting the value from keyboard*/
        /*finding the area by using the constant value of pi
        defined by #define*/
        area=pi*pow(r,2); /* pow() math function used for r to
                                  the power of 2*/
        printf("\n area of circle with radius %.2f =
                                  %.4f",r,area);
        /*gives the result with 2 & 4 decimal places*/
        getch();
}
```

Output:

enter radius of circle
6.52

area of circle with radius 6.52 = 133.5504

The following program finds the volume of the sphere.

```
/* Program name: intro12.c */
/* program to find volume of sphere */
#include<stdio.h>
#include<conio.h>
#include<math.h>
#define pi 3.142
void main()
{
        float r,v;/* r for radius and v for volume*/
        clrscr();
        printf("enter radius of sphere\n");
        scanf("%f",&r);/* inputting the value from keyboard*/
        v=4/3*pi*pow(r,3);
        /* pow() math function used for r to the power of 3*/
        /* the value of above expression won't gives correct
                        answer (4/3==>1) as 4 and 3 are
                        integer*/
        printf("\n volume of sphere with radius %.2f = %.4f",r,v);
        /*following gives the result with 2 & 4 decimal places*/
        v=4.0/3*pi*pow(r,3);
        /* the value of 4.0/3 leads to a correct answer can be
                        written as v=4*pow(r,3)*pi/3
                        priority of operators */
        printf("\n volume of sphere with radius %.2f = %.4f",r,v);
        /*gives the result with 2 & 4 decimal places*/
        getch();
}
```

Output:

enter radius of sphere
6.52

volume of sphere with radius 6.52 =870.7484

volume of sphere with radius 6.52 =1160.9978

The following program takes height and base of a triangle as input and finds its area.

```
/* Program name: intro13.c */
/* program to find area of triangle when height and base
are given */
#include<stdio.h>
#include<conio.h>
void main()
{
        float h, b, a;/* h for height, b for base and a for
                                  area*/
        clrscr();
        printf("enter height and base of triangle\n");
        scanf("%f%f", &h, &b);
        a=h*b/2;
        printf("\n area of triangle with height %.2f base %.2f
                                  is %.3f",h,b,a);
        getch();
}
```

Output:

enter height and base of triangle
4
3

area of triangle with height 4.00 base 3.00 is 6.000

Temperature can be represented either in Celsius or Fahrenheit. The following program takes temperature in degree Celsius and converts it to Fahrenheit.

```
/* Program name: intro14.c */
/* To convert the temperature from Celsius to Fahrenheit */
#include<stdio.h>
#include<conio.h>
void main()
{
        float c,f;/* c for celcious and f for Fahrenheit*/
        clrscr();
        printf("enter celcious\n");
        scanf("%f",&c);
        f=(c+32)*9/5;
        C*9/5+32;
        printf("\n temperature in Fahrenheit of celcious%.2f is
        %f", c, f);
        getch();
}
```

Output:

enter celcious
10.5

temperature in Fahrenheit of celcious 10.50 is 76.500000

The following program takes temperature in Fahrenheit and converts it to degree Celsius.

```
/* Program name: intro15.c */
/* To convert the temperature Fahrenheit to celcious */
#include<stdio.h>
#include<conio.h>
void main()
{
      float c,f;/* c for celcious and f for Fahrenheit*/
      clrscr();
      printf("enter Fahrenheit\n");
      scanf("%f", &f);
      c=f*(5/9-32); (f-32)*5/9
      printf("\n temperature in celcious of Fahrenheit%.2f is
                                            %f", f, c);
      getch();
}
```

Output:

enter Fahrenheit
100.34

temperature in celcious of Fahrenheit 100.34 is 23.744444

The following program calculates simple interest by taking principle amount, rate of interest and time in years as input.

```
/* Program name: intro16.c */
/* To find simple interest */
#include<stdio.h>
#include<conio.h>
void main()
{
      float p,t,r,si;/* p--> principle amount, t time in years,
                                      r rate of interest and si for
                                      calculated interest*/
      clrscr();
```

```
        printf("enter p, t, r\n");
        scanf("%f%f%f", &p, &t, &r);
        si=p*t*r/100;
        printf("\n simple interest is %.2f",si);
        getch();
}
```

Output:

enter p, t, r
5000
4
3

simple interest is 600.00

This program calculates the compound interest.

```
/* Program name: intro17.c */
/* To find compound interest */
#include<stdio.h>
#include<conio.h>
#include<math.h>
void main()
{
        float p, t, r, ci;/* p--> principle amount, t time in
        years, r rate of interest and ci for calculated interest*/
        clrscr();
        printf("enter p, t, r\n");
        scanf("%f%f%f", &p, &t, &r);
        ci=p*pow((1+r/100),t);/*gives compound amount, interest
                                        with principle amount*/
        printf("\n compound amount is %.2f\n",ci);
        ci=p*pow((1+r/100),t)-p;/*gives only compound interest*/
        printf("\n compound interest is %.2f\n",ci);
        getch();
}
```

Output:

enter p, t, r
5000
3
4

compound amount is 5624.32

compound interest is 624.32

This program performs all arithmetic operations on two integers.

```
/* Program name: intro18.c */
/* To perform all arithmetic operations on two integers */
#include<stdio.h>
#include<conio.h>
void main()
{
      int a, b, c;/* a, b for input and c for result*/
      clrscr();
      printf("enter two integers\n");
      scanf("%d%d", &a, &b);
      c=a+b; /* sum of two numbers*/
      printf("\n sum of %d and %d = %d", a, b, c);
      c=a-b; /* difference of two numbers*/
      printf("\n difference of %d and %d = %d", a, b, c);
      c=a*b; /* product of two numbers*/
      printf("\n product of %d and %d = %d", a, b, c);
      c=a/b; /* quiescent of two numbers*/
      printf("\n quiescent of %d divided by %d = %d", a, b,
                          c);
      c=a%b; /* remainder of two numbers*/
      printf("\n remainder after dividing %d by %d=%d", a, b,
                          c);
      getch();
}
```

Output:

enter two integers
20
6

sum of 20 and 6 = 26

difference of 20 and 6 = 14

product of 20 and 6 = 120

quiescent of 20 divided by 6 = 3

remainder after dividing 20 by 3 = 2

The following program illustrates the automatic data conversion from float to int. When a float value is assigned to an integer type variable, then only the integer part of that float value will be assigned to int type variable. The auto type conversion is common on the following.

int to float
float to int
int to char
char to int
int to long
long to int
float to long
long to float
float to double and
double to float

But whenever we are dealing with such auto conversions there is a chance of loosing precision and result may go wrong.

Here first we are assigning float value (amount) to int variable to get rupees separately, then the remaining result is assigned to int variable paise after multiplying it with 100.

```
/* Program name: intro19.c */
/* Program to take amount as Rupee and paise and print it
 as paise */
#include<stdio.h>
#include<conio.h>
void main()
{
      float rp;
      int r,p;
      clrscr();
      printf("\n Enter amount \n");
      scanf("%f",&rp);
      r=rp; /* assigns only integer part to r */
      p=(rp-r)*100; /* fraction part is multiplied by 100 to
                              get
      only 2 digits as integer part */
      r=r*100+p; /* total paise */
      printf("\n Total paise = %d\n",r);
      getch();
}
```

Output
Enter amount 12.50 Total paise = 1250

The following is an alternate solution to the above program. Here we are directly multiplying the float value by 100 and getting integer part to represent the paise for given rupee and paise.

```
/* Program name: intro20.c */
/* Program to take amount as Rupee and paise and print it
as paise */
#include<stdio.h>
#include<conio.h>
void main()
{
      float rp;
      int p;
      clrscr();
      printf("\n Enter amount \n");
      scanf("%f",&rp);
      p=rp*100; /* when multiplied by100 two digits of fraction
                              becomes integers and assigns
                              only integer part to p */
      printf("\n Total paise = %d\n",p);
      getch();
}
```

Output
Enter amount 10.50 Total paise = 1050

A sales man in a company is paid Rs.1000/- as salary and 20 percent bonus on sales amount. The following program calculates the sales man's gross salary based on the number of products he sales and their price.

```
/* Program name: intro21.c */
/* Program to calculate sales man's salary */
#include<stdio.h>
#include<conio.h>
void main()
{
      float amount, sal, price;
      int qty;
      clrscr();
      printf("\n Enter qty and price \n");
      scanf("%d%f",&qty,&price);
      amount=qty*price;
      sal=amount*0.20+1000;/* 20 % bonus and 1000 Rs fixed */
      printf(" Total amount = %.2f\n",amount);
      printf(" Total salary = %.2f\n",sal);
      getch();
}
```

Output

Enter qty and price
90 50
Total amount = 4500.00
Total salary = 1900.00

The distance travelled by a vehicle with initial velocity u meters per second, acceleration a meter per second^2, and time t in seconds is given by $d=ut+\frac{1}{2}at^2$. The following program finds the distance travelled by the vehicle.

```
/* Program name: intro22.c */
/* Program to calculate distance travelled by a vehicle */
/* u initial velocity, a is acceleration and t is time in
second */
#include<stdio.h>
#include<conio.h>
void main()
{
      float d,u,a;
      int t;
      clrscr();
      printf("\n Enter initial velocity, acceleration and time
                                  in seconds \n");
      scanf("%f%f%d",&u,&a,&t);
      d=u*t+a*t*t/2;
      printf(" Total distance travelled in %d seconds =%.2f
                                  Meters \n",t,d);
      getch();
}
```

Output

Enter initial velocity, acceleration and time in seconds
3
5
50
Total distance travelled in 50 seconds = 6400.00 Meters

An electrical company provides the electricity to its customers. The bill of the electricity consumed is calculated in the following program.

```
/* Program name: intro23.c */
/* Program to calculate electricity bill */
#include<stdio.h>
```

```
#include<conio.h>
void main()
{
      float bill,rate;
      int prev,prs,tu;/*previous meter reading, present meter
                              reading and total units */
      clrscr();
      printf("\n Enter previous mt reading, present mt reading
                              and rate per unit\n");
      scanf("%d%d%f",&prev,&prs,&rate);
      tu=prs-prev;
      bill=tu*rate;
      printf(" Total bill amount is = Rs %.2f \n",bill);
      getch();
}
```

Output
Enter previous mt reading, present mt reading and rate per unit 800 950 2.45 Total bill amount is = Rs 367.50

The following program illustrates common mathematical functions used in trigonometry. These functions are kept in math.h header file and take angle in radians as argument gives the result as float values.

```
/* Program name: intro24.c */
/* Program to illustrate trigonometric function */
#include<stdio.h>
#include<conio.h>
#include<math.h>
void main()
{
      int n;
      float f;
      clrscr();
      printf(" enter angle in degree \n");
      scanf("%d",&n);
      f=n*22.0/7.0/180;/* converting angle to radians*/
      printf("\nangle =%5d\nsin(%d) = %f\ncos(%d) = %f\ntan(%d)
                        =
      %f",n,n,sin(f),n,cos(f),n,tan(f));
      getch();
}
```

```
Output
enter angle in degree
30

angle =  30
sin(30) = 0.500183
cos(30) = 0.865920
tan(30) = 0.577631
```

2

Conditional Statements

2.1 Introduction

We have studied some of the preliminary concepts in C programming, which are essential for writing simple programs involving simple arithmetic expressions in the previous chapter. All the statements in a program are executed sequentially from statement 1 to statement n. Some times we need to change the control flow in a program in order to make certain decisions. Any structured languages like C provides statements that can alter the sequence in which the instructions are executed. We have two types of control structures to change the flow of control namely Conditional Branching and Looping. In this chapter we discuss conditional statements in detail and looping we will discuss in the next chapter. The relational and logical operators are used to make conditional expressions. The result of conditional expressions is either true or false.

2.2 Relational Operators

>, <, >=, <=, == and != are the six relational operators used in C language. These all are binary operators which take two operands and give the result as either true or false. Using these operators we can make relational conditions to check the operands as greater than, lesser than or equal to etc.

Ex: a> b x<y a==b etc.

2.3 Logical Operators

Now let us try to solve the more complex the conditional statements using logical operators. C provides three logical operators viz. && (AND), | | (OR) and ! (NOT) operators, which take relational expressions or other logical expressions as arguments and give the result as either True or False. By the use of logical operators we can improve the program logic and which may reduce the number of program statements or number of operations.

2.4 The if statement

if is a conditional statement, used to make decisions. It has number of formats. We will discuss the different formats of if statement one by one.

2.4.1 *Simple if*

Syntax:

if (conditional-expression)
Statement (s);

The statements will be executed only when the conditional expression gives true, otherwise those statements under if ( ) condition will not be executed.

In case of more than one statement if we want to execute depending on condition, then we need to make it compound statement by enclosing the statements within a pair of braces { }.

The following program which finds largest of two numbers shows the use of relational operators and if statement.

```
/*Program name: cond1.c*/
/* Largest of two numbers */
#include<stdio.h>
#include<conio.h>
void main()
{
     int a,b;/*for two numbers a & b*/
     clrscr();
     printf("Enter the numbers\n");
     scanf("%d%d",&a,&b);
     if(a>b) /* check for a is largest and gives true when a
                          is largest otherwise false*/
          printf("largest = %d\n",a);
     if(b>a) /* check for b is largest and gives true when b
                          is largest otherwise false*/
          printf("largest = %d\n",b);
     getch();
}
```

Output 1:	Output 2:
Enter the numbers 20 34 largest = 34	Enter the numbers 30 30 largest = 30

Here we need to think of logic. Our program logic should be such that it should have less number of statements, utilize less amount of memory, but it has to give accurate results. In the above program for finding the largest of two numbers, if we enter both the numbers same, then we will get one of them as great. This can be avoided in the following program by putting one more condition that checks for equality.

```
/*Program name: cond2.c*/
/* Largest of two numbers */
#include<stdio.h>
#include<conio.h>
void main()
{
        int a,b;/*for two numbers a & b*/
        clrscr();
        printf("Enter the numbers\n");
        scanf("%d%d", &a, &b);
        if(a>b) /* check for a is largest and gives true when
        a is largest otherwise false*/
              printf("largest = %d\n", a);
        if(b>a) /* check for b is largest and gives true when b
                                    is largest otherwise false*/
        printf("largest = %d\n",b);
        if(a==b) /* check for equality of a and b and gives true
                                    when equal otherwise false*/
        printf("both %d and %d are equal\n", a, b);
        getch();
}
```

Output 1:	Output 2:	Output 3:
Enter the numbers 20 30 largest = 30	Enter the numbers 40 30 largest = 40	Enter the numbers 20 20 both 20 and 20 are equal

In this case we are using conditions three times. It can be solved by just two conditions by the use of if…else statement, which is explained below.

The following program checks whether the given number is odd or even number.

```
/*Program name: cond3.c*/
/* Check for odd or even */
#include<stdio.h>
#include<conio.h>
void main()
{
        int a;/*for any integer*/
        clrscr();
        printf("Enter a number \n");
        scanf("%d", &a);
        if(a%2==0) /* checks for remainder is zero or not for
                                    even number it should be 0*/
              printf("%d is even number\n", a);
```

```
        if(a%2==1) /* checks for remainder is 1 or not for odd
                      number it should be 1*/
            printf("%d is odd number \n", a);
        getch();
}
```

Output 1:	Output 2:
Enter a number 20 20 is even number	Enter a number 13 13 is odd number

2.4.2 *if ... else statement*

Syntax:

```
if (conditional –expression)
    Statements1;
else
    Statements2;
```

Here, when conditional expression evaluates to true, statements1 gets executed, otherwise statements2 gets executed. We can have more than one statement under if & else parts. In such case we need to make it a compound statement. The following program explains the advantage of using if…else over if statement. It reduces one condition by introducing else. For example, We know when an integer is divided by 2 the remainder must be either 1 or 0. When it is not zero, no need to check for 1 because there is no alternative, it must be 1.

```
/*Program name: cond4.c*/
/* Check for odd or even */
#include<stdio.h>
#include<conio.h>
void main()
{
        int a;/*for any integer*/
        clrscr();
        printf("Enter a  number\n");
        scanf("%d", &a);
        if(a%2==0)
            printf("%d is even number\n",a);
        else
            printf("%d is odd number \n",a);
        getch();
}
```

Output 1:	Output 2:
Enter a number	Enter a number
3	4
3 is odd number	4 is even number

2.4.3 *else if-ladder*

When the number of alternatives are more than two, one can select one option from number of alternatives by using number of else if constructs. The general syntax is:

```
if(cond-1)
Statement(s);
else
if (cond-2)
Statements(s);
else
if (cond-3)
Statement(s);
....
....
```

Ex: Consider the program segment for printing the last digit of a number (n) in words.

```
if (n% 10 ==0)
printf( "zero");
else
if (n%10 ==1)
printf( "one");
...
...
if(n%10 ==8)
printf("eight");
else
printf("nine");
```

Now we can take again the same program of finding largest among two numbers, which we solved in two different methods above.

```
/*Program name: cond5.c*/
/* Largest of two numbers */
#include<stdio.h>
#include<conio.h>
void main()
{
        int a,b; /*for two numbers a & b*/
        clrscr();
        printf("Enter the numbers\n");
        scanf("%d%d", &a, &b);
```

```
        if(a>b)
              printf("largest = %d\n", a);
        else
        if(b>a)
              printf("largest = %d\n", b);
        else /* when first two conditions are false there is no
                                          need to check for third
                                          condition i.e. for equality*/
              printf("both %d and %d are equal\n", a, b);
        getch();
  }
```

Output 1:	Output 2:	Output 3:
Enter the numbers 20 30 largest = 30	Enter the numbers 40 30 largest = 40	Enter the numbers 20 20 both 20 and 20 are equal

The following programs are similar to above program in which we are checking for three possible conditions using else if.

```
  /*Program name: cond6.c*/
  /* program for checking a number is +ve, -ve or zero */
  #include<stdio.h>
  #include<conio.h>
  void main()
  {
        int a;
        clrscr();
        printf("Enter a number\n");
        scanf("%d",&a);
        if(a>0)
              printf("\n positive number\n");
        else if(a<0)
              printf("\n negative number\n");
        else
              printf("\n given number is zero\n");
        getch();
  }
```

Output 1:	Output 2:	Output 3:
Enter a number 20 positive number	Enter a number -5 negative number	Enter a number 0 given number is zero

```
/*Program name: cond7.c*/
/* program for finding the roots of quadratic equation */
#include<stdio.h>
#include<conio.h>
#include<math.h>
void main()
{
        float a,b,c,d,root1,root2;
        clrscr();
        printf("Enter a b c\n");
        scanf("%f%f%f", &a, &b, &c);
        d=b*b-4*a*c; /* finding determinant*/
        if(d==0)/* when d is 0 both the roots will be equal*/
                {
                printf("\n roots are equal\n");
                root1=root2=-b/(2*a);
                printf("root1=%.3f\nroot2=%.3f",root1,root2);
                }
        else
        if(d>0)/* roots are real and distinct*/
                {
                printf("\n roots are real and distinct\n");
                root1=(-b+sqrt(d))/(2*a);
                root2=(-b-sqrt(d))/(2*a);
                printf("root1=%.3f\nroot2=%.3f",root1,root2);
                }
        /* when d is -ve it is not possible to take the squareroot
                                of -ve number, we have to take
                                absolute value of d*/
        else
                {
                printf("\n roots are imaginary\n");
                root1=-b/(2*a);
                root2=sqrt(-d)/(2*a);
                printf("real part=%.3f \n imaginary part = %.3f",
                root1, root2);
                }
        getch();
}
```

Output 1:

Enter a b c
2 2 2
roots are imaginary
real part = -0.500
imaginary part = 0.866

Output 2:

Enter a b c
2 5 1
roots are real and distinct
root1 = -0.219
root2 = -2.281

Output 3:

Enter a b c
1 2 1
roots are equal
root1 = -1.000
root2 = -1.000

In the above program if we give the value for the variable 'a' as zero, then it becomes a non quadratic equation and we will get a run time error, the error that may occur at the time of execution of the program due to wrong input values. In the following program, which is the modification of above program we have taken care of data validation to avoid this run time error.

```
/*Program name: cond8.c*/
/* program for finding the roots of quadratic equation */
/* checking for runtime error that may happen when a is
zero*/
#include<stdio.h>
#include<conio.h>
#include<math.h>
void main()
{
      float a,b,c,d,root1,root2;
      clrscr();
      printf("Enter a b c\n");
      scanf("%f%f%f",&a, &b, &c);
      if(a==0)/* when a is 0 it leads to undetermined result,
                              because anything by 0 can not
                              be determined*/
            {
            printf(" not a quadratic equation\n");
            root1=-c/b;
            printf("\n the only root is %.3f\n",root1);
            }
      else
            {
            d=b*b-4*a*c; /* finding determinant*/
            if(d==0)/* when d is 0 both the roots will be
                                    equal*/
                  {
                  printf("\n roots are equal\n");
                  root1=root2=-b/(2*a);
                  printf("root1=%.3f\nroot2=%.3f",root1,root2);
                  }
            else
            if(d>0)/* roots are real and distinct*/
                  {
                  printf("\n roots are real and distinct\n");
                  root1=(-b+sqrt(d))/(2*a);
                  root2=(-b-sqrt(d))/(2*a);
                  printf("root1=%.3f\nroot2=%.3f",root1,root2);
                  }   /* when d is -ve it is not possible to
                                    take the square root
```

```
                                    of -ve number, we have
                                    to take absolute value
                                    of d */

        else
              {
              printf("\n roots are imaginary\n");
              root1=-b/(2*a);
              root2=sqrt(-d)/(2*a);
              printf("real  part=%.3f\nimaginary
                                    part=%.3f",root1,root2);
              }
        }
    getch();
}
```

Output 1:	Output 2:	Output 3:
Enter a b c 2 2 2 roots are imaginary real part = -0.500 imaginary part = 0.866	Enter a b c 0 2 3 not a quadratic equation the only root is –1.500	Enter a b c 1 2 1 roots are equal root1 = -1.000 root2 = -1.000

This program uses logical operators to find largest of three numbers.

```
/*Program name: cond9.c*/
/* Largest of three numbers */
/*In this program we are not checking for equality of 2 or
all 3 numbers*/
#include<stdio.h>
#include<conio.h>
void main()
{
      int a, b, c;
      clrscr();
      printf("Enter three numbers\n");
      scanf("%d%d%d", &a, &b, &c);
      if((a>b)&&(a>c)) /* use of logical &&, which gives true
                                only when both of its operands
                                are true*/
            printf("%d is largest\n", a);
      else /* when a is not largest */
      if((b>a)&&(b>c)) /* checks for b is larger than a and c
                                using logical operator */
            printf("%d is larger\n", b);
```

```
    else /* when both above  conditions are  false then c is
                             largest*/
        printf("%d is largest\n", c);

    getch();
}
```

Output 1:	Output 2:	Output 1:
Enter three numbers	Enter three numbers	Enter three numbers
2 4 8	7 4 7	2 2 2
8 is largest	7 is largest	2 is largest

In this program we are using the same logic as that of the above but one condition checking can be reduced without affecting the working of the program.

```
/*Program name: cond10.c*/
/* Largest of three numbers */
/*In this program we are not checking for equality of 2 or
all 3 numbers*/
#include<stdio.h>
#include<conio.h>
void main()
{
    int a,b,c;
    clrscr();
    printf("Enter three numbers\n");
    scanf("%d%d%d",&a,&b,&c);
    if((a>b)&&(a>c)) /* use of logical AND which gives true
                         only when both of its operands
                         are true*/
        printf("%d is largest\n",a);
    else
    if(b>c) /* when a is not largest then either b or c must
                         be largest */
        printf("%d is larger\n",b);
    else /* when both above  conditions are  false then c is
                         largest*/
        printf("%d is largest\n",c);
    getch();
}
```

Output 1:	Output 2.	Output 1:
Enter three numbers	Enter three numbers	Enter three numbers
2 4 8	7 4 7	2 2 2
8 is largest	7 is largest	2 is largest

This program finds the area of a triangle when three sides are given. Here we need to check the given three sides can make a triangle or not without which may lead to runtime error (incorrect input values lead to the problem of square root of a negative number).

```
/*Program name: cond11.c*/
/* program for finding the area of triangle when 3 sides
are given */
/* checking for formation of triangle which avoids runtime
error */
#include<stdio.h>
#include<conio.h>
#include<math.h>
void main()
{
      float a, b, c, s, area;
      clrscr();
      printf("Enter three sides a b c\n");
      scanf("%f%f%f", &a, &b, &c);
      if((a<=0)||(b<=0)||(c<=0))/* a side of a triangle can
                                   not be 0 or -ve number*/
            printf("\n given sides can not form a triangle\n");
      else
      if(((a+b)<=c)||((a+c)<=b)||((b+c)<=a))  /* to form a
                                   triangle sum of any two sides
                                   must greater than third side*/
            printf("\n given sides can not form a triangle\n");
      else /* there is possibility of triangle formation*/
            {
            s=(a+b+c)/2;
            area=sqrt(s*(s-a)*(s-b)*(s-c));
            printf("\n area = %.4f\n",area);
            }
      getch();
}
```

Output 1:	Output 2:
Enter three sides a b c 2 3 4 area = 2.9047	Enter three sides a b c 0 2 4 the given sides can not form a triangle

This program takes time as input in terms of seconds, minutes and hours and checks for its validity and increases the input time by one second.

```
/*Program name: cond12.c*/
/* program for updating the time by 1 second */
/* checks for validity of time by taking 12 hour clock */
#include<stdio.h>
#include<conio.h>
#include<math.h>
void main()
{
      int h, m, s;
      clrscr();
      printf("Enter time h m s\n");
      scanf("%d%d%d", &h, &m, &s);
      if((h<0)||(m<0)||(s<0))  /* hour or minute or seconds
                                 can not be  -ve number*/
            printf("\n invalid data\n");
      else
      if((h>12)||(m>59)||(s>59))  /* the extreme boundary
                                 condition*/
            printf("\n invalid time entry\n");
      else
            {
             s++; /* increase the seconds by one*/
            if(s>59)
            {
                  s=0; /* after increment when s becomes more
                                 than 59, minute
                                 changes by 1*/
                  m++;
            }
             if(m>59)
            {
                  m=0;
                  h++;
            }
            if(h>12)
                  h=1;
            printf("\n time updated by second is \n");
            printf("%4d%4d%4d",h,m,s);
      }
      getch();
}
```

Output 1:	Output 2:	Output 3:
Enter time h m s 2 59 59 the time updated by 1 second is 3 0 0	Enter time h m s -2 4 8 invalid data	Enter time h m s 2 59 65 invalid time entry

The following program finds largest of three numbers, uses simple logic with less number of condition checking and output statements. But this program will not check for equality of numbers.

```
/*Program name: cond13c*/
/* Largest of three numbers */
/*In this program we are not checking for equality of 2 or
all 3 numbers*/
#include<stdio.h>
#include<conio.h>
void main()
{
      int a, b, c, l; /* a, b, c for 3 numbers and l is for
                                                largest*/
      clrscr();
      printf("Enter three numbers\n");
      scanf("%d%d%d", &a, &b, &c);
      l=a;  /* assume a is largest and assign it to l */
      if(b>l)  /* check for b larger than l if true assign to
                                                l*/l=b;
      if(c>l)  /* check for c larger than l if true assign to
                                                l*/l=c;
      printf("%d is largest\n",l); /* print the largest which
                                                is stored in l*/
      getch();
}
```

Output 1:	Output 2:	Output 1:
Enter three numbers 2 4 8 8 is largest	Enter three numbers 7 4 7 7 is largest	Enter three numbers 2 2 2 2 is largest

This program uses similar logic as that of above program but checks for possibilities of all three numbers being equal or two numbers being equal and larger than the third.

```
/*Program name: cond14.c*/
/* Largest of three numbers */
/*In this program we are checking for equality of 2 or all
3 numbers*/
#include<stdio.h>
#include<conio.h>
void main()
{
      int a, b, c, l;/* a, b, c for 3 numbers and l is for
      largest*/
```

```
        clrscr();
        printf("Enter three numbers\n");
        scanf("%d%d%d", &a, &b, &c);
        l=a; /* assume a is largest and assign it to l */
        if(b>l) /* check for b larger than l if true assign to
                                    l*/l=b;
        if(c>l) /* check for c larger than l if true assign to
                                    l*/l=c;
        /* check all three are equal*/
        if((a==l)&&(b==l)&&(c==l))
              printf("\n all given three numbers are equal\n");
        else /* check for any 2 numbers are equal to large*/
        if(((l==a)&&(l==b))||((l==a)&&(l==c))||((l==b)&&(l==c)))
              printf("\n there are two numbers which are equal
        and larger among given three\n");
        else /* when above both conditions are false there will
                                    be only one largest*/
        printf("%d is largest\n",l);/* print the largest which
                                    is stored in l*/
        getch();
    }
```

Output 1:
Enter three numbers
2 4 8
8 is largest

Output 2:
Enter three numbers
7 4 7
there are two numbers which are equal and larger among given three

Output 3:
Enter three numbers
2 2 2
all given three numbers are equal

The following program checks the validity of the date input. It considers number of days in each month including special case in the month of February.

```
    /*Program name: cond15.c*/
    /* This program checks for validity of entered date*/
    #include<stdio.h>
    #include<conio.h>
    void main()
    {
          int d, m, y;
          clrscr();
```

```
printf("Enter date d, m, y\n");
scanf("%d%d%d", &d, &m, &y);
/*general condition*/
if((d<1)||(m<1)||(y<1)||(d>31)||(m>12))
        printf("\n invalid date\n");
else /*checking for months with maximum 30 days*/
if((d>30)&&((m==4)||(m==6)&&(m==9)&&(m==11)))
        printf("\n invalid date\n");
else /* checking for Feb month*/
if((m==2)&&(d>29))
        printf("\n invalid date\n");
else /* checking for Feb month*/
if((m==2)&&(d>28)&&(y%4!=0))
        printf("\n invalid date\n");
else /* when all above conditions are false the date
                                entered must be valid*/
        printf("\n given date is valid\n");
getch();
}
```

Output 1:	Output 2:	Output 3:
Enter date d m y 12 5 2002 given date is valid	Enter date d m y 29 2 2002 invalid date	Enter date d m y 31 9 2002 invalid date

2.4.4 *Nested if statement*

While solving complicated programs we need to check number of conditions, one within another. In such cases it is essential to use nested if conditions.

SYNTAX:

```
if (conditional-expression)
{
Statements;
if (conditional-expression)
{
Statements(s);
        if (conditional-expression)
        Statements(s);
        else
        Statements;
}
else
Statements(s);
```

```
}
else
Statements(s);
```

In case of nested conditions the inner condition executes only if outer condition is true. There may be corresponding else statement otherwise compound statements. We can nest the conditions to any depth.

This program finds the largest of three numbers using nested if statements.

```
/*Program name: cond16.c*/
/* Largest of three numbers */
/*In this program we are not checking for equality of 2 or
all 3 numbers*/
#include<stdio.h>
#include<conio.h>
void main()
{
        int a,b,c;
        clrscr();
        printf("Enter three numbers\n");
        scanf("%d%d%d",&a,&b,&c);
        if(a>b)  /* checks for a larger than b if true then
                            either a and c will be largest*/
            if(a>c)/*nested condition executes only when above
                                  condition is true*/
                printf("%d is largest\n",a);/* when inner
                                        condition is true a is
                                        largest*/
            else /* when inner condition is false then c is
                                  largest*/
                printf("%d is largest\n",c);
        else  /* else for outer condition, when that is false
                            then either b or c will be
                            largest*/
            if(b>c) /* checks for b is larger than c */
                printf("%d is larger\n", b);
            else /* when inner condition in else part is false
                                  then c is largest*/
                printf("%d is largest\n", c);
        getch();
}
```

Output 1:	Output 2:	Output 3:
Enter three numbers	Enter three numbers	Enter three numbers
2 4 8	7 4 7	2 2 2
8 is largest	7 is largest	2 is largest

This program finds not only the largest of three numbers but also the second largest using nested if statements.

```
/*Program name: cond17.c*/
/* Largest and second largest of three numbers */
/*In this program we are not checking for equality of 2 or all
        3 numbers*/
#include<stdio.h>
#include<conio.h>
void main()
{
        int a, b, c;
        clrscr();
        printf("Enter three numbers\n");
        scanf("%d%d%d", &a, &b, &c);
        if((a>b)&&(a>c)) /*checking for a is largest*/
                {
                printf("\n largest = %d", a);
                if(b>c)  /*when a is largest either b or c is
                                        second largest*/
                        printf("\n second largest = %d", b);
                else
                        printf("\n second largest = %d", c);
                }
        else
        if((b>a)&&(b>c))   /*checking for b is largest*/
                {
                printf("\n largest = %d", b);
                if(a>c)  /*when b is largest either a or c is
                                        second largest*/
                        printf("\n second largest = %d", a);
                else
                        printf("\n second largest = %d", c);
                }
        else  /*when a or b is not largest then c will be
                                largest*/
                {
                printf("\n largest = %d",c);
                if(a>b)  /*when c is largest either a or b is
                                        second largest*/
                        printf("\n second largest = %d",a);
                else
                        printf("\n second largest = %d",b);
                }
        getch();
}
```

Output 1:	Output 2:	Output 3:
Enter three numbers 248 largest = 8 second largest = 4	Enter three numbers 747 largest = 7 second largest = 7	Enter three numbers 2 2 2 largest = 2 second largest =2

In the following program we are checking for equality of 2 or 3 numbers while finding the largest and second largest of three numbers.

```
/*Program name: cond18.c*/
/* largest and second largest of three numbers */
/*in this program we are checking for equality of 2 or all 3
      numbers*/
#include<stdio.h>
#include<conio.h>
void main()
{
int a, b, c, l, sl ; /* a, b, c for 3 numbers and l is for
      largest*/
clrscr();
printf("Enter three numbers\n");
scanf("%d%d%d", &a, &b, &c);
l=a; /* assume a is largest and assign it to l */
if(b>l) /* check for b larger than l if true assign to l*/
      l=b;
if(c>l) /* check for c larger than l if true assign to l*/
      l=c;
/* Check all three are equal*/
if((a==l)&&(b==l)&&(c==l))
      printf("\n all given three numbers are equal\n");
else /* check for any 2 numbers are equal to large*/
if(((l==a)&&(l==b))||((l==a)&&(l==c))||((l==b)&&(l==c)))
      printf("\n there are two numbers which are equal and
                        larger among given three\n");
else /* when above both conditions are false there will be
      only one largest*/
      {
      printf("\n largest = %d\n", l);/* print the largest
                        which is stored in l*/
/*Finding second largest*/
if((a==l)&&(b>c))/* when a is largest then either b or c will
      be second largest*/
      sl=b;
else
      sl=c;
```

```
        if((b==l)&&(a>c))/* when b is largest then either a or c will
            be second largest*/
            sl=a;
        else
            sl=c;
        if((c==l)&&(a>b))/* when c is largest then either a or b will
            be second largest*/
            sl=a;
        else
            sl=b;
        printf("\n second largest =  %d\n", sl);
        }
        getch();
        }
```

Output 1:

Enter three numbers
2 4 8
8 is largest

Output 2:

Enter three numbers
7 4 7
there are two numbers which are equal and larger among given three

Output 3:

Enter three numbers
2 2 2
all given three numbers are equal

When three sides of a triangle are given and they construct a triangle then the triangle may be one of the three types based on the given sides, namely equilateral(all three sides equal), isosceles(any two sides are equal), or scalene(no sides are equal). Based on angles triangle may be one of the three types namely right angled triangle(any one angle should be 90 degree), obtuse angled triangle(any one angle should be greater than 90 degree) or acute angled triangle(all three angles should be less than 90 degree). This program takes three sides as input and checks whether they form a triangle or not. If they form a triangle then it gives the type of triangle formed by the given 3 sides as explained above.

```
/*Program name: cond19.c*/
/* Program for finding the type of triangle when 3 sides are
    given */
/* Checking for formation of triangle which avoids runtime
    error */
#include<stdio.h>
#include<conio.h>
#include<math.h>
void main()
{
float a, b, c;
clrscr();
```

```
printf("Enter three sides a b c of triangle\n");
scanf("%f%f%f", &a, &b, &c);
if((a<=0)||(b<=0)||(c<=0))/* a side of a triangle can not be 0
        or -ve number*/
        printf("\n given sides can not form a triangle\n");
else
if(((a+b)<=c)||((a+c)<=b)||((b+c)<=a)) /* to form a triangle
        sum of any two sides must greater than third side*/
        printf("\n given sides can not form a triangle\n");
else /* there is possibility of triangle formation*/
        {
        printf("\n given three sides forms a triangle\n");

                /* checking the triangle type by side */
        if((a==b)&&(a==c))/* when all three sides are equal*/
                printf("\n equilateral triangle\n");
        else
        if((a==b)||(a==c)||(b==c))/* when any two sides are
                        equal*/
                printf("\n isosceles triangle\n");
        else/* when all three sides are different*/
                printf("\n scalene triangle\n");

/* checking the triangle type by checking the angle*/
if((a*a==(b*b+c*c))||(b*b==(a*a+c*c))||(c*c==(a*a+b*b)))/
        *Pythagoras theorem */
        printf("\n right angle triangle");
else
        if((a*a>(b*b+c*c))||(b*b>(a*a+c*c))||(c*c>(a*a+b*b)))
                /* Pythagoras theorem*/
                printf("\n obtuse angle triangle");
        else/*when it is not right or obtuse angle it must be
                        acute angle triangle*/
                printf("\n acute angle triangle");
}
getch();
}
```

Output 1:

Enter three sides a b c of triangle
2 3 4
given three sides forms a triangle

scalene triangle

obtuse angle triangle

Output 2:

Enter three sides a b c of triangle
4 6 6
given three sides forms a triangle

isosceles triangle

acute angle triangle

Output 3:
Enter three sides a b c of triangle
3 4 5
given three sides forms a triangle

scalene triangle

right angle triangle

Output 4:
Enter three sides a b c of triangle
4 6 16
given sides can not form a triangle

2.4.5 *Conditional Operator ?*

C provides the only one ternary operator ?: to replace the simple if-else statement. The syntax is

(Conditional-expression)? Statement1: statement2;

When the conditional expression gives true, statement1 gets executed otherwise statement2 gets executed.

Example: For checking odd or even of a number a of type int.

(a%2==0)?printf("even number"):printf("odd number");

```
/*Program name: cond20.c*/
/* Program for updating the date by 1 day */
/* This program will not check for validity of entered date*/
#include<stdio.h>
#include<conio.h>
void main()
{
int d, m, y;
clrscr();
printf("Enter date d, m, y\n");
scanf("%d%d%d", &d, &m, &y);
/* Increase the day by 1*/
d++;
if(d>31)
      {
      d=1;
      m++;
      }
if((d>30)&&((m==4)||(m==6)||(m==9)||(m==11)))
      {
      d=1;
      m++;
      }
if((d>29)&&(m==2))
      {
```

```
            d=1;
            m++;
            }
        if((d>28)&&(m==2)&&(y%4!=0))
            {
            d=1;
            m++;
            }
        if(m>12)
            {
            m=1;
            y++;
            }
        printf("\n updated date is %4d%4d%8d",d,m,y);
        getch();
        }
```

Output 1: **Enter date d m y** 20 2 2002 **the updated date is 20 2 2002**	**Output 2:** **Enter date d m y** 32 3 2002 **the updated date is 1 4 2002**

As shown in the output 2 of the above program, the program will not check for validity of date. The following program checks for validity of the given date. When it is valid it updates the date otherwise it gives just the message "invalid date".

```
/*Program name: cond21.c*/
/* Program for updating the date by 1 day */
/* This program checks for validity of entered date*/
#include<stdio.h>
#include<conio.h>
void main()
{
int d, m, y;
clrscr();
printf("Enter date d, m, y\n");
scanf("%d%d%d", &d, &m, &y);
/*general condition*/
if((d<1)||(m<1)||(y<1)||(d>31)||(m>12))
      printf("\n invalid date\n");
else /*checking for months with maximum 30 days*/
if((d>30)&&((m==4)||(m==6)&&(m==9)&&(m==11)))
      printf("\n invalid date\n");
else /* checking for Feb month*/
```

```
if((m==2)&&(d>29))
        printf("\n invalid date\n");
else /* checking for Feb month*/
if((m==2)&&(d>28)&&(y%4!=0))
        printf("\n invalid date\n");
else /* when all above conditions are false the date entered
        must be valid*/
        {
        printf("\n given date is valid\n");
        /* increase the day by 1*/
        d++;
        if(d>31)
                {
                d=1;
                m++;
                }
        if((d>30)&&((m==4)||(m==6)||(m==9)||(m==11)))
                {
                d=1;
                m++;
                }
        if((d>29)&&(m==2))
                {
                d=1;
                m++;
                }
        if((d>28)&&(m==2)&&(y%4!=0))
                {
                d=1;
                m++;
                }
        if(m>12)
                {
                m=1;
                y++;
                }
        printf("\n updated date is %4d%4d%8d",d,m,y);
        }
getch();
}
```

Output 1:
Enter date d m y
20 2 2002
the given date is valid
the updated date is 20 2 2002

Output 2:
Enter date d m y
32 3 2002
invalid date

Output 3:	Output 4:
Enter date d m y	Enter date d m y
29 2 2000	31 12 2002
the given date is valid	the given date is valid
the updated date is 1 3 2000	the updated date is 1 1 2003

Consider the following program that finds the difference between two dates. The simple logic used here is to convert both the dates into number of days, then taking the difference by subtracting small number from the greater. The difference we get in terms of number of days will be re-converted into date format with appropriate arithmetic operations that gives quotient and remainders. In this program we have assumed 30 days in a month and not checked for date validation.

```
/*Program name: cond22.c*/
/* Program for finding difference of two dates */
/* This program will not check for validity of entered date*/
/* The answer may not be 100% correct as we have assumed 30
      days a month and 365 days a year*/
#include<stdio.h>
#include<conio.h>
void main()
{
int d1, m1, y1;/* first date*/
int d2, m2, y2;/* second date*/
int d, m, y;/* difference date*/
long a, b, c;
clrscr();
printf("Enter first date d, m, y\n");
scanf("%d%d%d",&d1,&m1,&y1);
printf("enter second date d, m, y\n");
scanf("%d%d%d",&d2,&m2,&y2);
a=d1+(m1-1)*30+(y1-1)*365; /* converting to total number of
      days assuming 30 days in month*/
b=d2+(m2-1)*30+(y2-1)*365;
if(a==b)
      printf("\n difference in given dates is zero\n");
else
      {
      if(a>b)
            c=a-b;
      else
            c=b-a;
     /* convert c into number of days, months and years*/
            y=c/365; /* quiescent gives number of years*/
            c=c%365;/* remainder gives number of days after
                                          making years*/
```

```
        m=c/30; /* quiescent gives number of months*/
        d=c%30;/* remainder gives number of days after
                                  making months*/
        printf("\n difference in date is %4d days %4d
        months  and %8d years",d,m,y);
      }
  getch();
  }
```

Output 1:	Output 2:
Enter first date d, m, y 34 3 1990 enter second date d, m, y 22 2 2002 difference in date is 23 days 10 months and 11 years	Enter first date d, m, y 20 2 2000 enter second date d, m, y 20 2 2000 difference in date is zero

2.5 switch () ... case statement

It is an alternative statement for else...if constructs. This statement makes program easily understandable and more readable. It is used to select one option from number of alternatives.

The general syntax is

```
switch (expression)
{
case value 1: Statements;
              break;
case value 2: Statements;
              break;
...
...
...
case value n: Statements;
              break;

default: Statements;
}
```

Expression can be an arithmetic expression or simply a constant. Depending on the value of expression the control goes through switch construct for searching that particular case value and executes statement block of that case, and the 'break;' statement at the end of the statement block in that case transfers the control to the end of the switch statement, if there is no match then the default case is executed and the switch statement terminates. However 'default' is optional and need not necessarily be included in the switch construct.

2.6 The 'break;' statement

This statement is used to break the compound or looping statement. It is mainly used in loops and switch() ...case statement. The syntax is

break;

The following program takes an integer value from keyboard and prints its last digit in words. The simple logic implemented here is by taking modulus of 10 with given number we will get last digit which will be selected and printed with the help of switch-case construct.

```
/*Program name: cond23.c*/
/* Program for printing the last digit of an integer in
      words */
/* This program uses switch case*/
#include<stdio.h>
#include<conio.h>
void main()
{
long no;
clrscr();
printf("\n Enter an integer \n");
scanf("%ld", &no);
switch(no%10)
{
case 0:
      printf("\n zero \n");
      break;
case 1:
      printf("\n one \n");
      break;
case 2:
      printf("\n two \n");
      break;
case 3:
      printf("\n three \n");
      break;
case 4:
      printf("\n four \n");
      break;
case 5:
      printf("\n five \n");
      break;
case 6:
      printf("\n six \n");
      break;
```

```
case 7:
     printf("\n seven \n");
     break;
case 8:
     printf("\n eight \n");
     break;
case 9:
     printf("\n nine \n");
  }
getch();
}
```

Output 1:	Output 2:
Enter an integer	Enter an integer
1234	123
four	three

The same program can be written by using only if…else…if constructs as follows.

```
/*Program name: cond24.c*/
/* Program for printing the last digit of an integer in
     words */
/* This program uses if...else...if constructs*/
#include<stdio.h>
#include<conio.h>
void main()
{
long no;
clrscr();
printf("\n Enter an integer \n");
scanf("%ld", &no);
if(no%10==0)
     printf("\n zero \n");
else
if(no%10==1)
     printf("\n one\n");
else
if(no%10==2)
     printf("\n two \n");
else
if(no%10==3)
     printf("\n three \n");
else
```

```
if(no%10==4)
      printf("\n four \n");
else
if(no%10==5)
      printf("\n five \n");
else
if(no%10==6)
      printf("\n six \n");
else
if(no%10==7)
      printf("\n seven \n");
else
if(no%10==8)
      printf("\n eight \n");
else
if(no%10== 9)
      printf("\n nine \n");
getch();
}
```

Output 1:	**Output 2:**
Enter an integer	Enter an integer
1297	1239
seven	nine

The following two programs are similar to the programs we have already discussed above. In these programs we are accepting two integer values from keyboard along with an arithmetic operator. The first program uses switch-case statement and the second program makes use of if…else…if construct.

```
/*Program name: cond25.c*/
/* Program for doing arithmetic operation on 2 integers based
      on an operator */
/* This program uses switch case*/
#include<stdio.h>
#include<conio.h>
void main()
{
int a, b;
char op; /* for storing operator +, -, *, /, % */
clrscr();
printf("\n Enter an arithmetic operator +, -, *, /, %\n");
op=getchar();
printf("\n enter two  integers \n");
```

```
scanf("%d%d", &a, &b);
switch(op)
{
case '+':
        printf("\n sum = %d \n", a+b);
        break;
case '-':
        printf("\n difference = %d \n",a-b);
        break;
case '*':
        printf("\n product = %d \n",a*b);
        break;
case '/':
        printf("\n quiescent = %d \n",a/b);
        break;
case '%':
        printf("\n remainder = %d \n",a%b);
        break;
default:
        printf("\n given operator is not an arithmetic
                                    operator\n");

}
getch();
}
```

Output 1:	Output 2:
Enter an arithmetic operator +,-,*,/,%	Enter an arithmetic operator +,-,*,/,%
+	=
enter two integers	enter two integers
20 4	20 4
sum is 24	given operator is not an arithmetic operator

```
/*Program name: cond26.c*/
/* Program for doing arithmetic operation on 2 integers based
        on operator */
/* This program uses if...else...if constructs */
#include<stdio.h>
#include<conio.h>
void main()
{
int a, b;
char op; /* for storing operator +, -, *, /, % */
clrscr();
printf("\n Enter an arithmetic operator +, -, *, /, %\n");
```

```
op=getchar();
printf("\n enter two  integers \n");
scanf("%d%d", &a, &b);
if(op=='+')
      printf("\n sum = %d \n", a+b);
else
if(op== '-')
      printf("\n difference = %d \n", a-b);
else
if(op== '*')
      printf("\n product = %d \n", a*b);
else
if(op== '/')
      printf("\n quiescent = %d \n",a/b);
else
if(op=='%')
      printf("\n remainder = %d \n", a%b);
else
      printf("\n  given  operator  is  not  an  arithmetic
                  operator\n");
getch();
}
```

Output 1:
Enter an arithmetic operator +,-,*,/,%
*
enter two integers
20 4
product is 80

Output 2:
Enter an arithmetic operator +,-,*,/,%
%
enter two integers
20 3
remainder is 2

An university gives the admission to the Ph.D. program on following conditions.

1. **Candidate must be a master degree holder or**
2. **Candidate must be a professional bachelor holder with minimum of 2 years experience or**
3. **Candidate must be a bachelor degree holder with minimum of 15 years of experience.**

The following program checks whether the candidate is eligible for the admission or not by inputting the degree, type of degree and number of years of experience. It makes use of string library functions for comparing the strings.

(Note strings are explained in detail in 'strings chapter').

```
/*Program name: cond27.c*/
/* Program for admission to the Ph.D. with certain Conditions
   */
```

```
/* Must be master degree or professional bachelor degree with
      2 year experience or bachelor degree with 15 year
      experience */
#include<stdio.h>
#include<conio.h>
#include<string.h>
void main()
{
char degree[20], typeofcourse[20];
int exp;
clrscr();
printf(" enter degree, type of of course and experience\n");
scanf("%s%s%d",degree,type_of_course,&exp);
if(strcmpi(degree,"Master")==0)
printf("eligible to Ph.D. \n");
else
if((strcmpi(degree, "bachelor")==0) &&(strcmpi
      (typeofcourse, "Professional")==0) &&(exp>=2))
printf("eligible to Ph.D. \n");
else
if((strcmpi(degree, "bachelor")==0)&&(strcmpi(typeofcourse,
      "Professional")==0)&&(exp>=15))
printf("eligible to Ph.D. \n");
else
printf("not eligible to Ph.D. \n");
getch();
}
```

```
Output
enter degree, type of of course and experience
bachelor
professional
4
eligible to PhD
```

The solution to the simultaneous equations

ax+by=c1
cx+dy=c2
Is given by
x=(c1d-c2b)/(ad-cb);
y=(c2a-c1c)/(ad-cb);

At the time of inputting the values for the coefficients a,b,c,d,c1 and c2 care should be taken that ad-cb should be zero. The following program implements this.

```
/*Program name: cond28.c*/
/* Program to solve simultaneous equations of 2 unknowns */
#include<stdio.h>
#include<conio.h>
void main()
{
int a,b,c,d,c1,c2;
float x,y;
clrscr();
xyz:
printf(" enter constants for first equation a,b,c1\n");
scanf("%d%d%d",&a,&b,&c1);
printf(" enter constants for second equation c,d,c2\n");
scanf("%d%d%d",&c,&d,&c2);
if(a*d==b*c)
{
printf("\n wrong inputs\n re-enter...\n");
goto xyz;
}
x=(c1*d-c2*b)/(float)(a*d-c*b);
y=(c2*a-c1*c)/(float)(a*d-c*b);
printf("\n unknown x = %f\n unknown y = %f",x,y);
getch();
}
```

Output
enter constants for first equation a,b,c1
2 3 10
enter constants for second equation c,d,c2
4 3 15

unknown x = 2.500000
unknown y = 1.666667

2.7 goto statement

goto is the unconditional looping statement. But it is used with conditional statements to do repeated operations. On executing the goto statement takes the program control to the specified label mentioned. The general syntax is

goto labelname;

where labelname is any user defied word and must be mentioned in the program line ended with colon (:). Using goto statement without conditions leads to infinite loop or may skips certain statements. Consider the following program segment.

.....
....
xyz:
....
....
goto xyz;
...

Here xyz is a label. On execution the goto statement transfers the control of the program execution to that label. When the execution of goto statement in the above program segment without condition definitely leads to infinite loop. Now consider the program segment given below.

.....
....
goto xyz;
....
....
xyz:
....

In this case all the statements between goto and label xyz will be totally skipped when goto is used unconditionally.

The following program illustrates the use of goto statement. Here we are inputting a fractional value with two digit precision from the keyboard. When the entered value is having more than two digits of precision then program asks for the input again.

```
/*Program name: cond29.c*/
/* Program to illustrate goto statement with condition */
/* read a float value with only two digit precision */
#include<stdio.h>
#include<conio.h>
void main()
{
int n;
float f;
clrscr();
xyz: /* label is declared */
printf(" enter a float value with 2 digit precision \n");
scanf("%f",&f);
n=f*100; /*takes integer part */
if(n!=f*100)
{
printf("\n wrong input re-enter \n");
goto xyz; /* control transfers to the xyz label */
}
printf("\n entered value is %.2f",f);
```

```
getch();
}
```

Output
enter a float value with 2 digit precision
12.505

wrong input re-enter
enter a float value with 2 digit precision
12.50

entered value is 12.50

The following program illustrates the goto statement. It prints all the numbers between 1 and n.

```
/*Program name: cond30.c*/
/* Program to illustrate goto statement for looping */
#include<stdio.h>
#include<conio.h>
void main()
{
int i,n;
clrscr();
printf(" enter n\n");
scanf("%d",&n);
i=1;
label:
        printf("%8d",i);
        i=i+1;
        if(i<=n)
        goto label;
getch();
}
```

Output
enter n
5
1 2 3 4 5

3

Looping Statements

3.1 Introduction

In some cases it is essential to execute certain set of statements repeatedly. Certain numerical equations can be solved by iterative methods. C provides looping statements to do repeated operations. We have three types of looping statements viz. for, while, and do while loops.

3.2 for ( ) loop.

General syntax

```
for ( initialization-expression; conditional-expression; update-expression)
Statement(s);
```

Where initialization-expression executes only once and initializes the starting value of loop counter. Conditional–expression checks the loop counter value with the target value. When the condition is true all the statements in the body of the loop get executed and the control advances to update-expression. Update-expression either increases or decreases the value of loop counter so that we are coming nearer to the solution in each and every step. Ex: 1.

```
int i;
for (i=1; i<=10; ++i ) printf("%d\n", i);
```

It prints all numbers between 1 and 10 (1,2,3…10)

Now we can see the following program, which prints first n natural numbers. Here we need to take the value of 'n' from keyboard. The value of loop counter has to be initialized to one as natural numbers starts from one. The condition becomes i<=n which gives either true or false. Until the condition is true the body of the loop keeps on executing. Each time the update expression increases the value of loop counter by one.

```
/* Program name: loop1.c */
/* Print 1 to n, using for loop*/
```

```
#include<stdio.h>
#include<conio.h>
main()
{
int i, n;/* i for loop counter, n for the extreme boundary*/
clrscr();
printf("\n Enter the upper limit\n");
scanf("%d", &n);
printf("\n Numbers from 1 to %d are \n", n);
for(i=1;i<=n; i++)   /* the loop which repeats 'n' times*/
      printf("%5d",i);  /* each time the condition gives true
      the value of 'i' gets printed. */
getch();
}
```

Output:
Enter the upper limit
10
Numbers from 1 to 10 are
 1 2 3 4 5 6 7 8 9 10

In the following program which is almost similar to the above one but the loop counter is initialized with value 'm' rather than 1, and prints all the numbers between 'm' and 'n' whose values are scanned from the keyboard.

```
/* Program name: loop2.c */
/* Prints all numbers from m to n, using for loop*/
#include<stdio.h>
#include<conio.h>
void main()
{
int i, n, m;/* i for loop counter, m is lower limit, n for
      upper limit*/
clrscr();
printf("\n Enter lower limit &  upper limit\n");
scanf("%d%d", &m, &n);
printf("\n Numbers from %d to %d are \n", m, n);
for(i=m; i<=n; i++)
      printf("%5d",i);
getch();
}
```

Output:
Enter the lower limit & upper limit
10 20
Numbers from 10 to 20 are
 10 11 12 13 14 15 16 17 18 19 20

Now look at the following two programs, which are having a conditional statement inside the loop body. It leads to a little complex operation compared to above programs. We can easily combine loops and conditions in the programs.

```
/* Program name: loop3.c */
/* Print all odd numbers from m to n, using for loop*/
#include<stdio.h>
#include<conio.h>
void main()
{
int i, n, m;/* i for loop counter, m is lower limit, n for
     upper limit*/
clrscr();
printf("\n Enter lower limit &  upper limit\n");
scanf("%d%d", &m, &n);
printf("\n Odd numbers from %d to %d are \n", m, n);
for(i=m; i<=n; i++)
     if(i%2==1) /* odd numbers are not divisible by 2*/
          printf("%5d",i);
getch();
}
```

Output:
Enter the lower limit & upper limit
10 20
Odd numbers from 10 to 20 are
11 13 15 17 19

```
/* Program name: loop4.c */
/* Print all even numbers from m to n, using for loop*/
#include<stdio.h>
#include<conio.h>
void main()
{
int i, n, m;/* i for loop counter, m is lower limit, n for
     upper limit*/
clrscr();
printf("\n Enter lower limit &  upper limit\n");
scanf("%d%d", &m, &n);
printf("\n Even numbers from %d to %d are \n", m, n);
for(i=m; i<=n; i++)
     if(i%2==0) /* even numbers are  divisible by 2*/
          printf("%5d",i);
```

```
getch();
}
```

Output:
Enter the lower limit & upper limit
10 20
Even numbers from 10 to 20 are
10 12 14 16 18 20

In the following program target value is constant (10), the inputted value is used to calculate the result. In printf() statement we can specify the arithmetic expressions, which gives the calculated values.

```
/* Program name: loop5.c */
/* Print multiplication table for any given number */
#include<stdio.h>
#include<conio.h>
void main()
{
int i, n;
      /* i for loop counter, n for given number for which, we
                              have print multiplication table
                              */
clrscr();
printf("\n Enter n\n");
scanf("%d", &n);
printf("\n Multiplication table for %d is: \n", n);
for(i=1;i<=10;i++)
      printf("%5d\n",i*n);
getch();
}
```

Output 1:
Enter n
8
Multiplication table for 8 is:
8 16 24 32 40 48 56 64 72 80

Output 2:
Enter n
12
Multiplication table for 12 is:
12 24 36 48 60 72 84 96 108 120

Let us make a minor modification to the above program for printing multiplication table, to get the output in more readable form.

```
/* Program name: loop6.c */
/* Print multiplication table for any given number */
```

```
/* The output will be shown as table of values*/
#include<stdio.h>
#include<conio.h>
void main()
{
int i, n; /* i for loop counter, n for given number for which
      we have print multiplication table */
clrscr();
printf("\n enter n\n");
scanf("%d", &n);
printf("\n Multiplication table for %d is: \n", n);
for(i=1;i<=10;i++)
      printf("%d  * %3d  =%4d\n",n,i,i*n);
getch();
}
```

Output:

```
Enter n
8
Multiplication table for 8 is:
   8 *  1 =  8
   8 *  2 = 16
   8 *  3 = 24
   8 *  4 = 36
   8 *  5 = 40
   8 *  6 = 48
   8 *  7 = 56
   8 *  8 = 64
   8 *  9 = 72
   8 * 10 = 80
```

The following program finds the sum of first 'n' natural numbers. The sum of first n natural numbers is given by the formula (sum=n*(n+1)/2). When we are using the formula, we can avoid number of calculations in the loop. Instead of formula if we are using looping statements, then it leads to number of computations.

```
/* Program name: loop7.c */
/* Finding sum of 1 to n */
/* This program uses formula without loop */
#include<stdio.h>
#include<conio.h>
void main()
```

```
{
int n;
long s; /* n for given number, s for sum */
clrscr();
printf("\n Enter n\n");
scanf("%d", &n);
s=n*(n+1)/2;
printf("sum of numbers from 1 to %d  = %ld\n", n, s);
getch();
}
```

Output	Output
Enter n	Enter n
5	9
sum of numbers from 1 to 5 = 15	sum of numbers from 1 to 9 = 45

The above program can be written using iterative method, as given below.

```
/* Program name: loop8.c */
/* Finding sum of 1 to n */
/* This program uses for loop */
#include<stdio.h>
#include<conio.h>
void main()
{
int n, i;
long s=0; /* n for given number, s for sum */
clrscr();
printf("\n Enter n\n");
scanf("%d", &n);
for(i=1;i<=n; ++i)
        s=s+i;
printf("sum of numbers from 1 to %d  = %ld\n", n, s);
getch();
}
```

Output	Output
Enter n	Enter n
5	9
sum of numbers from 1 to 5 = 15	sum of numbers from 1 to 9 = 45

Now we make some changes in the above program to display the intermediate results also.

```
/* Program name: loop9.c */
/* Finding sum of 1 to n */
/* This program uses for loop */
/* This program displays intermediate results also*/
#include<stdio.h>
#include<conio.h>
void main()
{
int n, i;
long s=0; /* n for given number, s for sum */
clrscr();
printf("\n Enter n\n");
scanf("%d", &n);
for(i=1;i<=n; ++i)
      {
      s=s+i;
      printf("sum of numbers from 1 to %4d = %ld\n", i, s);
      }
printf("\n sum of numbers from 1 to %4d  =  %ld\n", n, s);
getch();
}
```

Output
Enter n
5
sum of numbers from 1 to 1 = 1
sum of numbers from 1 to 2 = 3
sum of numbers from 1 to 3 = 6
sum of numbers from 1 to 4 = 10
sum of numbers from 1 to 5 = 15

sum of numbers from 1 to 5 = 15

After finding the sum of first 'n' natural numbers, now let us consider similar program for finding the sum of first 'n' terms of a series. In this program the step size is 3 instead of 1. The initial value remains 1 & the target is 'n'. Here we need to add first 'n' terms of the series, so we can use a separate variable for terms of the series and another variable for loop counter.

```
/* Program name: loop10.c */
/* Finding sum of series 1+4+7+10 up to n terms */
/* This program uses for loop */
#include<stdio.h>
```

```
#include<conio.h>
void main()
{
int n, i, j=1;
long s=0; /* n for given number, s for sum */
clrscr();
printf("\n Enter n\n");
scanf("%d", &n);
for(i=1;i<=n; i++)
    {
    s=s+j;
    j=j+3;         /* difference between each term is 3 */
    }
j=j-3;
printf("\n sum of numbers from 1 to %4d in steps of 3   =
%ld\n", j, s);
getch();
}
```

Output Enter n 20 sum of numbers from 1 to 58 in steps of 3 = 590

Output Enter n 10 sum of numbers from 1 to 28 in steps of 3 = 145

For easy understanding of the working of the program we are displaying the intermediate results of the above program.

```
/* Program name: loop11.c */
/* Finding sum of series 1+4+7+10 up to n terms */
/* This program uses for loop */
/* Program displays intermediate results*/
#include<stdio.h>
#include<conio.h>
void main()
{
int n, i, j=1;
long s=0; /* n for given number, s for sum */
```

```
        clrscr();
        printf("\n Enter n\n");
        scanf("%d", &n);
        for(i=1;i<=n; i++)
              {
              s=s+j;
              printf("sum of numbers from 1 to %4d  = %ld\n", j, s);
              j=j+3;         /* difference between each term is 3 */
              }
        j=j-3;
        printf("\n sum of numbers from 1 to %4d  =  %ld\n", j, s);
        getch();
        }
```

Output
Enter n
10
sum of numbers from 1 to 1 = 1
sum of numbers from 1 to 4 = 5
sum of numbers from 1 to 7 = 12
sum of numbers from 1 to 10 = 22
sum of numbers from 1 to 13 = 35
sum of numbers from 1 to 16 = 51
sum of numbers from 1 to 19 = 70
sum of numbers from 1 to 22 = 92
sum of numbers from 1 to 25 = 117
sum of numbers from 1 to 28 = 145

sum of numbers from 1 to 28 = 145

Now we can check the logic behind the following program, which displays series along with the result.

```
/* Program name: loop12.c */
/* Finding sum of series 1+4+7+10 up to n terms */
/* This program uses for loop */
/* This program prints the series also*/

#include<stdio.h>
#include<conio.h>
void main()
{
int n, i, j=1;
```

```
long s=0; /* n for given number, s for sum */
clrscr();
printf("\n Enter n\n");
scanf("%d", &n);
printf("\n sum of the series\n");
for(i=1;i<=n; i++)
    {
    s=s+j;
    printf("%d", j);
    if(i<n) /* when i reaches n we should not display + at
                                        end*/
            printf("+"); /* to print the '+' except at last*/
    j=j+3;       /* difference between each term is 3 */
    }
    printf(" =  %ld\n", s); /* to display the sum that is
                                        stored in s */
getch();
}
```

Output
Enter n
12
sum of the series
1+4+7+10+13+16+19+22+25+28+31+34 = 210

Output
Enter n
5
sum of the series
1+4+7+10+13 = 35

The program that follows makes use of little complicated logic. Here we need to take care of the fractional values. The proper type of variable or proper type casting is necessary whenever we are doing a division operation that gives fractions. The next two programs show this.

```
/* Program name: loop13.c */
/* Finding sum of 1/2+2/3+3/4+.... n/n+1 */
/* This program uses for loop */
#include<stdio.h>
#include<conio.h>
void main()
{
int n, i;
```

```
float  s=0; /*  s for sum which is a float value as division
      occurs */
clrscr();
printf("\n Enter n\n");
scanf("%d", &n);
for(i=1;i<=n; ++i)
      s=s+i/(i+1.0);  /* 1.0 because we have make it float
                           value otherwise result becomes
                           0*/
printf("sum of series = %.3f\n",s);
getch();
}
```

Output
Enter n
10
sum of the series = 7.980

```
/* Program name: loop14.c */
/* Finding sum of 1/2+2/3+3/4+.... n/n+1 */
/* This program uses for loop */
/* This program prints the series also */
#include<stdio.h>
#include<conio.h>
void main()
{
int n, i;
float  s=0; /*  s for sum which is a float value as division
      occurs */
clrscr();
printf("\n Enter n\n");
scanf("%d", &n);
printf("\n sum of series \n");
for(i=1;i<=n; ++i)
      {
      s=s+i/(i+1.0);  /* 1.0 because we have make it float
                           value otherwise result becomes
                           0*/
      printf("%d/%d",i,i+1);
      if(i<n)
      printf(" + ");
      }
printf(" = %.3f\n",s);
getch();
}
```

Output
Enter n
10
sum of series
½ +2/3 +3/4+4/5+5/6+6/7+7/8+8/9+9/10+10/11=7.980

In the programs that follows we are using complicated series. Here first we have to generalize the series, before writing the program. Consider the following series.

S= 1+4+9+16+25+... up to n terms. Here we have to think of the relationship between the terms. There is no constant change/difference between each consecutive terms. The relationship tells that the terms are the squares of first 'n' natural numbers. We can proceed by finding the squares of each loop counter value which varies from 1 to n and adding the results . The sum may be long integer as the square is a large value.

```
/* Program name: loop15.c */
/* Finding sum of 1+4+9+16+25... n terms(sum of squares) */
/* This program uses for loop */
#include<stdio.h>
#include<conio.h>
void main()
{
int n, i;
long  s=0;
clrscr();
printf("\n enter n\n");
scanf("%d", &n);
for(i=1;i<=n; ++i)
      s=s+i*i;
printf("\n sum of series = %ld \n", s);
getch();
}
```

Output
Enter n
10
sum of series = 385

In the following program we are printing the series along with the sum.

```
/* Program name: loop16.c */
/* Finding sum of 1+4+9+16+25... n terms(sum of squares) */
/* This program uses for loop */
```

```
#include<stdio.h>
#include<conio.h>
void main()
{
int n, i;
long  s=0;
clrscr();
printf("\n Enter n\n");
scanf("%d", &n);
printf("\n sum of series \n");
for(i=1;i<=n; ++i)
        {
        s=s+i*i;
        printf(" %d ",i*i);
        if(i<n)
                printf("+");
        }
printf(" = %ld", s);
getch();
}
```

Output
Enter n
10
sum of series

1+4+9+16+25+36+49+64+81+100 = 385

Now look at the series. S= 1 +8+27+64... upto n terms. This is a series of cubes of first 'n' natural numbers. The following program finds the sum of cubes. The next program is an alternative method of the following program, which prints the series with sum.

```
/* Program name: loop17.c */
/* Finding sum of 1+8+27+64+125..... n terms(sum of cube) */
/* This program uses for loop */
#include<stdio.h>
#include<conio.h>
void main()
{
int n, i;
long  s=0;
clrscr();
printf("\n Enter n\n");
```

```
scanf("%d", &n);
for(i=1;i<=n; ++i)
    s=s+i*i*i;
printf("\n sum of series = %ld \n", s);
getch();
}
```

> **Output**
> Enter n
> 10
> sum of series = 3025

```
/* Program name: loop18.c */
/* Finding sum of 1+8+27+64.... n terms (sum of cubes) */
/* This program uses for loop */
#include<stdio.h>
#include<conio.h>
void main()
{
int n;
long  s=0,i;
clrscr();
printf("\n Enter n\n");
scanf("%d", &n);
printf("\n sum of series \n");
for(i=1;i<=n; ++i)
    {
    s=s+i*i*i;
    printf(" %ld ",i*i*i);
    if(i<n)
            printf("+");
    }
printf(" = %ld", s);
getch();
}
```

> **Output**
> Enter n
> 8
> sum of series
> 1+8+27+64+125+216+343+512 = 1296

Let us consider the series s= 1+4+27+256... up to 'n' terms, we can observe that there is no constant change in between the terms. Here the first term which is 1, anything to the power of 1 remains one. The second term is 4, which is 2 to the power of 2. The third term is 27, which is 3 to the power of 3 and so on i.e. each term in the series is given by a natural number to the power of itself. The following two programs find the sum of this series. First program just finds the sum and prints it without intermediate results. The second program prints the sum along with intermediate results also. For storing the value of sum we have used 'double' data type, in which we can store large range of values, with general of scientific format.

```
/* Program name: loop19.c */
/* Finding sum of 1+4+27+256.... n terms */
/* This program uses for loop */
#include<stdio.h>
#include<conio.h>
#include<math.h>
void main()
{
int n, i;
double  s=0;
clrscr();
printf("\n enter n\n");
scanf("%d", &n);
for(i=1;i<=n; ++i)
        s=s+pow(i, i);
printf("\n sum of series = %g \n", s);
getch();
}
```

Output
Enter n
9
sum of series = 4.05071e+08

Output
Enter n
4
sum of series = 288

```
/* Program name: loop20.c */
/* Finding sum of 1+4+27+256.... n terms */
/* This program uses for loop */
/* Prints intermediate result*/
#include<stdio.h>
#include<conio.h>
#include<math.h>
void main()
{
int n, i;
double  s=0;
clrscr();
printf("\n Enter n\n");
```

```
scanf("%d", &n);
for(i=1;i<=n; ++i)
    {
    s=s+pow(i, i);
    printf("\n sum of series up to %3d = %g ",i, s);
              /*printing the intermediate results.*/
    }
printf("\n\n sum of series for first %3d terms = %g ",s);
    /* prints the final result*/
getch();
}
```

Output
Enter n
4
sum of series up to 1 = 1
sum of series up to 2 = 5
sum of series up to 3 = 32
sum of series up to 4 = 288

sum of series for first 4 terms = 288

Now look at the series s= 1-2+3-4+5-... up to 'n' terms. The series is simple, but the terms are changing their sign alternatively. In such cases we have to adopt the program logic, which can change the sign alternatively. There are two different ways for changing the sign. First one we can take the power of '-1' i.e., pow(-1,i) where 'i' takes the values from 0,1,2,3,4.... For each odd value of 'i' the value will be negative (-1) and for even values of i the value remains 1. Multiplying the term by 1 there is no change and multiplying by –1 the sign of the term changes. The following program, will not display intermediate results.

```
/* Program name: loop21.c */
/* Finding sum of 1-2+3-4+5-.... n terms  */
/* This program uses for loop */
#include<stdio.h>
#include<conio.h>
#include<math.h>
void main()
{
int n, i;
int  s=0;
clrscr();
printf("\n Enter n\n");
scanf("%d", &n);
```

```
for(i=1;i<=n; ++i)
     {
     s=s+ i*pow(-1,(i-1)); /* multiplying by 1 no change but
                            multiply by -1 one sign
                            change*/
     }
printf("\n sum of series up to %3d = %d ", n, s);
getch();
}
```

Output Enter n 5 sum of series up to 5 =3	Output Enter n 6 sum of series up to 6 = -3

The above program can be solved with different program logic for sign change. In this case we are taking a temporary term say 't' for which, we have assigned a value 1. When multiplying the term with 't' there is no change in the result. By putting the statement 't=-t;' the sign of the variable 't' keeps on changing alternatively. With this logic now we can solve the above program. In this program the header file 'math.h' is not necessary as the 'pow()' function that is used in the above program is not used by this logic.

```
/* Program name: loop22.c */
/* Finding sum of 1-2+3-4+5-.... n terms    */
/* This program uses for loop */
#include<stdio.h>
#include<conio.h>
void main()
{
int n, i, t=1;
int  s=0;
clrscr();
printf("\n Enter n\n");
scanf("%d", &n);

for(i=1;i<=n; ++i)
     {
     s=s+ i*t;  /* multiplying by 1 no change but multiply by
                                          -1 one sign changes*/
     t=-t;        /* sign of t value changes alternately*/
     }
printf("\n sum of series up to %3d = %d ", n, s);
getch();
}
```

Output
Enter n
5
sum of series up to 5 =3

Output
Enter n
6
sum of series up to 6 = -3

The following is an example of similar type of program that we have discussed above. The terms are different in this series.

```
/* Program name: loop23.c */
/* Finding sum of 1/2-2/3+3/4-4/5+5/6-.... n terms  */
/* This program uses for loop */
#include<stdio.h>
#include<conio.h>
#include<math.h>
void main()
{
int n, i, t=1;
float  s=0;
clrscr();
printf("\n Enter n\n");
scanf("%d", &n);
for(i=1;i<=n; ++i)
      {
      s=s+i/(i+1.0)*t;  /* multiplying by 1 no change but
                           multiply by -1 one sign
                           changes*/
      t=-t;/* changes sign alternatively*/
      }
printf("\n sum of series up to %3d = %.4f ", n, s);
getch();
}
```

Output
Enter n
5
sum of series up to 5 = 0.6167

Output
Enter n
6
sum of series up to 6 = -0.2405

In the following program that calculates factorial of a non-negative integer, we are taking f=1, (1 is multiplication constant) as the initial value. The type of the variable 'f' which, is used to store the result must be able to store the large value, so we have taken 'double' and printing without decimal places by putting 0.0lf in the format specifier. If we are taking type of 'f' as int, it is possible to store the factorial of up to 7 only. If it is of type unsigned int we can store up to factorial of 8, and

if it is of long type we can store up to factorial of 15. So it is necessary to take care of type of a variable whenever we are writing such programs.

```
/* Program name: loop24.c */
/* Finding factorial of a number*/
/* This program uses for loop */
#include<stdio.h>
#include<conio.h>
void main()
{
int n i;
double  f=1;
clrscr();
printf("\n enter n\n");
scanf("%d", &n);
for(i=1;i<=n; ++i)
      f=f*i; /* finds the factorial */
printf("\n factorial of  %3d = %.0lf ", n, f);
getch();
}
```

Output	Output
Enter n	Enter n
4	6
factorial of 4 = 24	factorial of 6 = 720

Now we make a little change in the above program to print the intermediate terms also. By printing the intermediate terms it becomes easy to understand the output.

```
/* Program name: loop25.c */
/* Finding factorial of a number */
/* This program uses for loop */
/* This program displays intermediate results */
#include<stdio.h>
#include<conio.h>
void main()
{
int n, i;
double  f=1;
clrscr();
printf("\n Enter n\n");
scanf("%d", &n);
printf("\n number                    factorial\n");
for(i=1;i<=n; ++i)
```

```
        {
        f=f*i;
        printf("%6d\t%30.0lf\n",i,f); /* for printing the number
                                        with its factorial. */
        }

    printf("\n factorial of  %3d = %.0lf ",n, f); /* for printing
        the final result */
    getch();
    }
```

```
Output
Enter n
6
number              factorial
     1              1
     2              2
     3              6
     4              24
     5              120
     6              720
  factorial of 6 = 720
```

In the following program we are considering a sequence that needs little difficult logic. The sequence in consideration is 'Fibonacci' sequence whose terms are given by 0, 1, 1, 2, 3, 5, 8, … . The first two terms i.e., 0 and 1 are given. The subsequent terms are given by adding previous two terms. By adding first two terms we can get 3rd term. Now by adding 2nd and 3rd term we can get 4th term and so on. While implementing such programs we have to think of when to add, which term to add and how to interchange the variable values, which are involved in the program implementation.

Here we are taking f0 for first term (0) and f1 for second term (1), the variable f2 is used for storing the sum of first two terms. After printing the first term, the value of f1 has to be shifted to f0(f0=f1) and the value of f2 will be shifted to f1(i.e. f1=f2), and finding the sum of these terms (f0 and f1) again and storing it in f2. This process continues for 'n' iterations and meanwhile each value of f0 will be printed in each iteration..

```
/* Program name: loop26.c */
/* Printing Fibonacci series for first n terms  */
/* This program uses for loop */
#include<stdio.h>
#include<conio.h>
void main()
{
int n, i;
```

```
        long f0=0,f1=1,f2;
        clrscr();
        printf("\n enter n\n");
        scanf("%d", &n);
        printf("\n Fibonacci series up to %d terms\n", n);
        for(i=1;i<=n; ++i)
             {
             printf("%10d",f0); /* printing the terms with considering
                                    10 digit number, which gives
                                    proper gap between each terms
                                    */
             f2=f0+f1; /* finding the next term */
             f0=f1; /* exchanging the terms to get next term of the
                                    sequence. */
             f1=f2;
             }
        getch();
        }
```

```
Output
Enter n
5
Fibonacci series up to 5 terms
     0     1     1     2     3
```

```
Output
Enter n
10
fibonacci series up to 10 terms
     0     1     1     2     3     5     8     13
     21    34
```

The following program finds the sum of first 'n' terms of Fibonacci series. It will not print the sequence, but prints only the sum of n Fibonacci terms.

```
/* Program name: loop27.c */
/* Sum of terms of Fibonacci series for first n terms */
/* This program uses for loop */
#include<stdio.h>
#include<conio.h>
void main()
{
```

```
int n, i;
long f0=0,f1=1,f2,s=0;
clrscr();
printf("\n enter n\n");
scanf("%d", &n);
for(i=1;i<=n; ++i)
    {
    s=s+f0;
    f2=f0+f1;
    f0=f1;
    f1=f2;
    }
printf("\n sum of first %d Fibonacci terms = %ld\n", n, s);
getch();
}
```

Output Enter n 5 sum of first 5 Fibonacci terms = 7	Output Enter n 12 sum of first 12 Fibonacci terms = 232

Here we made small change in the above program to print the intermediate results of the sum of series. The same Fibonacci series is considered again.

```
/* Program name: loop28.c */
/* Sum of terms of Fibonacci series for first n terms  */
/* This program uses for loop */
/* This program prints intermediate results also */
#include<stdio.h>
#include<conio.h>
void main()
{
int n, i;
long f0=0,f1=1,f2,s=0;
clrscr();
printf("\n enter n\n");
scanf("%d", &n);
printf("\n termsum up to that term\n");
for(i=1;i<=n; ++i)
    {
    s=s+f0;
    printf("\n%ld\t\t%ld",f0,s); /* for printing intermediate
                                  sums. */
    f2=f0+f1;
```

```
        f0=f1;
        f1=f2;
        }
printf("\n sum of first %d fibonacci terms = %ld\n", n, s);
getch();
}
```

Output	
Enter n	
8	
term	sum up to that term
0	0
1	1
1	2
2	4
3	7
5	12
8	20
13	33
sum of first 8 fibonacci terms = 33	

In the above programs for printing the fibonacci series, or finding the sum of terms of fibonacci series, we took the series from first term to n^{th} term. Now we are taking the program that prints fibonacci series from m^{th} term to n^{th} term. The following program implements this.

```
/* Program name: loop29.c */
/* Printing fibonacci series terms from m to n  */
/* This program uses for loop */
#include<stdio.h>
#include<conio.h>
void main()
{
int n, i, m;
long f0=0,f1=1,f2;
clrscr();
printf("\n Enter m, n\n");
scanf("%d%d", &m, &n);
printf("Fibonacci series terms from %d to %d are\n", m, n);
for(i=1;i<=n; ++i)
        {
        if(i>=m)
        printf("%10d",f0);
```

```
        f2=f0+f1;
        f0=f1;
        f1=f2;
        }
    getch();
    }
```

Output
Enter m, n
5 10
Fibonacci series terms from 5 to 10 are
3 5 8 13 21 34

Now we will consider the same program again in which, we are printing the terms of fibonacci series whose term values are in the range from m to n. The following program implements this.

```
/* Program name: loop30.c */
/* Printing fibonacci series terms whose values are in the
    range  m to n  */
/* This program uses for loop */
#include<stdio.h>
#include<conio.h>
void main()
{
int n, i, m;
long f0=0,f1=1,f2;
clrscr();
printf("\n Enter the range  m, n\n");
scanf("%d%d", &m, &n);
printf("\n Fibonacci  series terms whose values are in the
    range %d to %d are\n", m, n);
while(f0<=n)/* checking for the upper limit */
    {
    if((f0>=m)&&(f0<=n))  /* checking for upper and lower
                             limits for printing the terms*/
        printf("%10d",f0);
    f2=f0+f1;
    f0=f1;
    f1=f2;
    }
getch();
}
```

Output
Enter the range m, n
10 100
Fibonacci series terms whose values are in the range 10 to 100 are
13 21 34 55 89

Let us consider the following program which checks whether the given positive integer is prime or not. As we know prime number is one, which is not divisible by any other number but one and itself and must be greater than one(because 1 is neither prime nor complex). To check whether the number is prime or not, we can keep on dividing the given number from the numbers 2 to half of that number. In any case if the remainder after division becomes zero, the number is not prime, otherwise it is a prime number. For this we will introduce a flag whose value is set to some value. We can keep on dividing the number from 2 ,3,4,...n/2 and check for the remainder. When the remainder becomes zero the number is divisible and the flag can be changed to some other value, we can terminate the loop. After terminating the loop we print 'the number is prime' if the flag value is unchanged otherwise we print 'the number is not prime'.

In the following program we have taken t as the flag variable. The t is initialized to 0 before entering the loop. When the number gets divided the flag is changed to 1 inside the loop body. The flag value is checked after completing the loop.

```
/* Program name: loop31.c */
/* Check for given number is prime or not */
/* This program uses for loop */
#include<stdio.h>
#include<conio.h>
void main()
{
int n, i, t=0;/* t is used as flag, during process if any
    number divides n , then t changes to 1*/
clrscr();
printf("\n enter n\n");
scanf("%d", &n);
if(n<=1)
    printf("\n %d is not a prime number\n", n);
else
    {
    for(i=2;i<=n/2;++i)
    {
    if(n%i==0)
    t=1;
    }
if(t==0)
printf("\n %d is prime number ",n);
else
printf("\n %d is not a prime number", n);
}
getch();
}
```

Output	Output
Enter n	Enter n
5	68
5 is prime number	68 is not prime number

Now we will take a look at the following program that prints all perfect squares (the number without fractional square root). For solving such a simple program we have to use the concept of 'int' and 'float' conversion in which the fractional number with all fractional digits as 0's is equivalent to its integer part.

```
/* Program name: loop32.c */
/* Printing all perfect squares between 1 to n */
/* This program uses for loop */
#include<stdio.h>
#include<conio.h>
#include<math.h>
void main()
{
int n, i, m;
float p;
clrscr();
printf("\n enter n\n");
scanf("%d", &n);
printf("\n perfect squares are:\n");
for(i=1;i<=n; ++i)
     {
     m=sqrt(i); /* takes only integer part of square root*/
     p=sqrt(i); /* takes fractional part also*/
     if(m==p) /* when there is no fractional part the number
                                        is perfect square*/
     printf("\n %8d",i);
     }
getch();
}
```

Output
Enter n
10
perfect squares are
1
4
9

Output
Enter n
50
perfect squares are
1
4
9
16
25
36
49

3.3 while loop

Syntax;

```
Initial-expression;
while(conditional-expression)
{
Statement(s);
Update-expression;
}
```

In the for loop we have discussed earlier we know in advance how many iterations of the body of the loop we have to perform. But in some cases we do not have any idea about how many iterations we have to perform. In that case we use while loop. All programs that uses for loop can be solved by while loop also.

3.4 do-while loop

Syntax

```
Initial-expression;
do
{
Statement(s);
Update-expression;
} while (conditional-expression);
```

It is similar to while loop, but in this the body of the loop executes first and then the condition will be checked. The do-while loop executes at least one time.

3.5 Nested Loops

We can nest one loop within another to solve more complex problems. In such cases the inner loop executes completely for each change in outer loop. Ex:

```
for (int i =1; i<10; i+=2)
        for (int j=5; j>=3; ++j)
                printf("%d\t", j);
```

The output will be

5 4 3 5 4 3 ... 5 4 3

9 times

The same can be written using while loop as follows.

```
int i, j;
i=1;
while(i<10)
        {
                j=5;
                while(j>=3)
                        {
                        printf("%d\t", j);
                        j--;
                        }

                i++;
        }
```

With the help of do...while looping statement, the above code can be written as

```
int i, j;
i=1;
```

```
do
    {
        j=5;
        do
        {
            printf("%d\t",j);
                j--;
        }while(j>=3);
    i++;
    }while(i<10);
```

For each change in outer loop all possible changes takes place in inner loop. We can nest the loops to any extent but nesting to more depth will lead to more number of executions. Nested loops can be for loop within while loop, while loop within for loop, do...while within for or while loop and vice versa. When we are nesting the loops we have to take care of compound statements i.e. we need to clearly mark the body of each of the nested loops.

3.6 The continue statement

This statement is used to skip certain statements within the body of loop. The syntax is

```
continue;
```

Ex: Consider printing all the number between 1 & n that are divisible by five.

```
for(i=1; i<=n; ++i)
    {
    if(i%5!=0)
    continue;
    printf("%d\n", i);
    }
```

Where i & n are integers.

All the above programs can easily be solved with the help of while or do...while looping statements. When we know exactly how many times we have to execute the loop body, it is better to use for loop, otherwise use of while or do...while loop is advisable.

Now we can look at some of the programs, which can be easily solved by while statement. Consider the program for finding number of digits in a given integer number. Here we do not know how many digits are there, so we don't know how many times loop will repeat, but we know the initial and the target value of the loop counter.

```
/* Program name: loop33.c */
/*Program to count the number of digits in a given integer*/
/* This program uses while () loop*/
#include<stdio.h>
#include<conio.h>
void main()
{
```

```
long n;
int s=0;
clrscr();
printf("\n Enter a number\n");
scanf("%ld", &n);
while(n!=0)
     {
     s++;
     n=n/10; /* the number looses its last digit every time*/
     }
printf("\n number of digits = %d", s);
getch();
}
```

Output	Output
Enter a number	Enter a number
12	1223
number of digits = 2	number of digits = 4

By making a small change in the above program we find the sum of all digits of the given number. Here we need to separate the last digit by % operator and add it to the variable used for finding the sum then remove the last digit by using / operator i.e. dividing by 10. Our number system is decimal number system, so division by 10 removes the last digit on integers.

```
/* Program name: loop34.c */
/* Program to find the sum of digits in a given integer*/
/* this program uses while() loop*/
#include<stdio.h>
#include<conio.h>
void main()
{
long n;
int s=0;
clrscr();
printf("\n Enter a number\n");
scanf("%ld", &n);
while(n!=0)
{
        s=s+n%10;/* n%10 gives last digit of the number n */
        n=n/10; /* the number looses its last digit every time*/
}
printf("\n sum of digits = %d", s);
getch();
}
```

Output
Enter a number
1237
sum of digits = 13

Output
Enter a number
9394
sum of digits = 25

Again, here the change we make is small but the effect is big. The formula s=s*10+n%10;(in place of s=s+n%10 in the above program) inside the loop, gives the number in reverse order. As we are getting the last digit by %10, multiplying it by 10 changes the digit's position to its higher digit position. The following program reverses the given number.

```
/* Program name: loop35.c */
/* Program to find the reverse of the given integer*/
/* This program uses while () loop*/
#include<stdio.h>
#include<conio.h>
void main()
{
long n;
long s=0;
clrscr();
printf("\n Enter a number\n");
scanf("%ld", &n);
while(n!=0)
{
        s=s*10+n%10;/*n%10 gives last digit of the number n */
        n=n/10; /* the number looses its last digit every time*/
}
printf("\n reversed number = %ld", s);
getch();
}
```

Output
Enter a number
1203
reversed number = 3021

Output
Enter a number
122300
reversed number = 3221

When a number is reversed and it is equivalent to the original number after reversing then that number is said to be 'palindrome'. In the above program for reversing the number, we will get the reversed number(in variable s) when the original number (n) becomes zero, so it is necessary to keep the original value of given number in some other variable and at the end of the loop we can compare it with the reversed number. The following program checks the number for palindrome.

```
/* Program name: loop36.c */
/* Program to check for number palindrome*/
/* This program uses while () loop*/
#include<stdio.h>
#include<conio.h>
void main()
{
long n, m, s=0;
clrscr();
printf("\n Enter a number\n");
scanf("%ld", &n);
m=n; /* m contains the value of n */
while(n!=0)
{
        s=s*10+n%10;/*n%10 gives last digit of the number n */
        n=n/10;
}/* Now s contains reversed number and m contains original
        number*/
if(m==s)
        printf("\n given number is palindrome");
else
        printf("\n given number is not palindrome");
getch();
}
```

Output **Enter a number** **12021** **given number is palindrome**	**Output** **Enter a number** **1223** **given number is not palindrome**

All the above four programs which are similar in logic can be solved by one program, which is shown below.

```
/* Program name: loop37.c */
/* Program to find sum of digits, number of digits, reversing
        the number and check for number palindrome*/
/* This program uses while () loop*/
#include<stdio.h>
#include<conio.h>
void main()
{
long n, m, s=0;
int c=0, sd=0;/* c for count of digits, sd for sum of digits*/
clrscr();
```

```
printf("\n Enter a number\n");
scanf("%ld", &n);
m=n; /* m contains the value of n */
while(n!=0)
{
      s=s*10+n%10;
      c++;
      sd=sd+n%10;
      n=n/10;
}
printf("\n number of digits = %d", c);
printf("\n sum of digits = %d", sd);
printf("\n reversed number = %ld", s);
/* Now s contains reversed number and m contains original
      number*/
if(m==s)
printf("\n given number is palindrome");
else
printf("\n given number is not palindrome");
getch();
}
```

Output	Output
Enter a number	Enter a number
12021	1223
number of digits = 5	number of digits = 4
sum of digits = 6	sum of digits = 8
reversed number = 12021	reversed number = 3221
given number is palindrome	given number is not palindrome

After dealing with a single integral number in the above five programs, we will now consider the program that finds GCD of two integers. For finding the greatest common divisor (GCD), we can find all the factors of 1st and 2nd numbers, and then list all common factors and we take the common factor that is greatest among all common factors. For example consider the GCD of 24 & 18. The factors are given as:

24 = 1,2,3,4,6,8,12,24
18 = 1,2,3,6,9,18

Among all these factors the common factors are 1,2,3 & 6. The highest common factor is 6 so the GCD is 6. This method takes lot of time, calculations and memory for storing all factors. The same can be solved by dividing one number (say n) by other number (say m) getting the remainder. Now we can change the value of first number (n) with value of second number (m) and the value of second number by remainder. This process can be continued until the second number becomes zero. When second number becomes zero the other number contains GCD. This logic is implemented in the following program, which uses while loop.

```
/* Program name: loop38.c */
/* Program to find GCD of two numbers*/
/* This program uses while () loop*/
#include<stdio.h>
#include<conio.h>
void main()
{
long n, m, r; /* n ,m  for two numbers, r for remainder*/
clrscr();
printf("\n Enter two numbers\n");
scanf("%ld%ld", &n, &m);
while(n!=0)
{
      r=m%n;
      m=n;/* changing the numbers */
      n=r;
}
/* when n=0 the value of m will be GCD*/
printf("\n GCD = %ld", m);
getch();
}
```

Output	Output
Enter two numbers	Enter two numbers
20	12
24	29
GCD = 4	GCD = 1

In the following program we are finding the Least Common Multiplier (LCM) of two integer quantities. The LCM of two numbers m and n is given by:

LCM (n, m)=n*m/GCD (n, m)

When we are finding the GCD the original values of m and n changes (one becomes GCD and other becomes 0). To keep the original values the other two variables are used in the following program. This program also prints GCD.

```
/* Program name: loop39.c */
/* Program to find GCD & LCM of two numbers*/
/* This program uses while () loop*/
#include<stdio.h>
#include<conio.h>
void main()
{
long n, m, r, l, p, q; /* n ,m  for two numbers, r for
      remainder*/
clrscr();
```

```
printf("\n Enter two numbers\n");
scanf("%ld%ld", &n, &m);
p=n;
q=m;/*p & q contains original values of n & m */
while(n!=0)
{
      r=m%n;
      m=n;/* changing the numbers */
      n=r;
}
/* When n=0 the value of m will be GCD*/
printf("\n GCD of %ld & %ld = %ld", p, q, m);
l= p*q/m; /* calculates LCM */
printf("\n LCM of %ld & %ld = %ld", p, q, l);
getch();
}
```

Output	Output
Enter two numbers	Enter two numbers
30 45	20 18
GCD of 30 & 45 =15	GCD of 20 & 18 =2
LCM of 30 & 45 = 90	LCM of 20 & 18 = 180

The following program is the extension of the program for printing multiplication table for a given number(explained earlier in this chapter). Here we are displaying the multiplication table for all the numbers from 1 to n. We need nested loops in which the outer loop is for passing the numbers from 1 to n, one by one. The inner loop repeats for 10 times ranging from 1 to 10. The output will be displayed in such a way that the table for one number should fit in one line.

```
/* Program name: loop40.c */
/* Program to print multiplication table from 1 to n */
/* This program uses nested loop */
#include<stdio.h>
#include<conio.h>
void main()
{
int i, j, n;
clrscr();
printf("Enter n\n");
scanf("%d", &n);
for(i=1;i<=n; ++i)
{
      for(j=1;j<=10;++j)
            printf("%7d",i*j);
```

```
        printf("\n");
        }
getch();
}
```

Output

Enter n

6

1	2	3	4	5	6	7	8	9	10
2	4	6	8	10	12	14	16	18	20
3	6	9	12	15	18	21	24	27	30
4	8	12	16	20	24	28	32	36	40
5	10	15	20	25	30	35	40	45	50
6	12	18	24	30	36	42	48	54	60

We discussed about checking whether a number is prime or not. Now we are extending the same program for printing all the primes between m and n. We use the nested loops in which the inner loop for checking the prime number characteristic and outer loop for sending one number at a time to the inner loop. The flag is initialized inside the outer loop as it applies for inner loop. The flag value changed or not will be checked before closing the outer loop. The flag may change in the inner loop only. The proper use of break statement avoids number of unwanted calculations. If we are not using break statement then also program works correctly, but the number of unnecessary computations will increase.

```
/* Program name: loop41.c */
/* Program to print all primes between m and n */
/* This program uses nested for loop*/
#include<stdio.h>
#include<conio.h>
void main()
{
int n, m, i, j, t;
clrscr();
printf("\n Enter lower and upper limits\n");
scanf("%d%d", &m, &n);
printf("\n prime numbers between %d & %d are \n", m, n);
for(i=m; i<=n; ++i) /* the outer loop which passes all the
        numbers from m to n */
{ /* outer loop starts */
        t=0; /* the flag is set to zero */
        for(j=2;j<=i/2;++j) /* the inner loop to check each i is
                                        prime or not */
        if(i%j==0)
        {
```

```
                    t=1; /* when j divides i successfully flag changes
                                                   its value */
                    break; /* when divides no need to check further by
                                                   break    inner    loop
                                                   terminates*/
                }
                if((t==0)&&(i>1)) /* when t is not changed and number is
                                             greater than one then that
                                             number will be prime, and it
                                             will be printed on the screen
                                             */
                    printf("%10d",i);
                } /* Outer loop closes*/
            getch();
            }
```

Output
Enter lower and upper limits
10 25
prime numbers between 10 and 25 are
11 13 17 19 23

Output
Enter lower and upper limits
30 40
prime numbers between 30 and 40 are
31 37

The following three programs use little complex algorithms. In all these programs we need to calculate factorial. First one is simple which needs calculation of x^i along with factorial of i, where i changes from 0 to n. Here we have to consider double data type, as the values are fractional and large.

```
/* Program name: loop42.c */
/* Program to find e^x     e^x=1+x+x^2/2! +... */
/* This program uses nested for loop*/
#include<stdio.h>
#include<conio.h>
#include<math.h>
void main()
{
int n, i, j;
float x;
double ex=0, f;
clrscr();
printf("\n Enter upper limit n & value of x\n");
scanf("%d%f", &n, &x);
for(i=0;i<=n; ++i) /* the outer loop which passes all the
        numbers from 0 to n */
    { /* outer loop starts */
        f=1; /* the factorial is set to 1 */
```

```
        for(j=2;j<=i;  ++j)  /*  the  inner  loop  to  calculate
                                 factorial of i */
             f=f*j;
        ex=ex + pow(x, i)/f;
     } /* Outer loop closes*/
  printf("\n exp(%.4f)=%g", x, ex);
  getch();
  }
```

Output
Enter the upper limit n and value of x
10 3
exp(3.000) = 20.0797

Output
Enter the upper limit n and value of x
20 3
exp(3.000) = 20.0855

In the next two programs along with the calculation of factorial and x^i the terms change their sign alternatively. We need to think a while before writing such programs. We have to design the logic, write the flowchart or algorithm. First test the designed logic by taking some sample value for n and x. The angle must be taken in radians or can be converted to radians before using the value of x in the loop.

```
/* Program name: loop43.c */
/* Program to find sin (x) */
/* This program uses nested for loop*/
#include<stdio.h>
#include<conio.h>
#include<math.h>
void main()
{
int n, i, j, t=1;
float x, s=0;
double f;
clrscr();
printf("\n Enter upper limit n & value of x in degree\n");
scanf("%d%f", &n, &x);
x=x*3.142/180; /* converting degree to radians */
for(i=1;i<=n; i=i+2)
     {
     f=1; /* the factorial is set to 1 */
     for(j=2;j<=i; ++j)
          f=f*j;
     s=s+ pow(x, i)*t/f;
     t=-t; /* sign changes alternatively */
     } /* Outer loop closes*/
printf("\n  sin(%.4f)=%g",  x*180/3.142,s);/*print  angle  in
     degree*/
```

```
getch();
}
```

Output
Enter the upper limit n and value of x in degree
20 30
sin(30.0000) = 0.500059

Output
Enter the upper limit n and value of x in degree
30 60
sin(60.0000) = 0.866093

Just some small change in the initialization of outer loop counter value of the above program we get cos(x) series.

```
/* Program name: loop44.c */
/* Program to find cos (x) */
/* This program uses nested for loop*/
#include<stdio.h>
#include<conio.h>
#include<math.h>
void main()
{
int n, i, j, t=1;
float x, s=0;
double f;
clrscr();
printf("\n Enter upper limit n & value of x in degree\n");
scanf("%d%f", &n, &x);
x=x*3.142/180; /* converting degree to radians */
for(i=0;i<=n; i=i+2)
{ /* outer loop starts */
      f=1; /* the factorial is set to 1 */
      for(j=2;j<=i;  ++j)  /*  the  inner  loop  to  calculate
                                factorial of i */
            f=f*j;
      s=s + pow(x, i)*t/f;
      t=-t; /* sign changes alternatively */
} /* Outer loop closes*/
printf("\n cos(%.4f)=%g", x*180/3.142,s);/* to print the angle
      in degree*/
getch();
}
```

```
Output
Enter the upper limit n and value of x in degree
45 45
cos(45.0000) = 0.707035
```

```
Output
Enter the upper limit n and value of x in degree
30 30
cos(30.0000) = 0.865991
```

The series for the value of ? (can be given as (=v(6/1! + 6/2! +6/3! + ...). Like sin(), cos() and exp() it is also an infinite series. By taking some value for n we can calculate approximately the value of ?. The following program finds the approximate value.

```
/* Program name: loop45.c */
/* Program to find pie value   */
/* This program uses nested for loop*/
#include<stdio.h>
#include<conio.h>
#include<math.h>
void main()
{
float n, i;
float s=0;
clrscr();
printf("\n Enter upper limit n \n");
scanf("%f", &n);
for(i=1;i<=n; ++i)
      s=s+6/(i*i);
s=sqrt(s);
printf("\n value of pie = %f", s);
getch();
}
```

```
Output
Enter the upper limit n
30
value of pie = 3.110129
```

```
Output
Enter the upper limit n
50
value of pie = 3.122627
```

The result in the output of the above program is not maintaining accuracy properly. Taking required digits of precision into consideration can solve the problem. For this we need to use while loop instead of for loop, as we don't know after how many steps we will reach the required precision. Look at the following program, which calculates ? value correct to the required precision.

```
/* Program name: loop46.c */
/* Find pi value */
#include<stdio.h>
#include<conio.h>
#include<math.h>
void main()
{
float i, n, s=0,j,f,x;
clrscr();
printf("\n enter accuracy : ");
scanf("%f", &x);
n=22.0/7;
i=1;
f=n;
while(f>x)
{
      f=(6.0/(i*i));
      s=s+f;
      i++;
}
s=sqrt(s);
printf("actual value = %.3f\n calculated value = %.3f\n", n,
      s);
getch();
}
```

Output
Enter accuracy
0.0001
actual value of pie = 3.142 calculated value of pie 3.142

Now will write a program for finding all perfect numbers from 1 to n. A perfect number is one whose sum of all factors other than that number is equal to that number itself. (Example: 6 factors are 1,2,3 and 1+2+3=6). Here we need to use nested loops. The outer loop passes the values from 1 to n. The inner loop is used to find the sum of factors. After finding the sum of factors, in the outer loop body we are comparing that sum with outer loop counter value and when both are same we are printing the number, which is a perfect number.

```
/* Program name: loop47.c */
/* Program to print all perfect numbers between 1 to n  */
/* Whose sum of factors other than that number is equal to
      number itself*/
/* This program uses nested loop*/
#include<stdio.h>
```

```
#include<conio.h>
void main()
{
int n, i, j, s;
clrscr();
printf("\n Enter upper limit n \n");
scanf("%d", &n);
printf("\n perfect numbers between 1 to %d are\n", n);
for(i=1;i<=n; ++i)
    {
    s=0;
    for(j=1;j<=i/2;++j)
        if(i%j==0)
            s=s+j;
        if(s==i)
            printf("%d\n", i);
    }
getch();
}
```

Output
Enter upper limit n
10000
perfect numbers between 1 to 10000 are
6
28
496
8128

An Armstrong number is one whose sum of cubes of the digits is equal to that number itself. Example 1 is an Armstrong number. The number 153 is an Armstrong number ($153=1^3+5^3+3^3$). The following program prints such all Armstrong numbers from 1 to 'n'. For this we need nested loops, in which, outer loop gives each of the numbers between 1 to 'n' and inner while() loop is used to find the sum of cubes of the digits of each number. After completing the inner loop the sum will be checked with outer loop counter value, when matches we will get Armstrong number.

```
/* Program name: loop48.c */
/* Prints all Armstrong numbers between 1 to n  */
/* Whose sum of cubes of the digits is equal to number itself*/
/* This program uses nested loop*/
#include<stdio.h>
#include<conio.h>
#include<math.h>
void main()
{
```

```
int n, i, j, s;
clrscr();
printf("\n Enter upper limit n \n");
scanf("%d", &n);
printf("\n Armstrong numbers between 1 and %d are\n", n);
for(i=1;i<=n; ++i)
    {
    s=0;
    j=i;
    while(j!=0)
        {
        s=s+pow(j%10,3);
        j=j/10;
        }
    if(s==i)
    printf("%d\n", i);
    }
getch();
}
```

Output
Enter the upper limit n
1000
Armstrong numbers between 1 and 1000 are
1
153
370
371
407

To make the result more understandable we made change in the above program so as to print each cubes. Look at the following program.

```
/* Program name: loop49.c */
/* Prints all Armstrong numbers between 1 and n  */
/* It prints the cubes of each digit also for each Armstrong
    numbers*/
#include<stdio.h>
#include<conio.h>
#include<math.h>
void main()
{
int n, i, j, s;
clrscr();
printf("\n Enter upper limit n \n");
```

```
scanf("%d", &n);
printf("\n Armstrong numbers between 1 to %d are\n", n);
for(i=1;i<=n; ++i)
        {
        s=0;
        j=i;
        while(j!=0)
                {
                s=s + pow(j%10,3);
                j=j/10;
                }
        if(s==i)
                {
                /* For printing the cubes of digits, in reverse
                order from last digit to first digit*/
                j=i;
                while(j!=0)
                {
                        printf("%8.0f",pow(j%10,3));
                        j=j/10;
                }
                printf("       =%8d\n",i);
                }

        }
 getch();
 }
```

Output				
Enter the upper limit n				
10000				
Armstrong numbers between 1 to 10000 are				
1	=	1		
27	125	1	=	153
0	343	27	=	370
1	343	27	=	371
343	0	64	=	407

Consider the following program which prints all the numbers from 1 to 'n' that are divisible by 'm' and 'p'. The implementation of this program involves division of the number by 'm' and 'p' and checking whether the remainder is zero or not. Whenever the remainder is zero in both the cases the number will be printed. Just simple loop with logical condition is enough for solving this program.

```
/* Program name: loop50.c */
/* Program to print the numbers from 1 to n which are divisible
      by m & p */
```

```
/* This program uses loop*/
#include<stdio.h>
#include<conio.h>
void main()
{
int n, m, p, i;
clrscr();
printf("\n enter the numbers n m & p \n");
scanf("%d%d%d", &n, &m, &p);
for(i=1;i<=n; ++i)
        if((i%m==0)&&(i%p==0)) /* when I is divisible by both m
                                  and p condition gives true*/
              printf("%8d",i);
getch();
}
```

Output
Enter the numbers n m & p
100 3 5
15 30 45 60 75 90

Output
Enter the numbers n m & p
300 18 30
90 180 ·270

When the temperature is given in Fahrenheit, it will be converted to Celsius with the formula C=(f-32)5/9.

The following program prints the table of values for Fahrenheit and Celsius.

```
/* Program name: loop51.c */
/* Program to print Fahrenheit Celsius table */
#include<stdio.h>
#include<conio.h>
void main()
{
float c;
int i,f;
clrscr();
printf("\n Sl.No.  Fahrenheit        Celsius\n");
for(f=0,i=1;f<=100;f=f+10,i++)
{
c=(f-32)*5.0/9;
printf("\n%3d%12d%15.3f",i,f,c);
}
getch();
}
```

Output

Sl.No.	Fahrenhit	Celsius
1	0	-17.778
2	10	-12.222
3	20	-6.667
4	30	-1.111
5	40	4.444
6	50	10.000
7	60	15.556
8	70	21.111
9	80	26.667
10	90	32.222
11	100	37.778

The following program illustrates the use of type casting. It finds the sum of the series 1/I for I with values 1 to n. here we need to do proper type casting otherwise it leads to wrong results.

```
/* Program name: loop52.c */
/* Program to illustrate type casting summation of 1/i for i=1
    to n */
#include<stdio.h>
#include<conio.h>
void main()
{
float s=0;
int i,n;
clrscr();
printf(" enter n\n");
scanf("%d",&n);
for(i=1;i<=n;i++)
s=s+1/(float)i;/* type casting i becomes integer only
during operation */
printf("\nsum of series =%.3f",s);
getch();
}
```

Output
enter n
100

sum of series =5.187

The goto statement we already discussed in chapter 2. The following program illustrates how goto statement is used with for statement.

```
/* Program name: loop53.c */
/* Program to illustrate goto statement with for loop */
#include<stdio.h>
#include<conio.h>
void main()
{
int i,n;
clrscr();
printf(" enter n\n");
scanf("%d",&n);
for(i=1;i<=n;++i)
{
        if(i==(n/2))
        goto label;
        printf("%8d",i);
}
label:
getch();
}
```

Output
enter n
20

```
       1  2  3  4  5  6  7  8  9
```

The great mathematician Pythagoras gave a theorem on right angled triangle. The theorem tells that when square of one side of a triangle is equal to sum of squares of other two sides then it is a right-angled triangle. The following program checks and prints such a triplet, which comes first.

```
/* Program name: loop54.c */
/* Program to print first possible Pythagorean triplet */
/* This program uses nested loop*/
#include<stdio.h>
#include<conio.h>
#include<math.h>
void main()
{
int i, j, k, l, m, p, t=0;
clrscr();
printf("\n Combinations of three sides are\n");
i=1;
while(t==0)
```

```
{
        for(j=1;j<=i; ++j)
                for(k=1;k<=j; ++k)
                        if((i*i==(j*j+k*k))||(j*j==(i*i+k*k))||(k*k==(i*i+j*j)))
                        {
                        t=1;
                        printf("\n %5d  %5d   %5d",i,j,k);
                        }
        i++;
}
getch();
}
```

```
Output
Combinations of three sides are
5        4        3
```

The following program is the modification of the above program. In a given range there may be number of solutions for the above problem. The following program prints all such combinations of Pythagoras triplets, which forms a right-angled triangle.

```
/* Program name: loop55.c */
/* Program to print all possible Pythagorean triplets from 1
   to n */
/* This program uses nested loop*/
/* It prints all possible combinations of three sides */
#include<stdio.h>
#include<conio.h>
#include<math.h>
void main()
{
int n, i, j, k, l, m, p;
clrscr();
printf("\n Enter upper limit n \n");
scanf("%d", &n);
printf("\n Combinations of three sides are\n", n);
for(i=1;i<=n; ++i)
{
        for(j=1;j<=n; ++j)
                for(k=1;k<=n; ++k)
                        if((i*i==(j*j+k*k))||(j*j==(i*i+k*k))||(k*k
                            ==(i*i+j*j)))
                            printf("\n %5d  %5d   %5d",i,j,k);
}
```

```
getch();
}
```

Output		
Enter upper limit n		
10		
Combinations of three sides are		
3	4	5
3	5	4
4	3	5
4	5	3
5	3	4
5	4	3
6	8	10
6	10	8
8	6	10
8	10	6
10	6	8
10	8	6

The above program prints all possible combinations of 3 sides for right-angled triangle. By this same output repeats six times (for the combination 3,4,5 it will prints 3,4,5 and 3,5,4 and 4,3,5 and 4,5,3 and 5,3,4 and 5,4,3). The following program avoids this and gives just one solution for one combination of a triplet. For achieving this we have keep track of loop counter values. Let the outer loop start at 1 and goes up to 'n', but inner loops should go up to the loop counter value of its immediate outer loop, so that the duplicates will be avoided.

```
/* Program name: loop56.c */
/* It will not print all possible combinations,
prints just one combination */
#include<stdio.h>
#include<conio.h>
#include<math.h>
void main()
{
int n, i, j, k, l, m, p;
clrscr();
printf("\n Enter upper limit n \n");
scanf("%d", &n);
printf("\n Combinations of three sides are\n", n);
for(i=1;i<=n; ++i)
{
        for(j=1;j<=i; ++j)
        for(k=1;k<=j; ++k)
```

```
                if(i*i==(j*j+k*k))
                        printf("\n %5d  %5d   %5d",i,j,k);
}
getch();
}
```

Output		
Enter upper limit n		
20		
Combinations of three sides are		
5	4	3
10	8	6
13	12	5
15	12	9
17	15	8
20	16	12

The following program prints the ASCII character set for all 256 ASCII characters. It passes the values from 0 to 255 to the loop counter which are printed as characters by the use of suitable format specifier in the printf() statement. Certain ASCII characters are non-printable characters.

```
/* Program name: loop57.c */
/* Program for printing ASCII character set */
#include<stdio.h>
#include<conio.h>
void main()
{
int i;
clrscr();
printf(" ASCII character set\n");
for(i=0;i<=255;++i)
{
printf("%c   ",i);
}
getch();
}
```

The following is the little modification of previous program. It prints all the ASCII characters along with their code screen by screen.

```
/* Program name: loop58.c */
/* Program for printing ASCII character set with code screen
     by screen */
#include<stdio.h>
```

```
#include<conio.h>
void main()
{
int i;
clrscr();
printf(" ASCII character set\n");
for(i=0;i<=255;)
{
printf("\n\t%3d  %c",i,i);
i++;
if(i%20==0)
{printf("\n press any key ...");
getch();
clrscr();
}
}
getch();
}
```

Here let us consider a simple program to print the given integer in words (123 = one two three). We know by dividing a decimal number by 10 we will loose last digit of the number and the remainder will be the last digit. By using this concept we write the program for this problem as follows.

```
/* Program name: loop59.c */
/* Program to print the given number in words */
/* This program uses loop*/
/* Prints the result in the reverse order */
#include<stdio.h>
#include<conio.h>
void main()
{
long n;
clrscr();
printf("\n enter a number \n");
scanf("%ld", &n);
while(n!=0)
{
switch(n%10)
{
        case 0: printf(" zero"); break;
        case 1: printf(" one"); break;
        case 2: printf(" two"); break;
        case 3: printf(" three"); break;
        case 4: printf(" four"); break;
        case 5: printf(" five"); break;
```

```
        case 6: printf(" six"); break;
        case 7: printf(" seven"); break;
        case 8: printf(" eight"); break;
        case 9: printf(" nine");
    }
    n=n/10;
    }
    getch();
    }
```

Output	Output
Enter a number	Enter a number
2193	1020
three nine one two	zero two zero one

The main problem in the solution of above problem is 'the result is displayed in reverse order'. The reason for this is when we divide the number by 10 we will get the last digit as remainder, and that digit we are printing in words first, and then we are going for second last digit and so on. To avoid this we need to print the first digit of the number in words first, and then second digit and so on. Reversing the number and then applying the above procedure can do this. In the program that follows we are adapting this logic.

```
/* Program name: loop60.c */
/* Program to print the given number in words */
/* This program uses loop*/
/* Prints the result without considering the last zeroes */
#include<stdio.h>
#include<conio.h>
void main()
{
long n, m=0;
clrscr();
printf("\n Enter a number \n");
scanf("%ld", &n);

while(n!=0)
{
      m=m*10+n%10;
      n=n/10;
}
n=m;
while(n!=0)
{
switch(n%10)
{
```

```
        case 0: printf(" zero"); break;
        case 1: printf(" one"); break;
        case 2: printf(" two"); break;
        case 3: printf(" three"); break;
        case 4: printf(" four"); break;
        case 5: printf(" five"); break;
        case 6: printf(" six"); break;
        case 7: printf(" seven"); break;
        case 8: printf(" eight"); break;
        case 9: printf(" nine");
    }
    n=n/10;
    }
    getch();
    }
```

Output	**Output**
Enter a number	**Enter a number**
1220	**10002**
one two two	**one zero zero zero two**

The output of the above program may be correct or may not be as shown above. When a number contains zeros at the end, in the reversed number that zeros will not reflect (Eg. 1200 becomes 21). To solve this problem we have to store the entered number in a variable, then reverse the given number and print in words. Finally we have to print 'zero' number of times equal to number of zeros at the end of original number. This gives correct answer to the given problem, which is implemented in the following program.

```
/* Program name: loop61.c */
/* Program to print the given number in words */
/* This program uses loop*/
/* Prints the result clearly */
#include<stdio.h>
#include<conio.h>
void main()
{
long n, m=0,p;
clrscr();
printf("\n Enter a number \n");
scanf("%ld", &n);
p=n;
while(n!=0)
     {
     m=m*10+n%10;
```

```
        n=n/10;
        }
n=m;/* now n is reversed number */
while(n!=0)
{
switch(n%10)
{
        case 0: printf(" zero"); break;
        case 1: printf(" one"); break;
        case 2: printf(" two"); break;
        case 3: printf(" three"); break;
        case 4: printf(" four"); break;
        case 5: printf(" five"); break;
        case 6: printf(" six"); break;
        case 7: printf(" seven"); break;
        case 8: printf(" eight"); break;
        case 9: printf(" nine");
}
n=n/10;
}
while(p%10==0)
{
        printf(" zero");
        p=p/10;
}
getch();
}
```

Output Enter a number 12330 one two three three zero	Output Enter a number 1020 one zero two zero

The numbers 0's and 1's can be displayed as a triangle as given below.

```
1
0    1
0    1    0
1    0    1    0
```

The following program prints this triangle of alternate 0's and 1's for specified number of rows.

```
/* Program name: loop62.c */
/* Program for triangle of numbers */
#include<stdio.h>
#include<conio.h>
```

```
void main()
{
int n,i,j,t;
clrscr();
printf(" enter n\n");
scanf("%d",&n);
t=1;
for(i=1;i<=n;++i)
{
for(j=1;j<=i;++j)
{
printf("%3d",t);
if(t==0)
t=1;
else
t=0;
}
printf("\n");
}
getch();
}
```

Output
enter n
10

```
1
0 1
0 1 0
1 0 1 0
1 0 1 0 1
0 1 0 1 0 1
0 1 0 1 0 1 0
1 0 1 0 1 0 1 0
1 0 1 0 1 0 1 0 1
0 1 0 1 0 1 0 1 0 1
```

The following is the changed version of above triangle. It prints the triangle of numbers from both the sides of the screen.

```
/* Program name: loop63.c */
/* Program for triangle of numbers */
#include<stdio.h>
#include<conio.h>

void main()
{
int n,i,j,t;
clrscr();
printf(" enter n\n");
scanf("%d",&n);
t=1;
for(i=1;i<=n;++i)
{
for(j=1;j<=i;++j)
{
printf("%4d",t);
if(t==0)
t=1;
else
```

```
t=0;
}
t=1;
gotoxy(80-i*4,i+2);
for(j=1;j<=i;++j)
{
printf("%4d",t);
if(t==0)
t=1;
else
t=0;
}
printf("\n");
}
getch();
}
```

```
Output
enter n
9
1
0 1
1 0 1
0 1 0 1
1 0 1 0 1
0 1 0 1 0 1
1 0 1 0 1 0 1
0 1 0 1 0 1 0 1
1 0 1 0 1 0 1 0 1

                  1
                1 0
              1 0 1
            1 0 1 0
          1 0 1 0 1
        1 0 1 0 1 0
      1 0 1 0 1 0 1
    1 0 1 0 1 0 1 0 0
  1 0 1 0 1 0 1 0 1 1
```

This is similar program compared to previous two programs. It will prints the triangle of *'s in reverse order.

```
/* Program name: loop64.c */
/* Program for reverse triangle of *'s */
#include<stdio.h>
#include<conio.h>
void main()
{
int n,i,j;
clrscr();
printf(" enter n\n");
scanf("%d",&n);
for(i=n;i>=1;--i)
{
for(j=1;j<=(n-i);++j)
printf(" ");/* giving the space */

for(j=1;j<=i;++j)
printf(" * ");
printf("\n");
}
getch();
}
```

```
Output
enter n
10
* * * * * * * * * *
 * * * * * * * * *
  * * * * * * * *
   * * * * * * *
    * * * * * *
     * * * * *
      * * * *
       * * *
        * *
         *
```

Now we will consider the design on *'s in the next two programs. The first program makes the cross shape using *'s in the middle of the screen, and second program makes cross with plus sign.

```
/* Program name: loop65.c */
/* Program for design of *'s */
#include<stdio.h>
#include<conio.h>
void main()
{
int n,i,j;
clrscr();
printf(" enter n\n");
scanf("%d",&n);
for(i=0;i<n;++i)
{
gotoxy(40-i*3,13-i);
printf(" * ");
gotoxy(40+i*3,13-i);
printf(" * ");
gotoxy(40-i*3,13+i);
printf(" * ");
gotoxy(40+i*3,13+i);
printf(" * ");
}
getch();
}
```

```
Output
enter n
8

*                                   *
   *                             *
      *                       *
         *                 *
            *           *
               *     *
                  *  *
                    *
                  *  *
               *     *
            *           *
         *                 *
      *                       *
   *                             *
*                                   *
```

```
/* Program name: loop66.c */
/* Program for design of *'s */
#include<stdio.h>
#include<conio.h>
void main()
{
int n,i,j;
clrscr();
printf(" enter n\n");
scanf("%d",&n);
for(i=0;i<n;++i)
{
gotoxy(40-i*3,13-i);
printf(" * ");
gotoxy(40+i*3,13-i);
printf(" * ");
gotoxy(40-i*3,13+i);
printf(" * ");
```

```
Output
enter n
7

      *           *           *
        *         *         *
          *       *       *
            *     *     *
              *   *   *
                * * *
*  *  *  *  *  *  *  *  *  *  *  *  *
                * * *
              *   *   *
            *     *     *
          *       *       *
        *         *         *
      *           *           *
```

```
gotoxy(40+i*3,13+i);
printf(" * ");
gotoxy(40,13-i);
printf(" * ");
gotoxy(40,13+i);
printf(" * ");
gotoxy(40-i*3,13);
printf(" * ");
gotoxy(40+i*3,13);
printf(" * ");

}
getch();
}
```

The following program deals with printing a word as a triangle. The first line starts with single character from the word and next lines increases the characters by one upto length of string and then decreases upto first character.

```
/* Program name: loop67.c */
/* Program for triangle of word */
#include<stdio.h>
#include<conio.h>
#include<string.h>
void main()
{
char ch[' '];
int i,j;
clrscr();
printf(" enter a string \n");
gets(ch);
for(i=0;i<strlen(ch);++i)
{
for(j=0;j<strlen(ch)-i;++j)
printf("%c",ch[j]);
printf("\n");
}
for(i=strlen(ch)-2;i>=0;--i)
{
for(j=0;j<=strlen(ch)-i-1;++j)
printf("%c",ch[j]);
printf("\n");

}
getch();
}
```

Output

enter a string
prg skills
prg skills
prg skill
prg skil
prg ski
prg sk
prg s
prg
prg
pr
p
pr
prg
prg
prg s
prg sk
prg ski
prg skil
prg skill
prg skills

4

Arrays

4.1 Introduction

Array is a derived data type and is defined as a set of homogeneous data elements and this collection of elements are represented by the same name and individual elements are referred by using array index. Arrays are also called subscripted variables. All the array elements are stored in continues memory locations. Arrays can be one-dimensional or multi dimensional. The syntax for declaring array is given by,

For one dimensional array : Typename arrayname [size];

For multi-dimensional array : Typename arrayname [sizel][size2]...[sizen];

```
Ex: int a [10]; /* one dimensional array with size 10*/
float  b[10][20]; /* two dimensional array with size 200(10 rows and 20 columns)*/
```

Array elements can be stored and processed by using array index.

Ex: a[0] gives first value.
a[5] given sixth value.

4.2 Initialization of arrays

Arrays can be initialized at the time of declaration as follows.

```
int  xyz [5] = {1,5,3,8,0};

float  pqr[5] [10] = {{1,2,3}, {3,4,1},  {1,2,8,9,10}};
```

If sufficient values are not given then all other locations will remain empty.
We can also assign values to the array individually using array subscripts.

```
Ex: int  A[5];
         A[0]=5;
         A[1]=20;
```

A[2]=-100;
A[3]=0;
A[4]=-4; etc.

We can directly scan the values into an array by using input statements.

Ex: 1. int a[10], i;
for(i=0;i<10;++i)
scanf("%d",&a[i]);

2. int b[10] [5], i,j;
for(i=0; i<10;++i)
for(j=0 j<5; ++j)
scanf("%d",&b[i][j]);

When array is used with index then it will be used as simple variable of type array. We can use individual array elements in arithmetic expressions, conditional expressions etc.

Ex: a[I]=a[j];
if(a[I]> a[j])
Etc.

Arrays have wide scope in mathematical and scientific applications. One dimensional arrays can be used to handle lists(list of numbers, students, employees, books etc.) and two dimensional arrays are used for handling matrix applications(where data is stored in the form of table using rows and columns).

The main advantage of arrays is, it is simple to use. The main disadvantage is it uses static memory allocation which may lead to wastage of memory.

Let us consider few programs which illustrate the use of arrays and make the concept clear.

The following program reads the list of integers into an array and displays them on the screen.

```
/* Program name: arr1.c */
/* program to read and display a list of numbers*/
#include<stdio.h>
#include<conio.h>
main()
{
int n,i,a[100]; /* declares an array of size 100 and can store
        maximum 100 integers*/
clrscr();
printf("enter n\n");
scanf("%d",&n); /* the actual number of values you want to
        read,n must be less than or equal to 100 */
printf("\n enter %d numbers \n",n);
for(i=0;i<n; ++i)
        scanf("%d", &a[i]); /* reading the values into the array
                                        using subscripts*/
printf("entered numbers are\n");
```

```
for(i=0;i<n; ++i)
printf("%d\t", a[i]);/* displaying the array elements using
     subscripts*/
getch();
}
```

Output
Enter n
5
enter 5 numbers
10 30 40 20 5
entered numbers are
10 30 40 20 5

As we can see the values are read into the array using subscripts. All the values are stored in continuous memory locations. Here we have used only 5 locations out of 100 memory locations that we have declared. Remaining 95 locations remain unused.

In the following program we are assigning the values to the array elements instead of taking from the keyboard, at the time of declaration.

```
/* Program name: arr2.c */
/* program to read and display a list of numbers*/
/* it will assign the numbers instead of taking form keyboard*/
#include<stdio.h>
#include<conio.h>
main()
{
int i, a[100]={10,2,0,3,5,4,32,54,65,43}; /* assigning numbers
     to array*/
clrscr();
printf("the array elements are\n");
for(i=0;i<10;++i) /* by assigning it assigns from a[0] */
     printf("%d\t",a[i]);
getch();
}
```

Now consider the similar example that just reads and prints the list of integers in reverse order.

```
/* Program name: arr3.c */
/* program to read and display a list of numbers in reverse
     order */
#include<stdio.h>
#include<conio.h>
void main()
```

```
{
int n,i,a[100];
clrscr();
printf("enter n\n");
scanf("%d",&n);
printf("\n enter %d numbers \n",n);
for(i=0;i<n; ++i)
      scanf("%d", &a[i]);
printf("entered numbers in reverse order are\n");
for(i=n-1; i>=0;--i)/* array index referred from last element
      to the first element */
      printf("%d\n", a[i]);
getch();
}
```

Output
Enter n
5
enter 5 numbers
10 30 40 20 5
entered numbers in reverse order are
5 20 40 30 10

The following is another simple program. Here we are finding the sum of a list of random numbers. The input is not entered from the keyboard, instead it is automatically generated using the rand() function. The rand() function when it is called gives one positive integer value. So to get the list of random numbers we need to call the rand() several times. This function is kept in the header file stdlib.h, so we need to include this header file also.

```
/* Program name: arr4.c */
/* program to read and display a list of numbers also find sum
      of numbers */
#include<stdio.h>
#include<conio.h>
#include<stdlib.h>
void main()
{
int n,i,a[100];
long s =0; /* for finding the sum which may be a large value */
clrscr();
printf("enter n\n");
scanf("%d",&n); /* the actual number of elements we want */
      /* the actual number of elements we want */
for(i=0;i<n; ++i)
      a[i]=rand(); /* generates random number and assigns to
                      array */
```

```
printf("\n numbers are\n");
for(i=0;i<n; ++i)
{
printf("%d\t", a[i]);
s=s+a[i]; /* doing arithmetic with array element*/
}
printf("\n sum = %ld ",s);
getch();
}
```

```
Output
Enter n
5
numbers are
346     130     10982  1090    11656

sum = 24204
```

In the above program we have used the arithmetic operator '+' with an array element. Similarly we can also use the other arithmetic operators. Now in the following program, we can see the use of relational operator '<'. This program finds the largest element in the list. For this we are assuming first element of the list as large and comparing it with all other elements one by one. Whenever an element greater than the large element is found then that element becomes the large element.

```
/* Program name: arr5.c */
/* program to read and display a list of numbers also largest
      of list */
#include<stdio.h>
#include<conio.h>
void main()
{
int n,i,a[100],lar;
clrscr();
printf("enter n\n");
scanf("%d",&n);
printf("\n enter %d numbers \n",n);
for(i=0; i<n; ++i)
scanf("%d", &a[i]);

lar=a[0]; /* assuming the first element as large */
printf("entered numbers are\n");
for(i=0;i<n; ++i)
{
printf("%d\t", a[i]);
```

```
if(lar<a[i]) /* comparing contents of lar with other elements
     */
lar=a[i]; /* replacing the contents of lar with array element
     */
}
printf("\n largest = %d ", lar);
getch();
}
```

Output
Enter n
5
enter 5 numbers
10 530 40 3320 5
entered numbers are
10 530 40 3320 5
largest = 3320

Here first time the contents of lar variable becomes 10, when it is compared with 530, the content replaced with 530 and now lar contains 530. Next as loop advances the element is compared with 40 and condition fails, no change in lar. Next element to compare is 3320 which is larger than the present contents of lar (530) and is replaced by 3320. The last comparison gives the result false and the value of lar variable remains 3320, which will be the largest element and shown as output.

The following program is similar to the above, but here we are finding the smallest element instead of largest. The relational operator '>' is used with array element.

```
/* Program name: arr6.c */
/* program to read and display a list of numbers also smallest
     of list */
#include<stdio.h>
#include<conio.h>
main()
{
int n,i,a[100],small;
clrscr();
printf("enter n\n");
scanf("%d",&n);
printf("\n enter %d numbers \n",n);
for(i=0;i<n; ++i)
     scanf("%d", &a[i]);
small=a[0];
printf("entered numbers are\n");
for(i=0;i<n; ++i)
     {
     printf("%d\n", a[i]);
```

```
            if(small>a[i])
                  small=a[i];
            }
      printf("\n smallest = %d ",small);
      getch();
      }
```

Output
Enter n
5
enter 5 numbers
10 530 40 3320 5
entered numbers are
10 530 40 3320 5

The following program is the combination of above two programs. It finds the largest and smallest of a list of numbers.

```
      /* Program name: arr7.c */
      /* program to read and display a list of numbers also smallest
                & largest of list */
      #include<stdio.h>
      #include<conio.h>
      void main()
      {
      int n,i,a[100],small, lar;
      clrscr();
      printf("enter n\n");
      scanf("%d",&n);
      printf("\n enter %d numbers \n",n);

      for(i=0; i<n; ++i)
            scanf("%d", &a[i]);
      lar=a[0]; /* assuming first element as the largest*/
      small=a[0];/* assuming first element as the smallest */
      printf("entered numbers are\n");
      for(i=0;i<n; ++i)
      {
      printf("%d\t", a[i]);
      if(small>a[i])
      small=a[i];
      else
      if(lar<a[i])
```

```
lar=a[i];
}
printf("\n smallest = %d \n largest = %d\n", small, lar);
getch();
}
```

Output
Enter n
8
enter 8 numbers
100 530 840 320 3 12 43 121
entered numbers are
100 530 840 320 3 12 43 121
smallest = 5
largest = 840

In the following programs we are listing the odd and even numbers separately from the given list of numbers.

```
/* Program name: arr8.c */
/* program to read a list of numbers */
/* print the odd and even numbers separately*/
#include<stdio.h>#include<conio.h>
void main()
{
int n,i,a[100];
clrscr();
printf("enter n\n");
scanf("%d",&n);
printf("\n enter %d numbers \n",n);
for(i=0;i<n; ++i)
      scanf("%d", &a[i]);
printf("\n odd numbers are \n");
for(i=0;i<=n; ++i)
      {
      if(a[i]%2==1)
      printf("%d\t", a[i]);
      }
printf("\n even numbers are \n");
for(i=0;i<n; ++i)
      {
      if(a[i]%2==0)
      printf("%d\t", a[i]);
```

```
        }
getch();
}
```

```
Output
Enter n
8
enter 8 numbers
100 53 84 320 3 12 43 121
odd numbers are
53      3       43      121
even numbers are
100     84      320     12
```

The following program is similar to the above program but it prints odd and even numbers from the list in separate columns. The above program uses looping statements twice and this program makes use of only one loop.

```
/* Program name: arr9.c */
/* program to read a list of numbers */
/* prints the odd and even numbers separate columns*/
#include<stdio.h>
#include<conio.h>
void main()
{
int n,i,a[100];
clrscr();
printf("enter n\n");
scanf("%d", &n);
printf("\n enter %d numbers \n", n);
for(i=0;i<n; ++i)
        scanf("%d", &a[i]);
printf("\n      odd              even \n");
for(i=0;i<n; ++i)
        {
        if(a[i]%2==1)
                printf("%8d\n",a[i]);
        else
                printf(" %20d\n",a[i]);
        }
getch();
}
```

```
Output
Enter n
8
enter 8 numbers
100  530  840 320  3  12  43 121
         odd                even
                            100
                            530
                            840
                            320
          3
                            12
         43
        121
```

Linear Search

Searching is one of the important process every one needs in daily life. We can search the telephone numbers in the telephone directory, a student roll number in the student list, an employ name in the employees list etc. There are several searching methods available. The simplest among the searching algorithms is 'linear search' algorithm.

The algorithm works as follows.

Compare the search element with the first element of the list; if present display the position and continue otherwise continue comparing with successive elements. The following program implements this. This program finds all possible occurrences of the element.

```
/* Program name: arr10.c */
/* Program to read a list of numbers */
/* Search a given number in the list along with position*/
/* Use linear search method */
#include<stdio.h>
#include<conio.h>
void main()
{
int n, i, x, a[100];
clrscr();
printf("enter n\n");
scanf("%d", &n);
printf("\n enter %d numbers \n", n);
for(i=0;i<n; ++i)
      scanf("%d", &a[i]);
printf("\n enter a number to search\n");
scanf("%d", &x);
for(i=0;i<n; ++i)
      {
```

```
            if(a[i]==x) /* when this condition is true, i+1 gives
                                    the position */
                  printf(" \n number %d present in position %d of
                                          the list\n", x, i+1);
            }
      getch();
      }
```

Output	Output 2
Enter n 8 enter 8 numbers 12 20 4 33 55 10 5 33 enter a number to search 33 number 33 present in position 4 of the list number 33 present in position 8 of the list	Enter n 8 enter 8 numbers 12 20 4 33 55 10 5 33 enter a number to search 3

Note that the above program will not give any information when the search fails as shown in output 2. To get the information about unsuccessful search, we need to use a flag and set it when the element is present otherwise it remains with its original value. The following search program implements this.

```
       /* Program name: arr11.c */
       /* Program to read a list of numbers */
      /* Search a given number in the list along with position*/
      /* Use linear search method */
      #include<stdio.h>
      #include<conio.h>
      void main()
      {
      int n, i, x, a[100],flag=0; /*flag is set to 0 initially */
      clrscr();
      printf("enter n\n");
      scanf("%d", &n);
      printf("\n enter %d numbers \n", n);
      for(i=0;i<n; ++i)
            scanf("%d", &a[i]);
      printf("\n enter a number to search\n");
      scanf("%d", &x);
      for(i=0;i<n; ++i)
            if(a[i]==x) /* when this condition is true, i+1 gives
                                    the position */
            {
```

```
                printf(" \n number %d present in position %d of
                                   the list\n", x, i+1);
                flag=1; /* flag is changed to 1 on success */
            }
        if(flag==0)  /* when flag remains 0 the search becomes
            unsuccessful*/
            printf("\n unsuccessful search\n");
        getch();
        }
```

Output	Output 2
Enter n 8 enter 8 numbers 12 20 4 33 55 10 5 33 enter a number to search 33 number 33 present in position 4 of the list number 33 present in position 8 of the list	Enter n 8 enter 8 numbers 12 20 4 33 55 10 5 33 enter a number to search 3 unsuccessful search

The following program is a little modification of linear search program. It finds the frequency of occurrence of a number in a list.

```
/* Program name: arr12.c */
/* Program to read a list of numbers */
/* Prints the frequency of occurrence of a number in the
    list*/
#include<stdio.h>
#include<conio.h>
void main()
{
int n, i, x, c=0,a[100];
clrscr();
printf("enter n\n");
scanf("%d",&n);
printf("\n enter %d numbers \n",n);
for(i=0;i<n; ++i)
scanf("%d", &a[i]);
printf("\n enter a number to find frequency\n");
    scanf("%d", &x);
for(i=0;i<n; ++i)
    {
    if(a[i]==x)
        c++;
```

```
          printf("%8d",a[i]);
          }
    printf("\nnumber %d present %d times in the list\n", x, c);
    getch();
    }
```

Output
Enter n
8
enter 8 numbers
12 20 4 33 55 10 5 33
enter a number to find frequency
33
number 33 present 2 times in the list

Following program prints all the numbers from the given list that are divisible by a given number.

```
/* Program name: arr13.c */
/* program to read a list of numbers */
/*print all numbers from list which are divisible by x */
/* use linear search method */
#include<stdio.h>
#include<conio.h>
void main()
{
int n, i, x, a[100];
clrscr();
printf("enter n\n");
scanf("%d",&n);
printf("\n enter %d numbers \n",n);
for(i=0;i<n; ++i)
      scanf("%d", &a[i]);
printf("\n enter a number to divide\n");
scanf("%d", &x);
printf("\n the element of the array which are divisible by %d
      are \n",x);
for(i=0;i<n; ++i)
      {
      if(a[i]%x==0)
            printf(" %d\t", a[i]);
      }
getch();
}
```

Output
Enter n
8
enter 8 numbers
12 20 4 33 55 10 5 33
enter a number to divide
11
the element of the array which are divisible by 11 are
33 55 33

Already we have discussed about prime numbers in loops chapter. Here we are finding all the prime numbers from the given list of numbers. To do this we need to use nested loops. The outer loop executes n number of times for a list of n elements, which supplies numbers one by one to the inner loop. The execution of inner loop is based on the each individual element. The use of flag is essential in these kind of programs and breaking from the loop really reduces the unnecessary computation.

```
/* Program name: arr14.c */
/* Program to read a list of numbers */
/* print all prime numbers from the list*/
/* use linear search method */
#include<stdio.h>
#include<conio.h>
void main()
{
int n, i, a[100],t, j;
clrscr();
printf("enter n\n");
scanf("%d",&n);
printf("\n enter %d numbers \n",n);
for(i=0;i<n; ++i)
        scanf("%d", &a[i]);
printf("\n the element of the array which are primes \n");
for(i=1;i<=n; ++i)
        {
        t=0; /* flag t is made 0 for every element */
                for(j=2;j<=a[i]/2;++j)
                if(a[i]%j==0)
                {
                t=1;
                break;
                }
        if(t==0)  /* when the flag t remains unchanged, the
                                  element is not divisible by any
```

```
                                  other numbers and it will be
                                  printed*/
                  printf("\n %8d",a[i]);
          }
  getch();
}
```

Output
Enter n
8
enter 8 numbers
11 20 4 33 55 17 5 33
the elements of the array which are primes
11 33 17 5 33

Now we will concentrate on sorting techniques. Sorting means arranging the elements in order. When the elements in the list are in order (either ascending or descending) then it becomes easy to search the elements. Think of searching a telephone number in the telephone directory, if the directory is not arranged in order, then it is quite difficult to search. In that case we need to apply linear search technique for searching purpose. Linear search method is good if the size of the list is small. When the size of the list is big we need to go for the better searching methods such as 'binary search' or 'tree searches'.

In sorting also there are number of methods, like 'bubble sort' , 'selection sort', 'sequential sort', 'quick sort', 'heap sort', etc. Here we will consider some of these sorting techniques and their implementation.

'BUBBLE SORT'

This is one of the most popular sorting techniques available and widely used. In this technique we are comparing two consecutive elements of the list and exchanging them if they found out of order, and then repeating this process for all possible consecutive pairs. For a list of 'n' elements we need 'n-1' comparisons in each of 'n-1' passes. So the time complexity of this algorithm of order $O(n^2)$ approximately.

Consider the list of 5 numbers and arranging in ascending order.

5 8 1 9 3

First we have to compare 5 and 8 they are in order so exchange is not necessary. Then we can compare 8 and 1, now they are not in order, so exchange them. Continue this for all pairs (8,9) ,(9,3). At the end of this pass we will get the list as follows.

5 1 8 3 9.

Note that the largest element is at the end. Now repeat the above process on the new list, we will get.

1 5 3 8 9. in the second pass.
1 3 5 8 9. in the third pass.

Now all the elements are in order, so we can stop the process. In some cases it may take 'n-1' passes to complete the process. The following program implements 'Bubble Sort' method.

```
/* Program name: arr15.c */
/* program to arrange a given list of numbers in ascending
    order*/
/* using bubble sort method */
#include<stdio.h>
#include<conio.h>
void main()
{
int n, i, a[100],t, j;
clrscr();
printf("enter n\n");
scanf("%d", &n); /* the number of elements in the list */
printf("\n enter %d numbers \n",n);
/* for inputting numbers*/
for(i=1;i<=n; ++i)
      scanf("%d", &a[i]); /* reading all the elements of the
                                    list */
/*for arranging the numbers */
for(i=1;i<n; ++i)
      {
      for(j=1;j<=n-i; ++j)
            if(a[j]>a[j+1])
            {
            t=a[j];      /* exchange of numbers when they are
                                    not in order */
            a[j]=a[j+1];
            a[j+1]=t;
            }
      }
/* printing the arranged numbers */
printf("\nelement of the array in ascending order are \n");
for(i=1;i<=n; ++i)
      printf("%8d",a[i]);
getch();
}
```

Output
Enter n
8
enter 8 numbers
8 9 15 1 -3 78 12 -5
elements of the array in ascending order are
-5 -3 1 8 9 10 12 15 78

For better understanding of the algorithm we can print all the intermediate results after each pass. The following program is a modification of the above program, which prints the intermediate results, along with the final arranged list. Note that from the result at the end of each pass the corresponding largest elements will be in their final positions, i.e., at the end of 1st pass 1st largest will be in its final position, at the end of 2nd pass 1st and 2nd largest elements will be in their final positions of the list and so on.

```
/* Program name: arr16.c */
/* Program to arrange a given list of numbers in ascending
     order*/
/* Using bubble sort method */
/* this program prints intermediate results also after each
     pass */
#include<stdio.h>
#include<conio.h>
void main()
{
int n, i, a[100],t, j;
clrscr();
printf("enter n\n");
scanf("%d", &n); /* the number of elements in the list */
printf("\n enter %d numbers \n", n);
/* for inputting numbers*/
for(i=1;i<=n; ++i)
     scanf("%d", &a[i]); /* reading all the elements of the
                                  list */
/*for arranging the numbers */
for(i=1;i<n; ++i)
     {
     for(j=1;j<=n-i; ++j)
     if(a[j]>a[j+1])
     {
     t=a[j];
     a[j]=a[j+1];
     a[j+1]=t;
     }
     printf("\n After pass = %d \n", i);
     for(j=1;j<n  ;  ++j)/* this loop prints intermediate
                                  results */
          printf("%8d",a[j]);
     }
/* printing the arranged numbers */
printf("\nelements of array in ascending order are \n");
for(i=1;i<=n; ++i)
     printf("%8d",a[i]);
```

```
getch();
}
```

```
Output
Enter n
8
enter 8 numbers
8 9 15 1 -3 78 12 -5
After pass = 1
8     9     1     -3    15    12    -5    78
After pass = 2
8     1     -3    9     12    -5    15    78
After pass = 3
1     -3    8     9     -5    12    15    78
After pass = 4
-3    1     8     -5    9     12    15    78
After pass = 5
-3    1     -5    8     9     12    15    78
After pass = 6
-3    -5    1     8     9     12    15    78
After pass = 7
-5    -3    1     8     9     12    15    78

elements of  array in ascending order are
-3    1     8     9     10    12    15    78
```

'SELECTION SORT'

This is a simple sorting technique and is used widely. The logic behind this algorithm is simple, as given below.

Select the smallest element (largest in case of descending order) and place it in the first place by replacing the first element with it(place the largest element in the first position if you are sorting the list in descending order). Now consider remaining part of the array (excluding 1st element) as new list and find smallest and replace it with first element of the newly formed list. Repeat this until this list becomes in order. This algorithm takes at the most 'n-1' replacements, each and every time we have to find the smallest element.

Consider the list of 5 numbers.

30 22 5 99 -4

Now among these five we will find the smallest and replace with first element, we will get the new list as follows.

-4 22 5 99 30

Now take the new list excluding first element, find the smallest, and replace with first element of the newly considered list. We will get.

-4 5 22 99 30

Now leave first two elements (which are already in their final position) and apply the above method on the new list. We will get the new lists as

-4	5	22	99	30
-4	5	22	30	99

This method is implemented in the program as follows.

```
/* Program name: arr17.c */
/* Program to arrange a given list of numbers in ascending
     order*/
/* Using selection sort method */
#include<stdio.h>
#include<conio.h>
void main()
{
int n, i, a[100],t,t1,j;
clrscr();
printf("enter n\n");
scanf("%d", &n);
printf("\n enter %d numbers \n", n);
/* for inputting numbers*/
for(i=1;i<=n; ++i)
     scanf("%d", &a[i]);
/*for arranging the numbers */
for(i=1;i<n; ++i)
     {
     t=a[i];
     for(j=i+1;j<=n; ++j)
          if(a[j]<t) /* finding smallest */
               t=a[j];
               /*searching smallest and replacing with
                                   respective number*/
     for(j=i;j<=n; ++j)
          if(a[j]==t)
               {
               t1=a[i]; /* exchange of numbers */
               a[i]=a[j];
               a[j]=t1;
               }
     }
/* printing the arranged numbers */
printf("\n element of  array in ascending order are \n");
for(i=1;i<=n; ++i)
     printf("%8d",a[i]);
getch();
}
```

```
Output
Enter n
8
enter 8 numbers
8 9 15 1 -3 78 12 -5
 elements of  array in ascending order are
-5      -3      1       8       9       10      12      15      78
```

For better understanding of the algorithm we can easily print the intermediate results. We can understand any algorithm only if we are able to check what is happening in each and every step of the program. [There are number of other sorting techniques. The reader is advised to find and try to solve those methods.]

Binary Search

Now we will take a look at the most popular searching algorithm, 'Binary Search'. This algorithm needs all the elements of the list to be in order. Here we have to compare the element to be searched with the middle element of the list. If the search condition is true, search is successful and we can come out of the process. If the search is unsuccessful then there are other two possibilities, either the search element is larger than the middle element or smaller than the middle element. When it is larger than the middle element, then take next half of the list as new list, and repeat the entire procedure again with the new list. When it is smaller than the middle element then if it is present it must be in the first half of the list, and take first half as the new list and continue. Repeat this until search is successful or there is no list left, which indicates the search is unsuccessful.

Example,
3 10 18 30 34 56 123 233
Searching element x=123.
Now take low = 1 and high as 8(as number of elements is 8)
Find mid = (low + high)/2; which is 4 (integer)

Compare x with 4th element of the list, it is unsuccessful. The search element (x=123) is greater than middle element (30). Now there is possibility of x present in the second half of the list. So make low = mid+1 =5 and keep high (=8) as it is, now find the new mid = (low + high)/2=(5+8)/2 =6. Compare mid element of the array with x again, we find the search is unsuccessful again and x is larger than middle element. So now take low = mid+1=7 and find new mid=(low + high)/2=(7+8)/2=7. Now compare this element with x and we will get successful search, and the value of mid gives the position of the element in the list. In case we are not getting successful search, then we should stop the process when low variable value becomes more than value of variable high. The following program implements this algorithm.

```
/* Program name: arr18.c */
/* Program for Binary search */
#include<conio.h>
#include<stdio.h>
void main()
```

```
{
int a[50],x, I, j, low, high, mid,n;
clrscr();
printf("enter n\n");
scanf("%d",&n);
printf("enter %d numbers in ascending order\n",n);
for(I=1;I<=n;++I)
     scanf("%d",&a[I]);
printf("\n enter element to search\n");
scanf("%d",&x);
low=1;
high=n;
while(low<=high)
     {
               mid=(low+high)/2;
               if(a[mid]==x)
               {
               printf("\nsearch is successful\n element found at
                                   position %d\n",mid);
               break;
               }
               else if(a[mid]<x)
                    low=mid+1;
               else
                    high=mid-1;
     } /* end of while */
if(low>high)
printf("\n unsuccessful search\n");
getch();
}
```

Output 1
Enter n
6
enter 6 numbers in ascending order
10 14 18 19 30 34
enter the number to search
10
search is successful
element found at position 1

Output 2
Enter n
6
enter 6 numbers in ascending order
10 14 18 19 30 34
enter the number to search
35
unsuccessful search

4.3 Two-dimensional arrays

Two-dimensional arrays play a very important role in handling the situations where the elements are arranged in tables. We have already discussed some of the basics about two-dimensional arrays in the beginning of this chapter. Now we will look at the programs using two-dimensional arrays.

Let us start with a simple program for reading and printing a matrix in the matrix format. As we know the structure of a matrix is like a table, with specific number of rows and columns it can be expressed easily using two dimensional array. In the declaration of array to represent the matrix the first size always specifies rows and the second size specifies columns. For example,

int a[10][5];

Here 'a' is an array; it can store 50 integer values in 10 rows each with 5 elements.

To read a matrix we need to use two loops one for specifying rows (outer loop) and inner for columns. The loop counters can be used as array indices, as given below.

```
int a[10][5],i,j;
for(i=0;i<10;++i)
        for(j=0;j<5;++j)
                scanf("%d",&a[i][j]);
```

Here when i is having value 0 j changes from 0 to 4, reading the elements a[0][0], a[0][1], a[0][2], a[0][3] and a[0][4], after that i changes to 1 and j again repeats from 0 to 4. This continues for all possible values of i i.e., i=0 to 9.

For printing the matrix in the matrix format, we should know the proper use of newline character ('\n'). The statements

```
for(i=0;i<10;++i)
        for(j=0;j<5;++j)
                printf("%d", a[i][j]);
```

prints the matrix as a list. We need to leave a space in between each element, by using '\t' or specifying number of digits in the format (ex. "%10d"). The outer loop specifies the row, so after each row we need to advance the cursor to the next line.

```
for(i=0;i<10;++i)
{
        for(j=0;j<5;++j)
                printf("%8d", a[i][j]);
        printf("\n");
}
```

The second printf() statement works in the outer loop only and takes the cursor to the next line for every row. The complete program code for reading and displaying a matrix is given below.

```
/* Program name: arr19.c */
/* program to read and print the matrix in matrix format*/
#include<stdio.h>
#include<conio.h>
void main()
```

```
{
int n,m,i, j, a[10][10]; /* assuming maximum 10 rows and 10
     columns*/
clrscr();
printf("enter order of matrix\n");
scanf("%d%d", &n, &m);
printf("\n enter %d X %d matrix \n", n, m);
/* For inputting numbers*/
for(i=1;i<=n; ++i)
     for(j=1;j<=m; ++j)
          scanf("%d", &a[i][j]);
printf("\n given matrix\n"); /* For printing in the matrix
     format*/
for(i=1;i<=n; ++i)
     {
          for(j=1;j<=m; ++j)
               printf("%8d", a[i][j]);
          printf("\n");/* gives a line after every row*/
     }
getch();
}
```

Output
Enter order of the matrix
3 4
enter 3 X 4 matrix
1 2 3 4 5 6 7 8 9 10 11 12
given matrix

1	**2**	**3**	**4**
5	**6**	**7**	**8**
9	**10**	**11**	**12**

In a square matrix the sum of all main diagonal elements is called its trace.

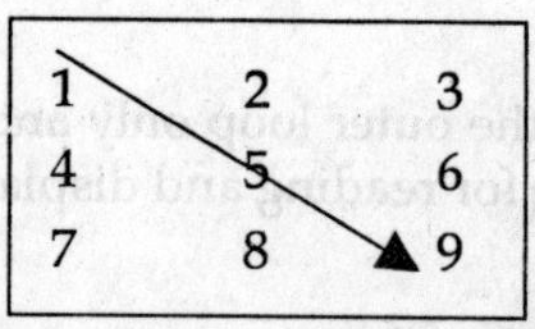

To find the trace of the matrix, we need to check whether the matrix is square matrix or not. The following program finds the trace of a matrix after reading and printing the matrix in matrix format.

```
/* Program name: arr20.c */
/* Program to read and print the matrix in matrix format*/
/* Find the trace of the matrix*/
        #include<stdio.h>
        #include<conio.h>
        void main()
        {
        int n, m, i, j, a[10][10],t=0;
        clrscr();
        printf("enter order of matrix\n");
        scanf("%d%d", &n, &m);
        printf("\n enter %d X %d matrix \n", n, m);
        /* For inputting numbers*/
        for(i=1;i<=n; ++i)
              for(j=1;j<=m; ++j)
                    scanf("%d", &a[i][j]);
        printf("\n given matrix\n");
        /* For printing in the matrix format*/
        for(i=1;i<=n; ++i)
              {
                    for(j=1;j<=m; ++j)
                          printf("%8d",a[i][j]);
                    printf("\n");/* gives a line after every row*/

              }
        if(m==n)
              {
              for(i=1;i<=n; ++i)
                    for(j=1;j<=m; ++j)
                          if(i==j)
                             t+=a[i][j];
              printf("\n\n trace of given matrix is  %d\n",t);
              }
        else
        printf("\n not a square matrix trace is not possible\n);
        getch();
        }
```

Output

Enter order of the matrix

1 4

enter 4 X 4 matrix

1 2 3 4 5 6 7 8 9 10 11 12 13 14 15 16

given matrix

1	2	3	4
5	6	7	8
9	10	11	12
13	14	15	16

trace of given matrix is 34

Although the above program gives correct answer, it performs unwanted computations while calculating the trace. We know that the array index for row and columns must be same along the main diagonal; we can replace the statements in the above program, to avoid unnecessary computations.

```
for(i=1;i<=n; ++i)
        for(j=1;j<=m; ++j)
                if(i==j)
                        t+=a[i][j];
```

the code for the same functionality can be written using single loop and without conditional statement as follows.

```
for(i=1;i<=n; ++i)
        t+=a[i][i];
```

Now we will discuss about identity matrix. The matrix in which all the elements other than the main diagonal are 0s and elements on main diagonal are 1s is called as an identity matrix. So it is clear that the matrix must be square matrix. We know that the indices of the array elements on the main diagonal, in a square matrix are equal, so we have to check for all other elements where indices are not equal. We need to use a flag variable that can change its value if an element other than main diagonal found to be non-zero. The following program implements this.

```
/* Program name: arr21.c */
/* Program to read and print the matrix in matrix format*/
/* Check for identity matrix*/
#include<stdio.h>
#include<conio.h>
void main()
{
int n, m, i, j, a[10][10], t=0; /* t is used as flag and set to
        0 */
clrscr();
printf("enter order of matrix\n");
scanf("%d%d", &n, &m);
printf("\n enter %d X %d matrix \n", n, m);
/* for inputting numbers*/
for(i=1;i<=n; ++i)
        for(j=1;j<=m; ++j)
                scanf("%d", &a[i][j]);
printf("\n given matrix\n");
/* for printing in the matrix format*/
for(i=1;i<=n; ++i)
        {
```

```
        for(j=1;j<=m; ++j)
                printf("%5d",a[i][j]);
        printf("\n");/* gives a line after every row*/
        }
    if(m==n) /* check for square matrix */
    {
        for(i=1;i<=n; ++i)
                for(j=1;j<=m; ++j)
                {
                if((i==j)&&(a[i][j]!=1)) /* checking identity for
                                            main diagonal */
                t=1;
                if((i!=j)&&(a[i][j]!=0))/*checking identity for
                                            all other elements */
                t=1; /* flag changes its value */
                }
                if(t==0)
                printf("\n\n matrix is  an identity matrix\n");
                else
                printf("\n\n matrix is not an identity matrix\n");
    }
    else
        printf("\n not a square matrix identity is not
                                    possible\n");
    getch();
    }
```

Output
Enter order of the matrix
3 3
enter 3 X 3 matrix
1 2 3 4 5 6 7 8 9
given matrix
1 2 3
4 5 6
7 8 9
matrix is not an identity matrix

Output
Enter order of the matrix
3 3
enter 3 X 3 matrix
1 0 0 0 1 0 0 0 1
given matrix
1 0 0
0 1 0
0 0 1
matrix is an identity matrix

A square matrix is said to be symmetric if and only if for all possible values of i and j a[i][j] must be equal to a[j][i]. In the following program we are implementing the same.

```
/* Program name: arr22.c */
/* program to read and print the matrix in matrix format*/
```

```
/* check for symmetric matrix*/
#include<stdio.h>
#include<conio.h>
void main()
{
int n, m, i, j, a[10][10],t=0;
clrscr();
printf("enter order of matrix\n");
scanf("%d%d", &n, &m);
printf("\n enter %d X %d matrix \n", n, m);
      /* for inputting numbers*/
for(i=1;i<=n; ++i)
      for(j=1;j<=m; ++j)
            scanf("%d", &a[i][j]);
printf("\n given matrix\n");
/* for printing in the matrix format*/
for(i=1;i<=n; ++i)
      {
      for(j=1;j<=m; ++j)
            printf("%5d",a[i][j]);
      printf("\n");/* gives a line after every row*/
      }
if(m==n)
      {
      for(i=1;i<=n; ++i)
            for(j=1;j<=m; ++j)
            if(a[i][j]!=a[j][i])  /* checking for symmetric
                                      and if not changing the
                                      flag */
            t=1;
            if(t==0)
            printf("\n\n  matrix is  a symmetric matrix\n");
            else
            printf("\n\n matrix is  not a symmetric matrix\n");
      }
else
      printf("\n  not  a  square  matrix  symmetric  is  not
                              possible\n");
getch();
}
```

```
Output
Enter order of the matrix
    3 3
enter 3 X 3 matrix
1 2 3 2 3 4 3 4 5
given matrix
 1      2      3
 2      3      4
 3      4      5
matrix is  a symmetric matrix
```

```
Output
Enter order of the matrix
    3 3
enter 3 X 3 matrix
1 2 3 4 5 6 7 8 9
given matrix
 1      2      3
 4      5      6
 7      8      9
matrix is not a symmetric matrix
```

In solving the simultaneous equations in mathematics matrices are frequently used. Gauss Elimination method is one of such popular method for solving a set of simultaneous equations. This method needs tringularization of equations. Upper triangle matrix and Lower triangle matrix are used for this. A square matrix, in which all the elements below the main diagonal are zeros, is called upper triangular matrix. The following figure shows the upper triangular matrix.

1	2	3
0	4	8
0	0	9

We can clearly observe that in a matrix a, if a_{ij}=0 for all i>j then the matrix will be upper triangular matrix. The following program illustrates this.

```
/* Program name: arr23.c */
/* program to read and print the matrix in matrix format*/
/* check for upper triangular matrix*/
#include<stdio.h>
#include<conio.h>
void main()
{
int n, m, i, j, a[10][10],t=0;
clrscr();
printf("enter order of matrix\n");
scanf("%d%d", &n, &m);
printf("\n enter %d X %d matrix \n", n, m);
/* for inputting numbers*/
```

```
for(i=1;i<=n; ++i)
        for(j=1;j<=m; ++j)
                scanf("%d", &a[i][j]);
printf("\n given matrix\n");
/* for printing in the matrix format*/
for(i=1;i<=n; ++i)
        {
        for(j=1;j<=m; ++j)
                printf("%8d",a[i][j]);
        printf("\n");/* gives a line after every row*/
        }
if(m==n) /* checks for square matrix*/
        {
        for(i=1;i<=n; ++i)
                for(j=1;j<=m; ++j)
                if((i>j)&&(a[i][j]!=0))  /* checking for upper
                                    triangular property of the
                                    matrix and changing the
                                    flag t if not */
                t=1;

        if(t==0) /* when flag t is not changed*/
                printf("\n\n  matrix is  an upper triangular
                                    matrix\n");
        else /* when changed */
                printf("\n\n  matrix is  not an upper triangular
                                    matrix\n");
        }
else
        printf("\n not a square matrix tringularization is not
                                possible\n");
getch();
}
```

Output
Enter order of the matrix
4 4
enter 4 X 4 matrix
1 2 3 2 3 4 3 4 5 4 2 3 4 5 2 1
given matrix
1 2 3 2
3 4 3 4
5 4 2 3
4 5 2 1
matrix is not an upper triangular matrix

Output
Enter order of the matrix
3 3
enter 3 X 3 matrix
1 2 3 0 3 4 0 0 5
given matrix
1 2 3
0 3 4
0 0 5
matrix is an upper triangular matrix

The lower triangular matrix is a square matrix in which all the elements above the main diagonal are zeros. This can be easily implemented by changing the condition (i>j) in the above program by (i<j).

```
/* Program name: arr24.c */
/* program to read and print the matrix in matrix format*/
/* check for lower triangular matrix*/
#include<stdio.h>
#include<conio.h>
void main()
{
int n, m, i, j, a[10][10],t=0;
clrscr();
printf("enter order of matrix\n");
scanf("%d%d", &n, &m);
printf("\n enter %d X %d matrix \n", n, m);
/* for inputting numbers*/
for(i=1;i<=n; ++i)
        for(j=1;j<=m; ++j)
                scanf("%d", &a[i][j]);
printf("\n given matrix\n");
/* for printing in the matrix format*/
for(i=1;i<=n; ++i)
{
        for(j=1;j<=m; ++j)
                printf("%5d",a[i][j]);
        printf("\n");/* gives a line after every row*/
}
if(m==n)
{
for(i=1;i<=n; ++i)
for(j=1;j<=m; ++j)
        if((i<j)&&(a[i][j]!=0))
        t=1;
if(t==0)
printf("\n\n  matrix is  a lower triangular matrix\n");
else
printf("\n\n  matrix is  not a lower triangular matrix\n");
}
else
printf("\n not a square matrix tringularization is not
        possible\n");

getch();
}
```

Output
Enter order of the matrix
3 4
enter 3 X 4 matrix
1 2 3 2 3 4 3 4 5 4 2 3
given matrix
1 2 3 2
3 4 3 4
5 4 2 3
not a square matrix tringularization is not possible

Output
Enter order of the matrix
3 3
enter 3 X 3 matrix
1 0 0 0 3 0 0 7 5
given matrix
1 0 0
0 3 0
0 7 5
matrix is a lower triangular matrix

Suppose we have the data pertaining to the company about sales or purchasing, year wise and region wise, as given below.

Year / Region	1998	1999	2000	2001	2002
East	1200	1390	1198	3048	3788
West	2000	2345	2780	4300	5076
South	1899	2990	1560	2300	2800
North	1775	1992	3990	2004	3200

When we want to calculate the total sales region wise for given 5 years or sum of sales in all regions in a particular year, it is essential to find the sum of each row and each column of the above data. This can be easily found when the data is represented in the matrix form. We can read the data in a matrix of desired number of rows and columns. As we know each row of a matrix is an array of one dimension, we can find the sum easily, by keeping the first index constant and varying the second index of the matrix for each of the rows. Similarly we can find the sum of each column by keeping the second index of the matrix constant and varying the first index for all the columns. The following program finds the sum of each row and prints the result along with the matrix.

```
/* Program name: arr25.c */
/* Program to read and print the matrix in matrix format*/
/* Find row sum print it along with row*/
#include<stdio.h>
#include<conio.h>
void main()
{
int n, m, i, j, a[10][10],s;
clrscr();
```

```
printf("enter order of matrix\n");
scanf("%d%d", &n, &m);
printf("\n enter %d X %d matrix \n", n, m);
/* for inputting numbers*/
for(i=1;i<=n; ++i)
   for(j=1;j<=m; ++j)
      scanf("%d", &a[i][j]);
printf("\n given matrix              row sum\n");
/* for printing in the matrix format*/
for(i=1;i<=n; ++i)
{
   s=0; /* for each row initializing sum as zero */
   for(j=1;j<=m; ++j)
   {
      printf("%8d",a[i][j]);
      s+=a[i][j]; /* adding the element to the sum s*/
   }
printf("%12d\n",s);/* printing the sum on the same row*/
}
getch();
}
```

Output

Enter order of the matrix
3 4
enter 3 X 4 matrix
1 2 3 2 3 4 3 4 5 4 2 3

given matrix				row sum
1	2	3	2	8
3	4	3	4	14
5	4	2	3	14

Now we can implement the program that finds sum of each column separately and prints along with the matrix. For implementing this program we need to take a temporary single-dimensional array, because the results must be printed only after printing the matrix. Also while calculating the sum of each column we need to execute outer loop equal to number of columns and inner loop number of times equal to number of rows. At the end of matrix printing we can print the contents of the temporary array that contains the sum of each column separately.

```
/* Program name: arr26.c */
/* Program to read and print the matrix in matrix format*/
/* Find column sum print it along with column*/
#include<stdio.h>
#include<conio.h>
void main()
```

```
{
int n, m, i, j, a[10][10],s[10]; /* s[10] is a temporary
    single-dimensional array to store results */
clrscr();
printf("enter order of matrix\n");
scanf("%d%d", &n, &m);
printf("\n enter %d X %d matrix \n", n, m);
/* for inputting numbers*/
for(i=1;i<=n; ++i)
   for(j=1;j<=m; ++j)
   scanf("%d", &a[i][j]);
printf("\n\t\t given matrix  \n");
/* for printing in the matrix format*/
fcr(i=1;i<=n; ++i)
{
   for(j=1;j<=m; ++j)
      printf("%8d",a[i][j]);
  printf("\n\t\t");
}
for(i=1;i<=m; ++i)
{
s[i]=0; /* initializing each column sum to zero */
for(j=1;j<=n; ++j)
      s[i]+=a[j][i]; /* sum of each column element to sum and
            storing it*/
}
printf("\n\n column sum ");
for(i=1;i<=m; ++i)
      printf("%8d",s[i]);
getch();
}
```

Output

```
Enter order of the matrix
  3 4
enter 3 X 4 matrix
1 2 3 2 3 4 3 4 5 4 2 3
              given matrix
              1      2      3      2
              3      4      3      4
              5      4      2      3

column sum    9      10     8      9
```

For the above sales data example some times it is essential to find the maximum sales or minimum sales in a particular year or region. This can be achieved by finding the largest/smallest element of the matrix along with its position in terms of rows and columns. Assume one of the elements of the matrix as largest or smallest; keep its position in terms of rows and columns in the temporary variables. Now compare this value with all other elements of the matrix and make changes as and when required. The following program finds the largest and smallest of the matrix elements along with their positions in terms of rows and columns.

```
/* Program name: arr27.c */
/* Program to read and print the matrix in matrix format*/
/* Find smallest and largest element in the matrix, along with
     position*/

#include<stdio.h>
#include<conio.h>
void main()
{
int n, m, i, j, a[10][10], small, lar, rs, cs, rl, cl;
clrscr();
printf("enter order of matrix\n");
scanf("%d%d", &n, &m);
printf("\n enter %d X %d matrix \n", n, m);
/* for inputting numbers*/
for(i=1;i<=n; ++i)
    for(j=1;j<=m; ++j)
        scanf("%d", &a[i][j]);
/*first element is assumed to be smallest and largest */
small=a[1][1];
lar =a[1][1];
rs=1;
cs=1;
rl=1;
cl=1;
printf("\n given matrix  \n");
/* for printing in the matrix format*/
for(i=1;i<=n; ++i)
{
for(j=1;j<=m; ++j)
{
    printf("%8d",a[i][j]);
    if(small>a[i][j]) /* checking any element is smaller than
        small */
    {
    small=a[i][j]; /* taking it as small when found and changing
        row and column values */
```

```
                rs=i;
                cs=j;
                }
                else if(lar<a[i][j]) /* checking any element is larger than
                    lar */
                {
                lar=a[i][j];
                rl=i;
                rc=j;
                }
            }
            printf("\n");
            }
            printf("\n\n smallest element  = %d  present at row = %d  and
                column = %d \n",small, rs, cs);
            printf("\n largest element   = %d  present at row = %d  and
                column = %d \n", lar, rl, cl);
            getch();
            }
```

Output
Enter order of the matrix
4 3
enter 4 X 3 matrix
10 22 3 12 23 4 -3 44 51 40 2 13
given matrix
10 22 3
12 23 4
-3 44 51
40 2 13

smallest element = -3 present at row = 3 and column = 1
largest element = 51 present at row = 3 and column = 3

Now we will consider other varieties of programs, we can arrange each row and column of the matrix in order. For arranging each row in an order we should take each row as an array of one-dimension and apply any of the sorting methods. We have to take care that each row is treated separately. The following program arranges each row of the given matrix in descending order of the elements, using bubble sort algorithm.

```
/* Program name: arr28.c */
/* Program to read and print the matrix in matrix format*/
/* Arrange each row in descending order*/
#include<stdio.h>
```

```
#include<conio.h>
void main()
{
int n, m, i, j, a[10][10], t, k;
clrscr();
printf("enter order of matrix\n");
scanf("%d%d", &n, &m);
printf("\n enter %d X %d matrix \n", n, m);
/* for inputting numbers*/
for(i=1;i<=n; ++i)
   for(j=1;j<=m; ++j)
      scanf("%d", &a[i][j]);
printf("\n given matrix  \n");
/* for printing in the matrix format*/
for(i=1;i<=n; ++i)
   {
   for(j=1;j<=m; ++j)
   printf("%8d", a[i][j]);
   printf("\n");
   }
/* arranging the matrix in descending row-wise*/
for(i=1;i<=n; ++i)
{
/* Arranging the ith row in order */
for(j=1;j<=m; ++j)
for(k=1;k<m; ++k)
if(a[j][k]<a[j][k+1])
   {
   t=a[j][k];
   a[j][k]=a[j][k+1];
   a[j][k+1]=t;
   }
printf("\n matrix after arranging row-wise\n\n");
/* for printing in the matrix format*/
for(i=1;i<=n; ++i)
{
   for(j=1;j<=m; ++j)
      printf("%8d",a[i][j]);
   printf("\n");
}
/* for arranging the matrix in column-wise*/
for(i=1;i<=n;++i)
{
for(j=1;j<=m;++j)
for(k=1;k<n; ++k)
```

```
if(a[k][i]< a[k+1][i])
   {
   t=a[k][i];
   a[k][i]=a[k+1][i];
   a[k+1][i]=t;
   }
printf("\n matrix after arranging column-wise\n it will not
      arranges the original matrix\n");
/* For printing in the matrix format*/
for(i=1;i<=n; ++i)
{
   for(j=1;j<=m; ++j)
      printf("%5d",a[i][j]);
   printf("\n");
}
getch();
}
```

Output

Enter order of the matrix

3 4

enter 3 X 4 matrix

10 6 8 9 19 12 1 2 3 22 33 41

given matrix

10	6	8	9
19	12	1	2
3	22	33	41

matrix after arranging row-wise

10	9	8	6
19	12	2	1
41	33	22	3

matrix after arranging column-wise
it will not arranges the original matrix

41	33	22	6
19	12	8	3
10	9	2	1

Now let us look at the output closely, we can observe that the program first arranges all the elements in each row of the given matrix in descending order. Then in case of arranging the matrix elements column-wise, we have taken the already arranged matrix as the input, so the output for column-wise arrangement is not based on the original given matrix. We need to think in such cases were the input to any process is already processed or not. To arrange the matrix column-wise on the original matrix, we have to keep a copy of the matrix in a temporary array before arranging it according to the row-wise. After arranging row-wise, we should take original array from the temporary array and apply our sorting algorithm. The following program implements this. This program arranges according to the ascending order on rows and columns.

```
/* Program name: arr29.c */
/* Program to read and print the matrix in matrix format*/
/* Arrange each row and column in ascending order*/
#include<stdio.h>
#include<conio.h>
void main()
{
int n, m, i, j, a[10][10], b[10][10], t, k; /* b[][] is a
      temporary array to keep original
matrix */
clrscr();
printf("enter order of matrix\n");
scanf("%d%d", &n, &m);
printf("\n enter %d X %d matrix \n", n, m);
/* for inputting numbers*/
for(i=1;i<=n; ++i)
   for(j=1;j<=m; ++j)
   {
   scanf("%d", &a[i][j]);
   b[i][j]=a[i][j];/* to preserve the original values */
   }
printf("\n given matrix  \n");
/* for printing in the matrix format*/
for(i=1;i<=n; ++i)
{
   for(j=1;j<=m; ++j)
      printf("%8d",a[i][j]);
   printf("\n");
}
/* for arranging row-wise */
for(i=1;i<=n; ++i)
for(j=1;j<=m; ++j)
for(k=1;k<m; ++k)
   if(a[j][k]>a[j][k+1])
   {
      t=a[j][k];
      a[j][k]=a[j][k+1];
      a[j][k+1]=t;
   }
printf("\n matrix after arranging row wise\n\n");
/* for printing in the matrix format*/
```

```
for(i=1;i<=n; ++i)
{
    for(j=1;j<=m; ++j)
        printf("%8d",a[i][j]);
    printf("\n");
}
/* for arranging column-wise on original matrix */
for(i=1;i<=n; ++i)
for(j=1;j<=m; ++j)
for(k=1;k<n; ++k)
    if(b[k][i]>b[k+1][i]) /* b[][] contains original data */
    {
    t=b[k][i];
    b[k][i]=b[k+1][i];
    b[k+1][i]=t;
    }
printf("\n matrix after arranging column-wise\n it arranges
        the original
matrix\n");
/* for printing in the matrix format*/
for(i=1;i<=n; ++i)
{
    for(j=1;j<=m; ++j)
        printf("%8d",b[i][j]);
    printf("\n");
}
getch();
}
```

```
Output
Enter order of the matrix
    3 4
enter 3 X 4 matrix
10 6 8 9 19 12 1 2 3 22 33 41
given matrix
10      6       8       9
19      12      1       2
3       22      33      41

matrix after arranging row-wise

6       8       9       10
1       2       12      19
3       22      33      41
matrix after arranging column-wise
it arranges the original matrix

3       6       1       2
10      12      8       9
19      22      33      41
```

The following program adds two matrices.

```
/* Program name: arr30.c */
/* Program to read and print the matrix in matrix format*/
/* Add two matrixes*/
#include<stdio.h>
#include<conio.h>
void main()
{
int n, m, p, q, i, j, a[10][10],b[10][10],c[10][10];
clrscr();
printf("enter order of first matrix\n");
scanf("%d%d",&n,&m);
printf("\n enter first  %d X %d matrix \n", n, m);
/* for inputting numbers for a matrix*/
for(i=1;i<=n; ++i)
for(j=1;j<=m; ++j)
scanf("%d", &a[i][j]);

printf("enter order of second matrix\n");
scanf("%d%d", &p, &q);
printf("\n enter second  %d X %d matrix \n", n, m);
/* for inputting numbers for b matrix*/
for(i=1;i<=p; ++i)
for(j=1;j<=q; ++j)
scanf("%d", &b[i][j]);

printf("\n first matrix  \n");
/* for printing in the matrix format*/
for(i=1;i<=n; ++i)
{
for(j=1;j<=m; ++j)
printf("%8d",a[i][j]);
printf("\n");
}

printf("\n second matrix  \n");
/* for printing in the matrix format*/
for(i=1;i<=p; ++i)
{
for(j=1;j<=q; ++j)
printf("%8d",b[i][j]);
printf("\n");
}

if((n==p)&&(m==q)) /*checking order of both matrices */
```

```
{
for(i=1;i<=n; ++i)
   for(j=1;j<=m; ++j)
      c[i][j]=a[i][j]+b[i][j];

printf("\n resultant matrix\n\n");
/* for printing in the matrix format*/
for(i=1;i<=n; ++i)
   {
   for(j=1;j<=m; ++j)
      printf("%8d",c[i][j]);
   printf("\n");
   }
}
else
printf("\n order of matrix are not same addition is not
      possible\n");
getch();
}
```

Output
enter order of first matrix
3 3
enter first 3 X 3 matrix
1 2 3 4 5 6 7 8 9
enter order of second matrix
3 3

enter second 3 X 3 matrix
5 6 7 8 9 0 1 2 3

first matrix

```
1  2  3
4  5  6
7  8  9
```

second matrix

```
5  6  7
8  9  0
1  2  3
```

resultant matrix

```
 6   8  10
12  14   6
 8  10  12
```

The following program multiplies two matrices.

```
/* Program name: arr31.c */
/* Program to read and print the matrix in matrix format*/
/* Multiply two matrixes*/
#include<stdio.h>
#include<conio.h>
void main()
{
int n, m, p, q, i, j, a[10][10],b[10][10],c[10][10],k;
clrscr();
printf("enter order of first matrix\n");
scanf("%d%d", &n, &m);
printf("enter first  %d X %d matrix \n", n, m);
/* for inputting numbers*/
for(i=1;i<=n; ++i)
for(j=1;j<=m; ++j)
scanf("%d", &a[i][j]);

printf("enter order of second matrix\n");
scanf("%d%d", &p, &q);
printf("enter second  %d X %d matrix \n", p, q);
/* for inputting numbers*/
for(i=1;i<=p; ++i)
for(j=1;j<=q; ++j)
scanf("%d", &b[i][j]);

printf(" first matrix  \n");
/* for printing in the matrix format*/
for(i=1;i<=n; ++i)
{
for(j=1;j<=m; ++j)
printf("%8d",a[i][j]);
printf("\n");
}
printf("second matrix  \n");
/* for printing in the matrix format*/
for(i=1;i<=p; ++i)
{
for(j=1;j<=q; ++j)
printf("%8d",b[i][j]);
printf("\n");
}

if((n==q)&&(m==p)) /*checking for multiplication condition on
        order */
{
for(i=1;i<=n; ++i)
```

```
for(j=1;j<=m; ++j)
{
c[i][j]=0;
for(k=1;k<=n; ++k)
c[i][j]+=a[i][k]*b[k][j];
}
printf("resultant matrix\n");
/* for printing in the matrix format*/
for(i=1;i<=n; ++i)
{
for(j=1;j<=m; ++j)
printf("%5d",c[i][j]);
printf("\n");
}
}
else
printf("\n order of matrix not allows multiplication\n");
getch();
}
```

Output

```
enter order of first matrix
2 2
 enter first 2 X 2 matrix
1 2 3 4
enter order of second matrix
2 2
 enter second 2 X 2 matrix
1 2 3 4
first matrix
  1  2
  3  4
second matrix
  1  2
  3  4
resultant matrix
  7  10
 15  22
```

Mean of the given list of numbers means the average of all the numbers in the list. The deviation means the difference of the number as compared to the overall list average i.e., its mean. The following program finds the mean and deviation of each elements from the given list of numbers.

```
/* Program name : arr32.c */
/* Program to deviation of each number from the average of the
     list */
#include<stdio.h>
#include<conio.h>
```

```
void main()
{
int n,i;
float a[100],avg=0;
clrscr();
printf("\n enter n \n");
scanf("%d",&n);
printf("enter %d numbers\n",n);
for(i=1;i<=n;++i)
{
scanf("%f",&a[i]);
avg+=a[i]; /*finding the sum */
}
printf("\n given list\n");
for(i=1;i<=n;++i)
printf("%8.3f",a[i]);
avg=avg/n; /* find average */
printf("\n average = %8.3f",avg);
printf("\n deviation of each numbers from average of the
        list\n");
for(i=1;i<=n;++i)
printf("%8.3f",avg-a[i]);
getch();
}
```

Output

```
enter n
6
enter 6 numbers
12 43 32 54 33 26

given list
 12.000  43.000  32.000  54.000  33.000  26.000
average =  33.333
deviation of each numbers from average of the list
 21.333 -9.667  1.333 -20.667  0.333  7.333
```

This program finds the mean, variance and standard deviation of the given list of numbers. 'mean' as we have seen already is the average of all the numbers in the list. 'Variance' is the sum of squares of the deviation of each number from its mean. The 'standard deviation' is the square root of variance.

```
/* Program name : arr33.c */
/* Program to find mean, variance and standard deviation of a
        list of numbers */
```

```
#include<stdio.h>
#include<conio.h>
#include<math.h>
void main()
{
int n,i;
float a[50],mean,var,stdd;
clrscr();
printf("\n enter n \n");
scanf("%d",&n);
printf(" enter %d numbers\n",n);
mean=0;
for(i=1;i<=n;++i)
{
scanf("%f",&a[i]);
mean+=a[i];
}
mean/=n;
printf("given list\n");
for(i=1;i<=n;++i)
{
printf("%.3f\t",a[i]);
var+=(mean-a[i])*(mean-a[i]);
}
var/=n;
stdd=sqrt(var);
printf("\nmean  =  %f\nVariance=%f\nstandard deviation =%f",
        mean, var, stdd);
getch();
}
```

Output

```
enter n
7
enter 7 numbers
12 34 45 43 23 121 54
given list
12.000 34.000 45.000 43.000 23.000 121.000 54.000
mean = 47.428570
Variance=1073.387817
standard deviation=32.762596
```

In a matrix the square root of the sum of squares of all the elements is called as norm of the matrix. The following program finds the norm of the matrix.

```
/* Program name : arr34.c */
/* Program to find norm of the matrix */
/* Norm is square root of the sum of squares of the elements */
#include<stdio.h>
#include<conio.h>
#include<math.h>
void main()
{
int n,m,i,j;
float a[10][10],sum=0;
clrscr();
printf("\n enter order of matrix \n");
scanf("%d%d",&m,&n);
printf(" enter matrix elements\n");
for(i=1;i<=m;++i)
for(j=1;j<=n;++j)
scanf("%f",&a[i][j]);
printf("given matrix is\n");
for(i=1;i<=m;++i)
{
for(j=1;j<=n;++j)
{
sum+=a[i][j]*a[i][j];
printf("%8.3f",a[i][j]);
}
printf("\n");
}
sum=sqrt(sum);
printf("\nnorm of the matrix = %f\n",sum);
getch();
}
```

Output

```
enter order of matrix
4 3
enter matrix elements
3 2 4 5 1 2 3 4 6 7 8 9
given matrix is
   3.000  2.000  4.000
   5.000  1.000  2.000
   3.000  4.000  6.000
   7.000  8.000  9.000

norm of the matrix = 17.720045
```

The transpose of a matrix means, making rows of the matrix into columns and columns into corresponding rows. For finding the transpose it need not be a square matrix. The following program finds the transpose of the matrix.

```
/* Program name : arr35.c */
/* Program to find transpose of the matrix */
#include<stdio.h>
#include<conio.h>
void main()
{
int n,m,i,j;
int a[10][10];
clrscr();
printf("\n enter order of matrix \n");
scanf("%d%d",&m,&n);
printf(" enter matrix elements\n");
for(i=1;i<=m;++i)
for(j=1;j<=n;++j)
scanf("%d",&a[i][j]);
printf("given matrix is\n");
for(i=1;i<=m;++i)
{
for(j=1;j<=n;++j)
printf("%8d",a[i][j]);
printf("\n");
}
printf("transposed matrix is\n");
for(i=1;i<=n;++i)
{
for(j=1;j<=m;++j)
printf("%8d",a[j][i]);
printf("\n");
}

getch();
}
```

Output

```
enter order of matrix
3 4
enter matrix elements
8 1 7 2 6 3 5 4 9 0 10 11
given matrix is
   8    1    7    2
   6    3    5    4
   9    0   10   11
transposed matrix is
   8    6    9
   1    3    0
   7    5   10
   2    4   11
```

5

Strings

5.1 Introduction

Character arrays with a null character (\0) at the end are called strings. Or a group of continuous characters with a null character at the end is a string.

General syntax for string declaration is:

char stringname [size];

```
Ex: char    s[10];
    char    name [20];
```

The maximum number of characters stored will be size-1, one character will be always '\0' stored at the end. So in the string variable 's' we can store maximum 9 characters and the string variable 'name' can hold maximum 19 characters.

The strings can be initialized at the time of declaration or at any point in the program. The following statement initializes the string during declaration.

```
char s[20] = "Bangalore city";
```

It is stored in the memory as shown below

B	a	n	g	a	l	o	r	e		c	i	t	y	\0

Individual characters of the string can be accessed using string index.

```
Ex: s[0]   is 'B'
    s[1]   is 'a' etc.
```

5.2 String I/O

To access the entire contents of one dimensional character array we directly refer string variable.

```
Ex: 1. char  name[20] ;
scanf("%s", name);
printf( "%s",name); etc.
```

NOTE: For strings %s format specifier is used and address operator (&) cannot be used, because array name itself specifies address.

We can declare strings as two-dimensional arrays.

Ex: char names[20][20];

'names' is an array of strings which can store 20 strings whose maximum length is of 19 characters each. Two dimensional arrays can be initialized at the time of declaration as follows.

Char names[20][20]={"Bangalore", "Chennai", "Hyderabad", "Delhi", "Calcutta"};

Here the first five storage locations are occupied with the given names and other storage locations remain empty.

To access the contents of a two dimensional character array we use array subscripts as shown below:

names[0] gives 'Bangalore',
names[1] gives "Chennai', and so on.

If we want to access individual characters of a particular string we need to use both the subscripts as shown below:

names[0][0] gives 'B',
names[4][2] gives 'l' etc.

Two dimensional arrays can be scanned from the key board using the functions scanf() and gets().

```
Eg.
char names[20][20] ;
for(i=0; i < 20; ++i)
scanf("%s",name[i]);
Etc.
```

scanf() function takes only a single word where as gets() function takes the entire line from the key board. But these two functions leave the enter key character(\n) in the input buffer. To clear the buffer the function fflush() is used which is present in the header file stdio.h.

For string output we use functions like puts() and printf().

```
Eg.
char names[20][20]={"Bangalore", "chennai"};
puts(names[0]);/*displays Bangalore.*/
printf("%s", names[1]);/*displays chennai*/
```

C language provides number of standard library functions to handle strings. All these functions are grouped under string.h header file.

5.3 Library Functions for String Manipulation

We have set of functions to deal with the input/output operations of individual characters.

Suppose 's' is a string variable, then

strlen(s) ; - gives length of string excluding \0.
strrev(s); - reverses the string.
strupr(s);- converts the string into its upper case.
strlwr(s);- converts to lower case.
strchr(s, C)- searches for a character 'C' in string s & returns its address if present otherwise returns zero.

Suppose; s1 & s2 are two strings then.

strcpy(s1, s2); – copies string s2 into s1.
strcat(s1 , s2); – combines string s2 at the end of string s1 & places \0 at the end of s1, s2 unaffected.
strcmp(s1,s2); -compares string s1 with s2 and gives 0 when both strings are same, gives > 0 when string s1 is greater than s2, and gives < 0 when string s1 is less than s2, lexicographically.
strcmpi(s1, s2) same as strcmp (s1, s2) but it ignores the case.
strncmp(s1, s2, n) – same as strcmp but it compares only first n characters of both the strings.
strncmpi(s1 , s2, n) – same as strcmpi( ) but it compares only first n characters of both strings.
strncpy(s1, s2, n); – copies first n characters of string s2 into string s1.
strncat(s1, s2, n); - copies first n characters of string s2 at the end of string s1.
strstr(s1, s2); searches for string s2 in string s1 if present returns the pointer to the first character of s2 in s1 otherwise returns NULL.

5.4 Character Related Functions

C provides certain functions that will work only on a single character; all these functions are stored in ctype.h header file.

Suppose C is a character variable, then C may contain any character, alphabet, digit, or any of the special characters such as , ; . ( ) = ? etc.

Following are few functions that take C as an argument and give the return value as either true or false.

isalpha(C) gives true if C contains alphabet.
isupper(C) gives true if C contains uppercase alphabet
islower(C) gives true if C is a lower case alphabet.
isdigit(C) gives true if C is a digit (o to 9)
isxdigit(C) gives true it C contains hexadecimal digit (0 –9 . a-f)
isspace(C) gives true if C is a space.
iscntl (C) gives true if C is control character.

Along with these, the other case conversion functions are

toupper(C); converts C to uppercase if it contains a lower case alphabet other wise no change.

tolower(C) ; converts C to lowercase if it contains a uppercase alphabet otherwise no change takes place.

5.5 Programs

The following program illustrates the use of getchar() and putchar() functions to read and display a single character.

```
/* Program name: str1.c */
/* reading and printing a single character */
/* illustrates getchar() and putchar() */
#include<stdio.h>
#include<conio.h>
void main()
{
  char c;
  clrscr();
  printf("\n enter a character\n");
  c=getchar();
  printf("\n the given character is\n");
  putchar(c);
  getch();
}
```

Output

enter a character
f

the given character is
f

This program illustrates the use of scanf() for string input. This function considers only the first word and leaves all the remaining words(if any) including enter key in the input buffer.

```
/* Program name: str2.c */
/* program to read and display a string */
/* uses scanf() and inputs one word only */
#include<stdio.h>
#include<conio.h>
void main()
{
char s[100];
clrscr();
printf("\n enter a string\n");
scanf("%s",s);
printf("given string is\n %s",s);
getch();
}
```

Output
enter a string
it is a string program
given string is
it

The function gets() takes the entire line of input until enter key. It leaves enter key value in the buffer.

```
/* Program name: str3.c */
/* program to read and display a string */
/* uses gets() and inputs one line */
#include<stdio.h>
#include<conio.h>
void main()
{
char s[100];
clrscr();
printf("\n enter a string\n");
gets(s);
printf("given string is\n %s",s);
getch();
}
```

Output
enter a string
it is a string program
given string is
it is a string program

This program takes single character input and changes its case. It makes use of ASCII codes.

Note: ASCII codes of upper case alphabets are 65 to 90 for A to Z respectively.
ASCII codes of lower case alphabets are 97 to 122 for a to z respectively.

```
/* Program name: str4.c */
/*  Program for checking a character as uppercase or lower
    case and changing its case without using library functions
    */
#include<stdio.h>
#include<conio.h>
void main()
{
char c;
```

```
clrscr();
printf("enter char\n");
c=getchar();
if((c>=65)&&(c<=90))
{
printf("upper case char\n its lower case is %c\n",c+32);
}
else
if((c>=97)&&(c<=122))
{
princf("lower case char\n its upper  case is %c\n",c-32);
}
else
printf("the given char %c is not an alphabet\n",c);
getch();
}
```

Output
enter char
N
upper case char
its lower case is n

String length is defined as the number of characters in the string excluding '\0'. To find the length it is essential to check and count all the characters till the end.

```
/* Program name: str5.c */
/* program to read and display a string */
/* get its length , uses library function strlen() */
#include<stdio.h>
#include<string.h>
#include<conio.h>
void main()
{
char s[100];
int n;
clrscr();
printf("\n enter a string\n");
gets(s);
n=strlen(s);
printf("given string is\n %s\n length = %d\n",s,n);
getch();
}
```

Output
enter a string
mohan is a good boy.
given string is
mohan is a good boy.
length = 19

In the above program we have used the library function strlen() to find the length of a string. In the program below we find the length of a string by writing the code.

```
/* Program name: str6.c */
/* program to read and display a string */
/* get its length, without using library function */
#include<stdio.h>
#include<string.h>
#include<conio.h>
void main()
{
char s[100];
int n=0;
clrscr();
printf("\n enter a string\n");
gets(s);
while(s[n]!='\0')
n++;
printf("given string is\n %s\n length = %d\n",s,n);
getch();
}
```

Output
enter a string
mohan is a good boy.
given string is
mohan is a good boy.
length = 19

The following program prints the given string in the reverse order.

```
/* Program name: str7.c */
/* program to read and display a string */
/* reverse the string , using library function */
#include<stdio.h>
#include<string.h>
```

```
#include<conio.h>
void main()
{
char s[50];
clrscr();
printf("\n enter a string\n");
gets(s);
printf("given string is\n %s\n",s);
  strrev(s);
printf("\n reversed string \n %s\n",s);
getch();
}
```

Output
enter a string
nothing is permanent in this world but change.
given string is
nothing is permanent in this world but change.

reversed string
.egnahc tub dlrow siht ni tnenamrep si gnihton

The string reverse can be achieved without using the library function by copying all the characters of the string into another string in the reverse order.

```
/* Program name: str8.c */
/* program to read and display a string */
/* reverse the string ,without using library function */
#include<stdio.h>
#include<string.h>
#include<conio.h>
void main()
{
char s[50],s1[50];
int n,i=0;
clrscr();
printf("\n enter a string\n");
gets(s);
s1[n]='\0';

while(s[i]!='\0')
{
s1[n-1-i]=s[i];
i++;
```

```
}
printf("given string is\n %s\n",s);
printf(" reversed string \n %s\n",s1);
getch();
}
```

Output
enter a string
changes are inevitable.
given string is
changes are inevitable.

reversed string
.elbativeni era segnahc

The string is said to be palindrome if we get the same string back after reversing it. For example 'malayalam', 'dad' etc.

```
/* Program name: str9.c */
/* check for string palindrome, using library function */
#include<stdio.h>
#include<string.h>
#include<conio.h>
void main()
{
char s[30],s1[30];
clrscr();
printf("\n enter a string\n");
gets(s);
strcpy(s1,s);
strrev(s);
if(strcmp(s,s1)==0)
printf("\n given string is palindrome\n");
else
printf("given string is not palindrome\n");
getch();
}
```

Output
enter a string
malayalam
given string is palindrome

This program checks whether the string is palindrome or not without using the library function. For this first we reverse and store the given string into another string and we check the reversed string and the original string for equality.

```
/* Program name: str10.c */
/* check for string palindrome, without using library function
     */
#include<stdio.h>
#include<string.h>
#include<conio.h>
void main()
{
char s[50];
int n=0,i,t=0;
clrscr();
printf("\n enter a string\n");
gets(s);
while(s[n]!='\0')
n++;
for(i=0;i<=n/2;++i)
if(s[i]!=s[n-i-1])
t=1;
if(t==0)
printf("\n given string is palindrome\n");
else
printf("given string is not palindrome\n");
getch();
}
```

Output
enter a string
Malayalam
given string is not palindrome

This program copies one string into another string. String copy means transferring the contents of one string to another. The contents of the source string remains unaffected and the contents of the destination string become the contents of source string.

```
/* Program name: str11.c */
/* copy a string onto another string, using library
function */
#include<stdio.h>
#include<string.h>
#include<conio.h>
```

```
void main()
{
char s[' '],s1[' '];
clrscr();
printf("\n enter a string\n");
gets(s);
strcpy(s1,s);
printf("\n given string \n %s\n",s);
printf("\n copied string \n %s\n",s1);
getch();
}
```

```
Output
enter a string
Computer
given string
computer
copied string
computer
```

Concatenation means joining two strings. Second string is copied at the end of first string. The following two programs implement this, one with the help of library function and another without using library function.

```
/* Program name: str12.c */
/* concatenation of two strings.  Using library function */
#include<stdio.h>
#include<string.h>
#include<conio.h>
void main()
{
char s[' '],s1[' '];
clrscr();
printf("\n enter first string\n");
gets(s);
printf("\n enter second string\n");
gets(s1);

printf("\n given first string \n %s\n",s);
printf("\n given second  string \n %s\n",s1);
strcat(s,s1);
printf("\n concatenated string \n%s",s);
getch();
}
```

```
Output
enter first string
Why to learn C
enter second string
To do programs

 given first string
Why to learn C

 given second  string
To do programs
 concatenated string
Why to learn CTo do programs
```

The following program concatenates two strings without using library function. It copies all the characters of second string one by one starting from the end of the string and at the end of the first string places '\0'.

```
/* Program name: str13.c */
/* concatenation of two strings. Without using library function
   */
#include<stdio.h>
#include<string.h>
#include<conio.h>
void main()
{
char s[' '],s1[' '];
int i,j;
clrscr();
printf("\n enter first string\n");
gets(s);
printf("\n enter second string\n");
gets(s1);

printf("\n given first string \n %s\n",s);
printf("\n given second  string \n %s\n",s1);
i=0;
j=0;
while(s[i]!='\0')
i++;
while(s1[j]='\0')
{
s[i]=s1[j];
i++;
```

```
        j++;
        }
        s[i]='\0';
        printf("\n concatenated string \n%s",s);
        getch();
        }
```

Output
enter first string
success is a journey
enter second string
not a destination

given first string
success is a journey
given second string
not a destination
concatenated string
success is a journey not a destination

The following program takes a line of text, using getchar() function. This program will not make use of string variable for storing text instead it makes use of buffer for temporary storage. For converting lowercase to uppercase it uses ternary operator(? :). This program converts only the characters in lowercase to uppercase and all other characters remain unchanged.

```
/* Program name: str14.c */
/*program to read a line of characters and convert them to
      upper case*/
/* to illustrate ternary operator*/
#include<stdio.h>
#include<conio.h>
#include<ctype.h>
void main()
{
    char c;
    clrscr();
    printf("\n enter  characters\n");
    while((c=getchar())!='\n')
    (islower(c))?printf("%c",toupper(c)):printf("%c",c);
    getch();
}
```

Output

enter characters
rew ww2344fsd fASDA fdg
REW WW2344FSD FASDA FDG

In a given line of text checking how many times a particular character is repeated is called its frequency of occurrence of that character.

```
/* Program name: str15.c */
/* frequency of occurrence of a character in a string*/
#include<stdio.h>
#include<conio.h>
#include<string.h>
void main()
{
   int n,c=0,i;
   char s[100],ch;
   clrscr();
      printf("\n enter a string\n");
      gets(s);
      fflush(stdin);/* clears the buffer */
      printf("\n enter a character\n");
      ch=getchar();
      n=strlen(s);
      for(i=0;i<n;++i)
      if(s[i]==ch)
      c++;
      printf(" given string is\n %s\n given character is =
                                %c\n      present      %d
                                times\n",s,ch,c);
  getch();
}
```

Output
enter a string A common man needs security an common man needs opportunity. enter a character e given string is A common man needs security an common man needs opportunity. given character is = e present 5 times

This program illustrates the use of strstr() function which searches for a string pattern in another string and returns the position of string in case it is present otherwise returns NULL.

```
/* Program name: str16.c */
/* search a string in another string*/
#include<stdio.h>
#include<conio.h>
#include<string.h>
void main()
{
  char s1[100],s2[100];
  clrscr();
    printf("\n enter first string\n");
    gets(s1);
    printf("\n enter second string\n");
    gets(s2);
    if(strstr(s1,s2)!=0)
    printf("\n  string %s is present  in  the  string
                              %s\n",s2,s1);

    else
    printf("\n  string %s is  not  present  in  the  string
                              %s\n",s2,s1);

    getch();
}
```

Output

enter first string
she sells sea shells in the sea shore

enter second string
shells in the sea

string shells in the sea is present in the string she sells sea shells in the sea shore

The following program makes use of two dimensional string arrays to read 'n' different words individually and prints them in a sentence with '.' at the end.

```
/* Program name: str17.c */
/* input n words and print them as a sentence */
#include<stdio.h>
#include<conio.h>
#include<string.h>
void main()
{
   char s[100][20];
```

```
int n,i;
clrscr();
   printf("\n enter n\n");
   scanf("%d",&n);
   printf("\n enter %d words\n",n);
   for(i=0;i<n;++i)
   scanf("%s",s[i]);
   printf("\n given words as a sentence is\n");
   for(i=0;i<n;++i)
   printf(" %s",s[i]);
   printf(".");
   getch();
```

Output

enter n
5

enter 5 words
bangalore
is
a
garden
city

given words as a sentence is
bangalore is a garden city.

This program takes a line of text as an input and illustrates the use of different character related functions such as islower(), isupper(), isdigit() etc. to count the number of lowercase alphabets, uppercase alphabets, digits and other characters in the given text.

```
/* Program name: str18.c */
/* count number of digits, upper case , lower case and
other characters*/
#include<stdio.h>
#include<conio.h>
#include<string.h>
#include<ctype.h>
void main()
{
   int n,i,uc=0,dc=0,lc=0,oc=0;
   char s[100];
   clrscr();
```

```
    printf("\n enter a string\n");
    gets(s);
    n=strlen(s);
    for(i=0;i<n;++i)
    {
    if(islower(s[i]))
    lc++;
    else
    if(isupper(s[i]))
    uc++;
    else
    if(isdigit(s[i]))
    dc++;
    else
    oc++;
    }
    printf("no. of uppercase = %d\n",uc);
    printf("no. of lowercase = %d\n",lc);
    printf("no. of digits = %d\n",dc);
    printf("no. of others = %d\n",oc);
    getch();
}
```

Output

enter a string
#175, 3rd Cross, 11th Main, Jayanagar, B'lore.
no. of uppercase = 4
no. of lowercase = 23
no. of digits = 6
no. of others = 13

This program counts the number of each of the five vowels(a,e,i,o,u) in a given line of text. It considers both cases of the characters (it is not case sensitive).

```
/* Program name: str19.c */
/* count vowels in a line of text */
#include<stdio.h>
#include<conio.h>
#include<string.h>
void main()
{
   int n,i,ac=0,ec=0,ic=0,cc=0,uc=0;
   char s[100];
   clrscr();
```

```
        printf("\n enter a string\n");
        gets(s);
        n=strlen(s);
        for(i=0;i<n;++i)
        {
        switch(s[i])
        {
        case 'a':
        case 'A': ac++; break;
        case 'e':
        case 'E': ec++; break;
        case 'i':
        case 'I': ic++; break;
        case 'o':
        case 'O': oc++; break;
        case 'u':
        case 'U': uc++; break;
        }
        }
        printf("no. of a  = %d\n",ac);
        printf("no. of e  = %d\n",ec);
        printf("no. of i  = %d\n",ic);
        printf("no. of o  = %d\n",oc);
        printf("no. of u  = %d\n",uc);
        getch();
}
```

Output

enter a string
If you waste time, time wastes you and it quits.
no. of a = 3
no. of e = 4
no. of i = 5
no. of o = 2
no. of u = 3

The following program arranges the given list of names in ascending order using bubble sort. It makes use of library functions strcmp() and strcpy().

```
/* Program name: str20.c */
/* arranging n names in order*/
#include<stdio.h>
```

```
#include<conio.h>
#include<string.h>
void main()
{
    int n,i,j;
    char t[20],a[100][20];
    clrscr();
        printf("\n enter n \n");
        scanf("%d",&n);
        printf("\n enter %d names\n",n);
        for(i=1;i<=n;++i)
        scanf("%s",a[i]);
        for(i=1;i<n;++i)
        for(j=1;j<n;++j)
        if(strcmp(a[j],a[j+1])>0)
        {
        strcpy(t,a[j]);
        strcpy(a[j],a[j+1]);
        strcpy(a[j+1],t);
        }
        printf("\n arranged names are\n");
        for(i=1;i<=n;++i)
        printf("\n%s",a[i]);
        getch();
}
```

Output

enter n
5

enter 5 names
Jyothi
Shreyas
Kalam
Stalin
Tom

arranged names are

Jyothi
Kalam
Shreyas
Stalin
Tom

This program converts all uppercase characters to lowercase and lowercase characters to uppercase from the given line of text. It makes use of ternary operator. In case the entered characters are not alphabets then they remains unchanged.

```
/* Program name: str21.c */
/* program to read a line text */
/* convert all upper case to lower case and vice versa*/
#include<stdio.h>
#include<conio.h>
#include<ctype.h>
void main()
{
char s[' '];
int i;
clrscr();
printf("\n enter a line of text\n");
gets(s);
printf("\n given string is \n %s\n",s);
printf("changed string is \n");
i=0;
while(s[i]!='\0')
{
printf("%c",(isupper(s[i])?tolower(s[i]):(islower(s[i])?
      toupper(s[i]):s[i])));
i++;
}
getch();
}
```

Output

```
enter a line of text
C Is A ProGramming Language.

given string is
C Is A ProGramming Language.
changed string is
c iS a pROgRAMMING lANGUAGE.
```

Usually there will be one space in between each word in a sentence. In such cases just by counting the number of spaces we get total number of words in a given line of text. There may be more than one space in between words in a sentence. In that case we need different approach to count the number of words in a sentence. In the following program we count the number of words in a line of text by considering the first case.

```
/* Program name: str22.c */
/* program to read a line text */
/* count the number of words*/
/* it will not considers multiple spaces */
#include<stdio.h>
#include<conio.h>
#include<ctype.h>
void main()
{
char s[' '];
int i,c=0;
clrscr();
printf("\n enter a line of text\n");
gets(s);
printf("\n given string is \n %s\n",s);
i=0;
while(s[i]!='\0')
{
if(isspace(s[i])) /* can be written as if(s[i]!=' ') */
c++;
i++;
}
if(i!=1) /* when i is 1 the string contains only null and no
        words. Otherwise the number of spaces will be one less
        than the number of words */
c++;
printf("\n number of words = %d",c);
getch();
}
```

Output

enter a line of text
Stand up, Be Strong, Be Bold, Take the Whole responsibility on your own Shoulders.

given string is
Stand up, Be Strong, Be Bold, Take the Whole responsibility on your own Shoulders.

number of words = 16

As we have seen in the output of the above program considering each space as a separation of the words in a sentence may lead to wrong assumption if there are more than one space in between words. In the following program we are taking care of such consecutive spaces in between words. We also consider the possibility of spaces in the beginning of the sentence and at the end of the sentence while calculating actual number of words in a given sentence.

```
/* Program name: str23.c */
/* program to read a line text */
/* count the number of words*/
/* it  consider multiple spaces */
#include<stdio.h>
#include<conio.h>
#include<ctype.h>
void main()
{
char s[' '];
int i,c=0;
clrscr();
printf("\n enter a line of text\n");
gets(s);
printf("\n given string is \n %s\n",s);
i=0;
/* to handle starting spaces*/
while(s[i]==' ')
i++;
while(s[i]!='\0')
{
if((isspace(s[i]))&&(!(s[i+1]==' ' || s[i+1]== '\0')))
/*to avoid multiple space in between words */
c++;
i++;
}
if(i!=1) /* when i is 1 the string contains only null and no
    words. Otherwise the number of spaces will be one less
    than the number of words */
c++;
printf("\n number of words = %d",c);
getch();
}
```

Output

enter a line of text
Arise,   Awake and Stop not Till the Goal is Reached.

given string is
Arise,   Awake and Stop not Till the Goal is Reached.

number of words = 10

This is a simple program which searches a name in a given list of names. It makes use of linear search which we have already discussed earlier.

```
/* Program name: str24.c */
/* search a name from a list of n names*/
#include<stdio.h>
#include<conio.h>
#include<string.h>
void main()
{
    int n,i,j=0;
    char t[20],a[100][20];
    clrscr();
      printf("\n enter n \n");
      scanf("%d",&n);
      printf("\n enter %d names\n",n);
      for(i=1;i<=n;++i)
      scanf("%s",a[i]);
      printf("\n enter name to search\n");
      scanf("%s",t);
      for(i=1;i<n;++i)
      if(strcmp(a[i],t)==0)
      {
      printf("\n the name %s present at position %d \n",t,i);
      j=1;
      }
      if(j==0)
      printf("\n the name %s is not present \n");
      getch();
  }
```

Output

```
enter n
5

enter 5 names
TOM
DICK
JERRY
HARRY
JACK

enter name to search
HARRY

the name HARRY present at position 4
```

This program removes all the blanks (spaces) in the given sentence. It makes use of very simple approach that keeps on printing all the characters from the given string when they are not spaces.

```
/* Program name: str25.c */
/* program to read a line text */
/* squeeze out all blanks*/
#include<stdio.h>
#include<conio.h>
#include<ctype.h>
void main()
{
char s[' '];
int i;
clrscr();
printf("\n enter a line of text\n");
gets(s);
printf("\n given string is \n %s\n",s);
printf("changed string is \n");
i=0;
while(s[i]!='\0')
{
if(!(isspace(s[i]))) /* can be written as if(s[i]!=' ') */
printf("%c",s[i]);
i++;
}
getch();
}
```

Output

enter a line of text
Until Truely Loved I Was Alone

given string is
Until Truely Loved I Was Alone
changed string is
UntilTruelyLovedIWasAlone

The string operation 'extract' means taking certain portion of the sub string from the given string. This program takes the main string, the starting character and the number of characters we extract as input from the keyboard and displays the extracted sub string on the screen.

```
/* Program name: str26.c */
/* program to extract a substring from main string*/
#include<stdio.h>
#include<conio.h>
#include<string.h>
void main()
{
   int n,i,pos,n1;
   char s[100];
   clrscr();
   printf("\n enter a string\n");
   gets(s);
   printf("\n enter position of the substring \n");
      scanf("%d",&pos);
      printf("enter number of characters to extract\n");
      scanf("%d",&n);
      n1=strlen(s);
      if(pos+n-1>n1)
      printf("\n invalid position\n");
      else
      {
      printf("Sub string is \n");
      for(i=pos-1;i<pos+n-1;++i)
      printf("%c",s[i]);
      }
      getch();
 }
```

Output

enter a string
Programming
enter position of the substring
4
enter number of characters to extract
4
Sub string is
gram

6

Structures, Unions and Bit Fields

6.1 Introduction

Structure is a user defined data type in which we can group number of data values of same type or of different types into a single variable. The use of structure is a two fold process. First we have to define a structure, which acts as a blue print, to declare the variables of its type.

The general syntax for defining a structure is.

```
struct  structurename
{
members-declarations;
members-declarations;
...
...
};
```

The members may be of any fundamental data types or user defined data types such as string, arrays, or other structures.

In a structure all the members must be data members and by default all members are public in scope i.e., they can be accessed from any where outside the body of the structure. Scope of members cannot be changed.

```
Ex: struct    emp
              {
              int  eno;
              char name[20];
              char addr[40];
              float sal;
              };
```

Here emp is a structure name. It has four data members.

Once structure is defined we can easily declare the variables of type structure. The structure name becomes a new data type for declaring the variables of that type.

Ex: struct emp e;

The keyword 'struct' is must while declaring variables.

The structure variables may be declared during structure definition or later in the program. Structure can be defined within the body of a function (local) or outside the body of a function (global).

```
Ex:
struct student
{
int rno;
char name[20] ;
char subject[25]; /* branch */
} s1 ={ 20," sneha", "bbm"},s2;
```

Here s1 and s2 are two-structure variables declared along with definition of the structure. Structure variable s1 is initialized with the values rno as 20, name as sneha and subject as bbm where as s2 variable is just declared and its data members are not initialized.

6.2 Arrays and Structures

We can declare an array of structure variables as follows.

Ex: struct student s[100];

Using array index and membership operator (.) we can easily access the particular member of a structure.

Ex: s[0].rno gives rno of first student.
s[10] gives all the information of 10th student.

We can do any kind of operations on members of structures.

Ex: s[i] = s[i+1];

Assigns $(i+1)^{th}$ structure variable value to i^{th} variable.

strcpy(s[i]. name, "sagar");

assigns the value "sagar" to the member 'name' of ith structure variable.

if (strcmp(s[i].name, s[i+1].name)>0)

Compares values of the member 'name' of structure variables s[i] and s[i+1].

6.3 Memory allocations

Structures can be allocated the memory only when structure variables are declared. Just by defining a structure memory will not be allocated to it.

6.4 Programs

Let us look at some sample programs explained below to make the concept clear.

This program illustrates the definition and usage of structures.

```
/* Program name: stru1.c */
/* Program to illustrate structure */
/* Program to declare a simple local structure */
/* Initialize values for structure members and print them*/
#include<stdio.h>
```

```
#include<conio.h>
void main()
{
    struct sample /* defining a structure */
    {
        int num1;
        float num2;
        char c;
    };
    struct sample s; /* structure variable declaration*/
    clrscr();
    s.num1=10; /* initializing the values to structure members*/
    s.num2=20.55;
    s.c='A';
    printf("\n int value = %d",s.num1);
    printf("\n float value = %f",s.num2);
    printf("\n character = %c",s.c);
    getch();
}
```

output
int value = 10
float value = 20.550000
character = A

The following program declares a simple structure. The size of a structure means the sum of sizes of all the members. Using sizeof() operator for the structure variable we get the size of structure variable.

```
/* Program name: stru2.c */
/* Program to illustrate size of the structure */
/* program to declare a simple global structure */
/* initialize values for structure members and print them*/
/* also print size of the structure variable*/
#include<stdio.h>
#include<conio.h>
struct sample /* defining a structure */
{
    int num1;
    float num2;
    char c;
};
```

```
void main()
{
   struct sample s={10,20.123,'A'};
   /*structure variable declaration and initialization*/
   clrscr();
   printf("\n int value = %d",s.num1);
   printf("\n float value = %f",s.num2);
   printf("\n character = %c",s.c);
   printf("\n size of structure sample in bytes = %d",
        sizeof(sample));
   getch();
}
```

output
int value = 10
float value = 20.123000
character = A
size of structure sample in bytes = 7

In the above two programs we have given static input to the members of the structure. In the following programs let us discuss the dynamic input to the members of a structure. The structure has three data members in which two of them are derived data types(strings) and one is fundamental data type(int).

```
/* Program name: stru3.c */
/* structure illustration through dynamic input */
#include<stdio.h>
#include<conio.h>

struct student /* defining a structure */
{
int roll_num;
char name[20];
char address[30];
};

void main()
{
struct student s;
clrscr();
printf(" enter roll number name and address\n");
scanf("%d%s%s", &s.roll_num,s.name,s.address);/* dynamic input
     to structure members */
printf("\n roll number = %d",s.roll_num);
printf("\n name = %s",s.name);
```

```
printf("\n address = %s",s.address);
printf("\n size of structure student in bytes = %d", sizeof(s));
getch();
}
```

```
output
enter roll number name and address
1234 keshav Bangalore
roll number = 1234
name = keshav
address = Bangalore
size of structure student in bytes = 52
```

The following program makes use of built in structure called 'time' which is given in the header file 'dos.h'. This structure contains four data members of type integer namely ti_hour, ti_min, ti_sec and ti_hund to represent hours, minutes, seconds and fractions of seconds respectively. By using library function 'gettime()' we can access the system time and display it on the screen. The gettime() function takes single argument which is a pointer to the 'time' structure variable(pointers are dealt later in this book).

```
/* Program name: stru4.c */
/* program to get system time using built-in function */
#include<stdio.h>
#include<conio.h>
#include<dos.h>
void main()
{
struct time t; /* variable of built-in structure 'time'*/
clrscr();
gettime(&t);/* to get the system time */
printf("The current time is : %2d:%02d:%02d.%02d\n",
t.ti_hour, t.ti_min, t.ti_sec, t.ti_hund);
getch();
}
```

```
Output
The current time is : 02:30:50.54
```

The following program gets the system date on the screen, which makes use of built-in structure 'date' and library function getdate(). The date structure has three members da_year, da_day and da_mon to represent year, day and month respectively. The getdate() function takes a single argument of type pointer to structure 'date'. This structure and getdate() function are predefined in dos.h header file.

```
/* Program name: stru5.c */
/* program to get system date using built-in function */
#include<stdio.h>
#include<conio.h>
#include<dos.h>
void main()
{
struct date d;
clrscr();
getdate(&d);/* to get system date */
printf("The current year is: %d\n", d.da_year);
printf("The current day is: %d\n", d.da_day);
printf("The current month is: %d\n", d.da_mon);
getch();
}
```

```
Output
The current year is : 2003
The current day is : 11
The current month is : 7
```

The following program changes the current system date and again sets back to the original date. This program uses built-in function setdate() for setting the new date in the system which is defined in dos.h.

```
/* Program name: stru6.c */
/* program to change/set the system date using built-in function
     */
#include<stdio.h>
#include<conio.h>
#include<dos.h>
void main()
{
struct date r;
struct date s;
clrscr();
getdate(&s);/* to get the current system date */
printf("Original date :\n");
printf("%d:%d:%d\n",s.da_day,s.da_mon,s.da_year);
r.da_year = 2002;
r.da_day = 2;
r.da_mon = 10;
setdate(&r);/* to change the current system date */
printf("Date after setting :\n");
```

```
getdate(&r);
printf("%d:%d:%d\n",r.da_day,r.da_mon,r.da_year);
setdate(&s);/* setting the original date */
printf("Back to original date :\n");
getdate(&s);/* gives the current date */
printf("%d:%d:%d\n",s.da_day,s.da_mon,s.da_year);
getch();
}
```

Output
Original date :
10:10:2003
Date after setting :
2:10:2002
Back to original date :
10:10:2003

The following program takes the time(hh mm ss) as input from the user and checks for validity. It also updates the given time by one second.

```
/* Program name: stru7.c */
/* program to input the user time and check for validity,
   update it by one second and print it */
/* consider 24 hour clock*/
#include<stdio.h>
#include<conio.h>
struct T
{
int h,m,s;
}t;

void main()
{
clrscr();
printf("enter time hours, minutes and seconds\n");
scanf("%d%d%d",&t.h,&t.m,&t.s);
printf("\nentered time %d:%02d:%02d\n",t.h,t.m,t.s);
/* checking for validity */
if(t.h<0 || t.m<0 || t.s<0 || t.h>23 || t.m>59 || t.s>59)
   printf("\n entered time is wrong\n");
else /* updates the time by one second*/
   {
   t.s++;
   if(t.s>59)
```

```
        {
                t.s=0;
                t.m++;
        }
        if(t.m>59)
        {
                t.m=0;
                t.h++;
        }
        if(t.h>23)
        t.h=0;
printf("\n updated time %d:%02d:%02d\n", t.h, t.m, t.s);
    }
getch();
}
```

Output 1	**Output 2**
enter time hours, minutes and seconds	**enter time hours, minutes and seconds**
20 60 78	**20 59 59**
enterd time is wrong	**updated time 21:00:00**

As shown in the output 1 of the above program, when wrong time is entered by the user, the program checks for validity and displays the message, but it will not ask for correct time. The following program is a bit modification of the above program to do the same.

```
/* Program name: stru8.c */
/* program to input the user time and check for validity,
   update it by one second and print it */
/* consider 24 hour clock*/
/* keeps on taking input until correct input*/
#include<stdio.h>
#include<conio.h>
struct T
{
int h,m,s;
}t;
void main()
{
int flag;
clrscr();
do
{
flag=0;
printf("enter time hours, minutes and seconds\n");
```

```
scanf("%d%d%d",&t.h,&t.m,&t.s);
printf("\nentered time %d:%02d:%02d\n",t.h,t.m,t.s);
/* checking for validity */
if(t.h<0 || t.m<0 || t.s<0 || t.h>23 || t.m>59 || t.s>59)
{
printf("\n entered time is wrong\n re-enter\n");
flag=1;
}
}while(flag==1);
/* update the time by one second*/
{
t.s++;
if(t.s>59)
{
t.s=0;
t.m++;
}
if(t.m>59)
{
t.m=0;
t.h++;
}
if(t.h>23)
t.h=0;
printf("\n updated time %d:%02d:%02d\n",t.h,t.m,t.s);
}
getch();
}
```

Output
enter time hours, minutes and seconds
20 60 78
enterd time is wrong
re-enter
enter time hours, minutes and seconds
20 30 40
updated time 20:30:41

The following program is similar to the above program but here we have considered date validation and updation instead of time.

```
/* Program name: stru9.c */
/* Program to input the user date and check for validity,
      update it by one day and print it  */
/* Keeps on taking input until correct input*/
```

```
#include<stdio.h>
#include<conio.h>
struct D
{
int d,m,y;
}d;
void main()
{
int flag;
clrscr();
do
{
flag=0;
printf("enter date: day, month and year\n");
scanf("%d%d%d",&d.d,&d.m,&d.y);
printf("\n entered date %02d:%02d:%4d\n",d.d,d.m,d.y);
/* checking for validity */
if(d.d<1 || d.m<1 || d.y<1 || d.d>31 || d.m>12)
flag=1;
if((d.d>30)&&(d.m==4 || d.m==6 || d.m==9 || d.m==11))
flag=1;
if(d.d>29 && d.m==2)
flag=1;
if(d.d>28 && d.m==2 && d.y%4!=0)
flag=1;

if(flag==1)
printf("\n entered date is wrong\n re-enter\n");
}while(flag==1);
 /* update the date by one day*/
{
d.d++;
if(d.d>31)
{
d.d=1;
d.m++;
}
if((d.d>30)&&(d.m==4 || d.m==6 || d.m==9 || d.m==11))
{
d.d=1;
d.m++;
}
if(d.d>29 && d.m==2)
{
d.d=1;
```

```
d.m++;
}
if(d.d>28 && d.m==2 && d.y%4!=0)
{
d.d=1;
d.m++;
}
if(d.m>12)
{
d.m=1;
d.y++;
}
printf("\n updated date %02d:%02d:%d\n",d.d,d.m,d.y);
}
getch();
}
```

```
Output
enter date: day, month and year
30 2 2002
entered date is wrong
re-enter
20 3 2003
updated date 21:03:2003
```

In the following program we define a structure called 'student'. We declare an array of structure variables for storing information about a list of students. We have written the following program to get the formatted output in rows and columns.

```
/* Program name: stru10.c */
/* program for student information */
/* input the information for n number of students and print
     them with format*/
#include<stdio.h>
#include<conio.h>

struct student /* defining a structure */
{
int roll_num;
char name[20];
char address[30];
};

void main()
{
```

```
struct student s[50]; /* s[50] is an array variable. it can
        store maximum 50 student information*/
int n,i;
clrscr();
printf("\n enter n \n");
scanf("%d",&n);
for(i=0;i<n;++i)
{
printf(" enter roll number name and address of student
        %d\n",i+1);
scanf("%d%s%s", &s[i].roll_num,s[i].name,s[i].address);
}
printf("\n-----------------------------------------\n");
printf(" Roll-noName        Address\n");
printf("-----------------------------------------\n");
for(i=0;i<n;++i)
printf("%6d%15s%15s\n", s[i].roll_num, s[i].name,
        s[i].address);
printf("-----------------------------------------\n");
getch();
}
```

Output

```
Enter n
4
enter roll number name and address of student 1
1234 keshav bangalore
enter roll number name and address of student 2
1235 saju chennai
enter roll number name and address of student 3
1220 simi kochin
enter roll number name and address of student 4
1230 jeena hydrabad

--------------------------------------------
Roll-no Name      Address
--------------------------------------------
1234       keshav bangalore
1235       saju        chennai
1220       simi        kochin
1230       jeena       hydrabad
--------------------------------------------
```

The following program is same as the above program but a small addition to its functionality that it searches for a particular student based on roll number that we input. It uses linear search algorithm.

```
/* Program name: strull.c */
/* Program for searching a student in the list*/
/* program for student information */
/* input the information for n number of students and print
    them with format*/

#include<stdio.h>
#include<conio.h>

struct student /* defining a structure */
{
int roll_num;
char name[20];
char address[30];
};

void main()
{
struct student s[50];
int n,i,x,flag=0;
clrscr();
printf("\n enter n \n");
scanf("%d",&n);

for(i=0;i<n;++i)
{
printf(" enter roll number name and address of student  %d\n",
    i+1);
scanf("%d%s%s", &s[i].roll_num,s[i].name,s[i].address);
}
printf("\n enter the roll number to search\n");
scanf("%d",&x);
/*giving the header format*/
printf("\n-------------------------------------------\n");
printf(" Roll-noName          Address\n");
printf("-------------------------------------------\n");
/* printing the students information*/

for(i=0;i<n;++i)
```

```
printf("%6d%15s%15s\n", s[i].roll_num, s[i].name,
    s[i].address);
printf("--------------------------------------------\n");
/* searching for the rollnumber*/
for(i=0;i<n;++i)
if(s[i].roll_num==x)/* on success change the flag */
{
printf("\n Search is successful at position %d\n",i+1);
flag=1;
}
if(flag==0)/* checking the flag */
printf("\n unsuccessful search\n");
getch();
}
```

```
Output
Enter n
4
 enter roll number name and address of student 1
1234 keshav bangalore
 enter roll number name and address of student 2
1235 saju chennai
 enter roll number name and address of student 3
1220 simi kochin
 enter roll number name and address of student 4
1230 jeena hydrabad
enter the roll number to search
1230
------------------------------------------------
 Roll-no Name      Address
------------------------------------------------
1234          keshav  bangalore
1235          saju         chennai
1220          simi         kochin
1230          jeena        hydrabad
------------------------------------------------
Search is successful at position 4
```

The following program is same as the above program but a small addition to its functionality that it arranges the student records based on roll number in ascending order. It uses bubble sort algorithm.

```
/* Program name: stru12.c */
/*program for arranging student information in order */
#include<stdio.h>
#include<conio.h>
struct student /* defining a structure */
{
int roll_num;
char name[20];
char address[30];
};
void main()
{
struct student s[50],t;
int n,i,j;
clrscr();
printf("\n enter n \n");
scanf("%d",&n);
for(i=0;i<n;++i)
{
printf(" enter roll number name and address of student %d\n",
      i+1);
scanf("%d%s%s", &s[i].roll_num,s[i].name,s[i].address);
}
/* sorting using bubble sort according to roll numbers*/
for(i=0;i<n-1;++i)
for(j=0;j<n-1-i;++j)
if(s[j].roll_num>s[j+1].roll_num) /* checking two consecutive
      roll numbers*/
{
t=s[j]; /* exchanging when they are not in order*/
s[j]=s[j+1];
s[j+1]=t;
}
/*giving the header format*/
printf("\n----------------------------------------------\n");
printf(" Roll-noName         Address\n");
printf("----------------------------------------------\n");
/* printing the students information*/
for(i=0;i<n;++i)
printf("%6d%15s%15s\n", s[i].roll_num,s[i].name, s[i].address);
printf("----------------------------------------------\n");
getch();
}
```

```
Output
Enter n
4
enter roll number name and address of student 1
1234 keshav bangalore
enter roll number name and address of student 2
1235 saju chennai
enter roll number name and address of student 3
1220 simi kochin
enter roll number name and address of student 4
1230 jeena hydrabad

---------------------------------------------------
Roll-no Name      Address
---------------------------------------------------
1220      simi      kochin
1230      jeena     hydrabad
1234      keshav    bangalore
1235      saju      chennai
```

The following program not only reads and displays the student information but also calculates the total marks, percentage and their results. The result calculation is based on the average marks.

```
/* Program name: stru13.c */
/* program for student marks and result information */
/* result calculation only based on % marks*/
#include<stdio.h>
#include<conio.h>
#include<string.h>

struct student /* defining a structure */
{
int roll_num;
char name[20];
int m1,m2,m3; /* three subject marks*/
int tm,avg;    /* total marks and average marks*/
char result[20];
};
void main()
{
```

```
struct student s[50];
int n,i;
clrscr();
printf("\n enter n \n");
scanf("%d",&n);
for(i=0;i<n;++i)
{
printf(" enter roll number name marks1, marks2 and marks3 of
    student  %d\n",i+1);
scanf("%d%s%d%d%d",  &s[i].roll_num,s[i].name,  &s[i].m1,
    &s[i].m2,&s[i].m3);
/* calculate total and average marks and result*/
s[i].tm=s[i].m1+s[i].m2+s[i].m3;
s[i].avg=s[i].tm/3;
if(s[i].avg<35)
strcpy(s[i].result,"Fail");
else
if(s[i].avg>=35 && s[i].avg<50)
strcpy(s[i].result,"Pass Class");
else
if(s[i].avg>=50 && s[i].avg<60)
strcpy(s[i].result,"Second Class");
else
if(s[i].avg>=60 && s[i].avg<75)
strcpy(s[i].result,"First Class");
else
strcpy(s[i].result,"Distinction");
}
/*giving the header format*/
printf("\n-----------------------------------------------------
---------------------\n");
printf(" Roll-no   Name marks1   marks2   marks3 tmarks  %
     marks  result\n");
printf("-----------------------------------------------------
--------------------\n");
/* printing the students information*/
for(i=0;i<n;++i)
printf("%6d%10s%7d%7d%7d %7d  %7d%15s\n",
   s[i].roll_num,s[i].name,s[i].m1,s[i].m2,s[i].m3,
   s[i].tm,s[i].avg,s[i].result);
printf("-----------------------------------------------------
--------------------\n");
getch();
}
```

```
Output
Enter n
3
 enter roll number name marks1 marks2 and marks3 of student 1
1234 charley 50 60 70
enter roll number name marks1 marks2 and marks3 of student 2
1235 dawn 70 25 85
enter roll number name marks1 marks2 and marks3 of student 3
1236 rayudu 48 45 57

-----------------------------------------------------------------------
Roll-no Name      mark1     mark2  mark3  tmark  %marks  result
-----------------------------------------------------------------------
1234    charley 50          60     70     180    60      First Class
1235    dawn    70          25     85     180    60      First Class
1236    rayudu 48           45     57     150    50      Second Class
-----------------------------------------------------------------------
```

In the above program we have not considered individual subject marks. Note that the second person(in the above output)is passed with first class even though he scored only 25 marks in one subject. There is a minimum marks to pass in each subject. So how do we go about doing this? Check out the following program which implements the same. It also arranges the student records according to ascending order of their names using bubble sort technique.

```
/* Program name: stru14.c */
/* program for student marks and result information */
/* result calculation based on % marks and checks for individual
      subject failure*/
/* prints the information on ascending order of names */
#include<stdio.h>
#include<conio.h>
#include<string.h>
struct student /* defining a structure */
{
int roll_num;
char name[20];
int m1,m2,m3; /* three subject marks*/
int tm,avg;     /* total marks and average marks*/
char result[20];
};
void main()
{
```

```
struct student s[50],t;
int n,i,j;
clrscr();
printf("\n enter n \n");
scanf("%d",&n);
for(i=0;i<n;++i)
{
printf(" enter roll number name marks1, marks2 and marks3 of
     student %d\n",i+1);
scanf("%d%s%d%d%d",   &s[i].roll_num,s[i].name,
     &s[i].m1,&s[i].m2,&s[i].m3);
s[i].tm=s[i].m1+s[i].m2+s[i].m3;
s[i].avg=s[i].tm/3;
if(s[i].m1<35 || s[i].m2<35 || s[i].m3<35)
strcpy(s[i].result,"Fail");
else
if(s[i].avg>=35 && s[i].avg<50)
strcpy(s[i].result,"Pass Class");
else
if(s[i].avg>=50 && s[i].avg<60)
strcpy(s[i].result,"Second Class");
else
if(s[i].avg>=60 && s[i].avg<75)
strcpy(s[i].result,"First Class");
else
strcpy(s[i].result,"Distinction");
}
for(i=0;i<n-1;++i)
for(j=0;j<n-1-i;++j)
if(strcmpi(s[j].name,s[j+1].name)>0)
{
t=s[j]; /* exchanging when they are not in order*/
s[j]=s[j+1];
s[j+1]=t;
}
printf("\n-------------------------------------------------
---------------------\n");
printf(" Roll-no    Name marks1   marks2   marks3 tmarks  %
     marks   result\n");
printf("-------------------------------------------------
--------------------\n");
/* printing the students information*/
for(i=0;i<n;++i)
printf("%6d%10s%7d%7d%7d %7d  %7d%15s\n", s[i].roll_num,
   s[i].name,s[i].m1,s[i].m2,s[i].m3,s[i].tm,
```

```
        s[i].avg,s[i].result);
    printf("-------------------------------------------------
    -------------------\n");
    getch();
    }
```

Output
Enter n
3
enter roll number name marks1 marks2 and marks3 of student 1
1235 dawn 70 25 85
enter roll number name marks1 marks2 and marks3 of student 2
1234 charley 50 60 70
enter roll number name marks1 marks2 and marks3 of student 3
1236 rayudu 48 45 57

Roll-no	Name	mark1	mark2	mark3	tmark	%marks	result
1234	charley	50	60	70	180	60	First Class 1235
	dawn	70	25	85	180	60	Fail
1236	rayudu	48	45	57	150	50	Second Class

An electricity board charges for its customers according to the following rules.

Upto 100 units Rs.150.

101 to 200 units Rs.2 per unit.

201 to 500 units Rs.3 per unit.

And above 500 units Rs.5 per unit.

The following program takes the customer information like customer no., name, previous meter reading, present meter reading and calculates total units consumed and the bill amount.

```
/* Program name: stru15.c */
/* program for electricity bill information */
/* input the information for n number of customers*/
/* calculates units consumed, total bill and print them with
     format*/
/* prints the information on ascending order of customer
     numbers */
#include<stdio.h>
#include<conio.h>
#include<string.h>

struct electricity /* defining a structure */
```

```
{
int cust_num;
char name[20];
int prv_mt_read, prs_mt_read, tot_unit;
long bill; /* previous meter reading, present meter reading ,
     units consumed and bill*/
};

void main()
{
struct electricity s[50],t;
int n,i,j;
clrscr();
printf("\n enter n \n");
scanf("%d",&n);
for(i=0;i<n;++i)
{
printf(" enter cust number, name, prev mt reading,pres mt
     reading of customer %d\n",i+1);

scanf("%d%s%d%d", &s[i].cust_num, s[i].name, &s[i].prv_mt_read,
     &s[i].prs_mt_read);
/* calculate total units and bill*/
s[i].tot_unit=s[i].prs_mt_read-s[i].prv_mt_read;
if(s[i].tot_unit<=100)
s[i].bill=150;
else
if(s[i].tot_unit>100 && s[i].tot_unit<=200)
s[i].bill=s[i].tot_unit*2;
else
if(s[i].tot_unit>200 && s[i].tot_unit<=500)
s[i].bill=s[i].tot_unit*3;
else
s[i].bill=s[i].tot_unit*5;
}
/* sorting using bubble sort according to cust_num*/
for(i=0;i<n-1;++i)
for(j=0;j<n-1-i;++j)
if(s[j].cust_num>s[j+1].cust_num)
{
t=s[j]; /* exchanging when they are not in order*/
s[j]=s[j+1];
s[j+1]=t;
}
```

```
/*giving the header format*/
printf("\n--------------------------------------------
-------------------\n");
printf(" Cust-no     Name prevmtreadprsmtreadtotunit
bills  \n");
printf("---------------------------------------------
------------------\n");

/* printing the students information*/
for(i=0;i<n;++i)
printf("%6d%10s      %7d     %7d     %7d     %10ld\n",
    s[i].cust_num,s[i].name,s[i].prv_mt_read,
    s[i].prs_mt_read,s[i].tot_unit,s[i].bill);
printf("---------------------------------------------
------------------\n");
getch();
}
```

Output
Enter n
3
enter cust number name prev mt reading and pres mt reading of customer 1
345 kanti 1234 1320
enter cust number name prev mt reading and pres mt reading of customer 1
346 jahan 6540 7010
enter cust number name prev mt reading and pres mt reading of customer 1
123 amit 5050 6250

Cust-no	Name	prevmtread	prsmtread	totunit	bills
123	amit	5050	6250	1200	6000
345	kanti	1234	1320	86	150
346	jahan	6540	7010	470	1410

The following program is a modified version of the above program. It calculates the bills category wise. The billing rules for different category are as given below.

For domestic category.

Upto 100 units Rs.150.

101 to 200 units Rs.2 per unit.

201 to 500 units Rs.3 per unit.

And above 500 units Rs.5 per unit.

For institutional category.

Upto 100 units Rs.250.

101 to 200 units Rs.3 per unit.

201 to 500 units Rs.4 per unit.

And above 500 units Rs.6 per unit.

For industrial category.

Upto 500 units Rs.750.

501 to 1000 units Rs.4 per unit.

1001 to 5000 units Rs.5 per unit.

And above 5000 units Rs.7 per unit.

```
/* Program name: stru16.c */
/* program for electricity bill information with category*/
/* input the information for n number of customers*/
/* calculates units consumed, total bill and print them with
     format*/
/* prints the information on ascending order of customer
     numbers */
#include<stdio.h>
#include<conio.h>
#include<string.h>

struct electricity /* defining a structure */
{
int cust_num;
char name[20],cat[20];
int prv_mt_read, prs_mt_read, tot_unit;
long bill; /* previous meter reading, present meter reading ,
     units consumed and bill*/
};
void main()
{
struct electricity s[50],t;
int n,i,j;
clrscr();
printf("\n enter n \n");
scanf("%d",&n);
for(i=0;i<n;++i)
{
printf(" enter cust number, name,Category, prev mt reading,
     pres mt reading of customer %d\n",i+1);
scanf("%d%s%s%d%d", &s[i].cust_num,s[i].name,s[i].cat,
     &s[i].prv_mt_read, &s[i].prs_mt_read);
```

```
/* calculate total units and bill*/
s[i].tot_unit=s[i].prs_mt_read-s[i].prv_mt_read;
if(strncmpi(s[i].cat,"domestic",4)==0)
{
if(s[i].tot_unit<=100)
s[i].bill=150;
else
if(s[i].tot_unit>100 && s[i].tot_unit<=200)
s[i].bill=s[i].tot_unit*2;
else
if(s[i].tot_unit>200 && s[i].tot_unit<=500)
s[i].bill=s[i].tot_unit*3;
else
s[i].bill=s[i].tot_unit*5;
}
else
if(strncmpi(s[i].cat,"institutional",4)==0)
{
if(s[i].tot_unit<=100)
s[i].bill=250;
else
if(s[i].tot_unit>100 && s[i].tot_unit<=200)
s[i].bill=s[i].tot_unit*3;
else
if(s[i].tot_unit>200 && s[i].tot_unit<=500)
s[i].bill=s[i].tot_unit*4;
else
s[i].bill=s[i].tot_unit*6;
}
else
if(strncmpi(s[i].cat,"industrial",4)==0)
{
if(s[i].tot_unit<=500)
s[i].bill=750;
else
if(s[i].tot_unit>500 && s[i].tot_unit<=1000)
s[i].bill=s[i].tot_unit*4;
else
if(s[i].tot_unit>1000 && s[i].tot_unit<=5000)
s[i].bill=s[i].tot_unit*5;
else
s[i].bill=s[i].tot_unit*7;
}
}
```

```
/* sorting using bubble sort according to cust_num*/
for(i=0;i<n-1;++i)
for(j=0;j<n-1-i;++j)
if(s[j].cust_num>s[j+1].cust_num)
{
t=s[j]; /* exchanging when they are not in order*/
s[j]=s[j+1];
s[j+1]=t;
}
/*giving the header format*/
printf("\n-------------------------------------------------------
-------------------------\n");
printf(" Cust-no    Name category prevmtread prsmtread totunit
     bills  \n");
printf("-------------------------------------------------------
-------------------------\n");
/* printing the students information*/
for(i=0;i<n;++i)
printf("%6d%10s%10s     %7d     %7d     %7d     %10ld\n",
   s[i].cust_num,s[i].name,s[i].cat,s[i].prv_mt_read,
   s[i].prs_mt_read,s[i].tot_unit,s[i].bill);
printf("-------------------------------------------------------
-------------------------\n");
getch();
}
```

Output
Enter n
3
enter cust number name category prev mt reading and pres mt reading of customer 1
345 kanti domestic 1234 1320
enter cust number name category prev mt reading and pres mt reading of customer 1
346 jahan institu 6540 7010
enter cust number name category prev mt reading and pres mt reading of customer 1
123 amit indust 5050 6250

Cust-no	Name	category	prevmtread	prsmtread	totunit	bills
123	amit	indust	5050	6250	1200	6000
345	kanti	domestic	1234	1320	86	150
346	jahan	institu	6540	7010	470	1880

6.5 Nested Structures

We can easily nest one structure within another structure by making it as a member.

Ex:

```
struct comp
{
int  modelno;
char type[10];
char memory[20];
};
```

Now we can declare a structure 'person' with a structure 'comp' as one of its member as given below.

```
struct person
{
char name[20] ;
char address [40] ;
struct comp C;
};
```

The variables of a structure can be declared normally as
struct person p;
Here 'p' is simple variable of structure 'person'.
'p.name' gives 'name' of person.
'p.address' gives 'address' person
'p.C.modelno' gives 'modelno' of computer.
'p.C.memory' gives 'memory' of computer.

The following program illustrates the concept of nested structures.

```
/* Program name: stru17.c */
/* program for nested structure*/
#include<stdio.h>
#include<conio.h>
struct computer
{
char proc[20],speed[20],mem[20];
};
struct person
{
char name[20],addr[20];
struct computer c; /* member is of type structure computer*/
};

void main()
{
```

```
struct person p;
clrscr();
printf("\n enter person details\n name , address\n");
scanf("%s%s",p.name,p.addr);
printf("\ncomputer details\nprocessor,speed and memory \n" );
scanf("%s%s%s",p.c.proc,p.c.speed,p.c.mem);
printf("\n complete details\n");
printf("\nperson name               :%s",p.name);
printf("\nperson address            : %s",p.addr);
printf("\ncomputer processor        : %s",p.c.proc);
printf("\ncomputer speed            : %s",p.c.speed);
printf("\ncomputer memory           : %s",p.c.mem);
getch();
}
```

Output
enter person details
name , address
srinivas mysore
scanf("%s%s",p.
srinivas mysore

computer details
processor , speed and memory
celeron 300mhz 128mb

complete details
person name : srinivas
person address : mysore
computer processor : celeron
computer speed : 300mhz
computer memory : 128mb

6.6 Unions

Union is a user defined data type similar to that of a structure. Unions are declared and used in the same way as structures. The general syntax for declaring union is,

```
union unionname
{
member declaration;
member declaration;
...
};
```

For example,

```
union student
{
    int rollno;
    char name[' '];
    char corse[' '];
};
```

Once the union is defined the variables of its type are declared as follows.

union student s1,s2;

Here s1 and s2 are two union variables by which we can access the members of the union with the help of membership operator (.). For example,

s1.rollno=10;
scanf("%s",s1.name); etc.

The major differences between union and structure are

1. In case of structure the memory is allotted to all the members according to their size. But in case of union the memory allotted is equal to the size of one of its member which takes highest number of bytes so all the members of union share the same storage area within the computer's memory.
2. In structure all the members can be assigned with values at a time but in case of unions all the members cannot be assigned the values at a time. Since the memory allotted to the union is just the memory required for one of its member it will not have enough memory to store the values of all of its members. So union members can be assigned a value one at a time.
3. Unions conserve memory.
4. Structures are useful when we need to assign the values for all the members at a time. Unions are useful for the applications involving multiple members, where values need not be assigned to all the members at a time.

```
Eg. union sample
{
    int n;
    float f;
    char c;
}var1;
```

The size of the above union variable var1 is 4 bytes. Because it is assigned the amount of storage area that is equal to the highest sized member. The following program illustrates the use of unions.

```
/* Program name: stru18.c */
/* Program for reading and printing an integer, a char and a
    float value using union */
#include<stdio.h>
#include<conio.h>
void main()
```

```
{
union s
{
int a;
char b;
float c;
}x;
clrscr();
printf(" enter a character\n");
x.b=getchar();
princf(" given character is %c\n",x.b);
printf(" enter an integer value\n");
scanf("%d",&x.a);
printf(" given number is %d\n",x.a);
printf(" enter a float value\n");
scanf("%f",&x.c);
printf(" given number is %f\n",x.c);
getch();
}
```

Output

enter a character
k
given character is k
enter an integer value
10
given number is 10
enter a float value
20.2
given number is 20.200000

6.7 Bit fields

To utilize the storage space efficiently it is necessary to pack several objects into a single variable. C allows us to split the number of bits required by an integer field into different members of a structure or union by specifying the number of bits for each member, is called bit fields.

For example,

```
struct sample
{
int num1: 6; /*num1 can store maximum 6 bits data*/
int num2: 6; /*num2 can store maximum 6 bits data*/
int num3: 4; /*num3 can store maximum 4 bits data*/
};
```

In this sample structure three data members can share 2 bytes that are necessary for an integer. By this in a single integer space we can store three small integers. The members of this structure are accessed normally as other structure members without bit fields. We can initialize the members as follows.

```
struct sample s;
s.num1=10;
s.num2=23;
s.num3=7;
```

While initializing bit field members care should be taken that the size required for the value should not exceed the number of bits assigned for the member. Suppose if we give the statement s.num1=70; the result stored in the num1 member will not be correct because the size allotted for num1 is 6 bits and the number 70 needs more than 6 bits.

6.8 typedef

The typedef feature allows us to define new data types that are equivalent to existing data types. The general syntax is,

```
typedef datatype newtype;
For example
typedef int a;
```

Now 'a' becomes a new type name for int. using 'a' we can declare integer variables.

a b, c, d=10; declares b, c and d as three integer variables and assigns a value 10 to variable d.

This feature is essential mainly in case of user defined data types because it makes the declaration of variables simple and easy. For example, when we are using a structure in different functions of a program we need to declare it several times in different functions. For declaring a structure the struct keyword and structure tag name is essential. Instead of using these lengthy statements for declaration, we can declare it as a new type using typedef and use that name for declarations of that structure wherever necessary.

```
struct employee
{
int empno;
char name[20];
char designation[20];
};
```

typedef struct employee emp;/* emp becomes a new data type by which we can declare the employee structure variables*/

6.9 enum.

The enumeration data type is used whenever we need to give character constants which can be accessed with the help of their name or numeric constants. All the character constants will get different values starting from 0. The general syntax for declaring enumeration data type is,

```
enum tagname {member1, member2, member3,......membern};
eg. enum Boolean{false, true};
Boolean b;/*b is a variable of type enum Boolean*/
```

'b' can take value either true or false depending on its numerical value 0 or 1 respectively.

7

Pointers

7.1 Introduction

A pointer is a variable containing the address of another variable. The address of a non pointer variable can be obtained using the address operator (&). Consider the simple statement given below which displays the value as well as address of an integer variable.

```
int a=10;
printf("value of a = %d",a); /* prints the value of a */
printf("the address of a = %d",&a); /* prints the address of a */
```

Now the question arises without a pointer variable when we are able to get the address as well as value then what is the need for pointers? The pointers are essential in several cases when we want to traverse through the addresses to get the different values stored in the continuous memory locations. The pointer makes use of the memory dynamically, so that program can assign the memory to the variable during execution. In case of arrays as we have discussed earlier the memory is allotted during the declaration of the array variable by mentioning the size of the array. In the program we may or may not use all the memory allotted to the array. In some cases when we are not using all the locations results in wastage of memory and in other cases when we need to store number of values greater than the number of memory locations allotted results in shortage of memory. In such cases dynamic allocation of memory is essential which allocates the required amount of memory at the time of execution which results in neither shortage nor wastage of computer memory.

In some cases we may not be knowing the required size of the memory needed to store certain objects like images on the screen or files etc. In such cases the use of pointer is essential without which data processing becomes very difficult. The memory can be allocated to the pointer variables with the help of 'malloc()' function. The allotted memory can be removed from the variable by 'free()' function. These two functions are defined in the header file alloc.h. For example,

```
int *ptr;
ptr=malloc(imagesize(10,10,30,30));
```

This statement allocates the memory necessary to store an image drawn on the screen with 20*20 pixels screen area. The memory allotted can be removed by the statement free(ptr);.

For declaring the pointer variable we have to use the following syntax.

```
typename *variablename;
int *n;
float *f;
struct emp *e;
```

The above statements declare n as integer pointer, f as float and e as pointer to the structure emp.

To access the values of a pointer variable we need to use * and just pointer variable name gives address.

```
Eg. int *a;
    *a=10;
    printf("value of a = %d",*a);
    printf("the address of a = %d",a);
```

7.2 Arrays and Pointers.

Once the pointer variable is declared we can extend the memory allocated to the pointer variable by using the arithmetic operations on pointer. The following program statement reads a list of n numbers into a single float pointer.

```
float *a;
int n,i;
scanf("%d",&n);
for(i=1;i<=n;i++)
{
scanf("%f",a);
a++;/* increases the pointer to point to the next memory
        location*/
}
```

During compilation of the above program segment the memory of a single float will be allocated to pointer 'a'. But during execution the size of pointer 'a' changes according to the value of n. Now consider displaying the values of pointer variable 'a'(inputted from the keyboard by the above program segment).

```
a=a-n;/*takes the pointer to the starting location where first
        data is stored*/
for(i=1;i<=n;i++)
{
printf("%d\n",*a);
a++;
}
```

The first statement (a=a-n;) is essential because by the time data inputting is over pointer is pointing to the nth location, so it is essential to make it to point to the first location in order to access the inputted values from the beginning of the list. By a++ the value of pointer 'a' is not increased by one instead its address is increased by 4 because 'a' is a pointer to the float which takes 4 bytes of memory.

7.3 Strings and Pointers.

Pointers are commonly used to handle strings. Without declaring as a pointer if we have declared the size of a string dynamically then it automatically becomes a pointer. For example,

```
char s[20];/* declares s as a character array of size 20*/
char s[' '];/* declares s as a string of dynamic size */
char *s;/* declares s as a string pointer with dynamic size*/
```

7.4 Structures and Pointers

To handle the complicated data structures such as linked list, stacks, queues, trees etc. pointers are used with structures. In case of array of structures, declaring the size statically may lead to large amount of memory wastage because the size of a single structure may take large number of bytes to store values of its members. In such cases we use pointers to the structures. For example,

```
struct item
{
int icode;
char iname[20];
float price;
}*ptr1;
```

To access the members of a structure through pointer variable the membership operator(->) is used.

```
ptr1->icode=10;
strcpy(ptr1->iname, "mouse"); etc.
```

7.5 Functions and Pointers

For passing the parameters to the function definition by 'call by reference' we need to use the pointers. When we are passing the parameter by reference, the variable acts as a global variable even it is defined locally. That means any changes made by the function in the reference variable will reflect in the calling function. We will discuss about functions with pointers in detail in the next chapter.

7.6 Files and Pointers

In C language the files can be handled with the help of file pointer. That we will discuss later in the files chapter in detail.

7.7 Programs

Following are few programs to illustrate the concept and the use of pointers.

This program prints the values and address of a simple variable. Just the variable name gives the value and variable prefixed with ampersand(&) gives the address of variable where the memory is allocated.

```
/* Program name: ptr1.c */
/* printing value and address of simple variable */
#include<stdio.h>
#include<conio.h>
void main()
{
int n;
clrscr();
n=10;
printf("\n Value = %d",n);
printf("\n Address = %ld",&n);
getch();
}
```

Output

Value = 10
Address = 720884

The above program can be modified to make use of pointers to get the address and value of a pointer variable. In case of pointers the variable with * gives the value and just variable name gives the address.

```
/* Program name: ptr2.c */
/* printing value and address of pointer variable */
#include<stdio.h>
#include<conio.h>
void main()
{
int *n;/* declaration needs * should be prefixed with variable
      */
clrscr();
*n=10;/* while assigning or accessing the value * should be
      prefixed with variable*/
printf("\n Value = %d",*n);
printf("\n Address = %ld",n);/* the variable name specify
      address */
getch();
}
```

Output

Value = 10
Address = 56886116

The following program adds two numbers by using pointers. Note that at the time of operation if we are not prefixing the variable with *, then instead of adding their values their addresses will be added. This care should be taken whenever we deal with pointers.

```
/* Program name: ptr3.c */
/* adding two numbers with pointer variables */
#include<stdio.h>
#include<conio.h>
void main()
{
int *a,*b,*c; /* three pointer variables */
clrscr();
printf("\n enter two numbers\n");
scanf("%d%d",a,b);/* & is not needed while scanning because
      pointer itself is an address*/
*c=*a+*b;
printf("\n sum of %d and %d = %d\n",*a,*b,*c);
getch();
}
```

Output

```
enter two numbers
10 20

sum of 10 and 20 = 30
```

When we use pointers with strings we need not have to mention the size of a string. The memory will be allotted to the string pointer dynamically during execution of the program if it is necessary. While dealing with individual characters in a string pointer either an index will be added to the string variable or the string variable itself will be increased or decreased to access the next or previous character.

```
/* Program name: ptr4.c */
/* reading and printing a string using pointer variables */
/* finds the length of string */
#include<stdio.h>
#include<conio.h>
void main()
{
char *s; /* size should not be mentioned for one-dimensional
      string in pointer */
int i=0;
clrscr();
```

```
printf("\n enter a string\n");
gets(s);
while(*(s+i)!='\0')
i++;
printf("\n given string is \"%s\"\n",s);
printf("length of string = %d",s,i);
getch();
}
```

Output

enter a string
tomorrow never dies

given string is "tomorrow never dies"
length of string = 19

This program concatenates two strings using pointers. The normal index is used to access the successive characters of the first string till the end. Then we are accessing individual characters from the second string and adding it to the first string one by one. Note that during adding characters the index of both strings should be increased and when the addition gets over NULL will be attached at the end of the first string.

```
/* Program name: ptr5.c */
/* combining two strings */
#include<stdio.h>
#include<conic.h>
void main()
{
char *s1,*s2;
int i=0,j=0;
clrscr();
printf("\n enter first string\n");
gets(s1);
printf("\n enter second string\n");
gets(s2);
while(*(s1+i)!='\0')
i++;
while(*(s2+j)!='\0')
{
*(s1+i)=*(s2+j);/* copying second string at the end of first
        string*/
i++;
j++;
}
*(s1+i)='\0'; /* marking the end of string with NULL */
```

```
printf("\n concatenated string is \"%s\" \n",s1);
printf("length of combined string = %d",s1,i);
getch();
}
```

Output

```
enter first string
silicon

enter second string
valley

concatenated string is "siliconvalley"
```

The following program illustrates arrays as pointers. In case of arrays without pointers the size has to be mentioned statistically during its declaration(i.e. static memory allocation). There is chance of wastage or shortage of computer memory. The following program avoids this by dynamically allocating memory.

```
/* Program name: ptr6.c */
/* reading and printing a list of n numbers by pointers */
#include<stdio.h>
#include<conio.h>
void main()
{
int *a,i=0,n;
clrscr();
printf("\n enter n\n");
scanf("%d",&n);
printf("\n enter %d numbers\n",n);
for(i=0;i<n;++i)
scanf("%d",(a+i));
printf("\n given numbers are\n");
for(i=0;i<n;++i)
printf("%6d",*(a+i));
getch();
}
```

Output

```
enter n
10

enter 10 numbers
1 2 3 4 5 6 7 8 9 10

given numbers are
     1     2     3     4     5     6     7     8     9    10
```

This program illustrates the use of pointers to the structures. While accessing the members of the structure with pointer variables we have to use the membership operator(->).

```
/* Program name: ptr7.c */
/* Program to illustrate the use of structures with pointers
     */
/* inputs an int, and a string and prints them */

#include<stdio.h>
#include<conio.h>
struct sample
{
int n;
char s[' '];
}*s;
void main()
{
clrscr();
printf(" enter an int\n");
scanf("%d", &s->n);
printf(" enter a string\n");
fflush(stdin);
gets(s->s);
printf("\n given int = %d", s->n);
printf("\n given string = %s", s->s);
getch();
}
```

Output
enter an int
12
enter a string
shreyas

given int = 12
given string = shreyas

8

Functions

8.1 Introduction

Function is a building block of a program. Every executable program should have at least one function ('main()' function as we know), from where the execution of a program starts. When we have a big task in hand it is difficult to solve by a single person. It is also difficult to understand and debug the program when we write the solution within a single function. So instead of making a big single function, we divide the program into small sub modules and assign each module to a particular user for writing and executing. When different users complete all the modules then we combine all the modules into one program, which carries out our task. It is easy to write each module separately, each module is called a function.

If we want to do same operations or process repeatedly, using different values then you must write a module or function, which carries out that process. Call that function with different arguments; it saves the space as well as time by calling a function repeatedly instead of writing function statements repeatedly. So functions reduce duplication of code(or code redundancy).

Function enables us to make the program structured. By structured programming we actually mean, whenever the programs are too big, it is necessary to split the program into number of parts, each part must be used for a specific sub task within the entire solution of the program. Each part becomes a function.

There are two types of functions.

1. Standard library functions.
2. User defined functions.

8.2 Standard library functions

These are certain functions, which are very commonly used in programming. All such commonly used functions are kept ready for the use by the programmer, in appropriate header files. By including the respective header files we can use the library functions just by calling them with necessary arguments.

Ex: printf( ), scanf( ), strlen( ), etc.

8.3 User defined functions

These are the modules written to carry out sub tasks within the programs defined by the user according to his needs. Writing any user defined function in C involves three steps.

1. Declare the function,
2. Define the function and
3. Call the defined function by passing required values or references to the values.

8.3.1 Function prototype/declaration

The function declaration specifies the name of the function, its return value and type and number of arguments it takes(i.e. the function signature).

General syntax:

Returntype functionname (argument types);

Ex:

1. int xyz(int , int);
2. void abc (int , float);
3. void dis(void);

The first statement declares a function 'xyz' which takes two integer arguments and returns a value of type integer. The second statement declares a function 'abc' which takes two arguments of type int and float but it returns no value. The third statement declares a function 'dis' which neither takes any argument nor returns any value.

The word 'void' indicates nothing, means the function with return type as void will not return any value.

8.3.2 Function definition

The function definition contains the program statements that are necessary to perform the required action from the function. The 'return (variablename);' statement is optional and if it is present it returns the specified value to the calling function.

General syntax

```
Returntype functionname (arguments and types)
{
Body of function;
return(variable/value);    /*  optional    */
}
```

```
Ex:  1.
int   xyz (int  a,  int  b)
{
int  C;
C=a+b;
return(C);
}
```

This simple function definition takes two arguments a and b, adds them and stores the result in the variable C. The statement return(C); returns the value of C to the calling function.

Ex 2.

```
void dis(void)
{
```

```
printf( "wel come to C \n";
}
```

Here the function 'dis' takes no arguments and returns no value. It just displays the message on the screen.

There may be any number of return ( ) statements in one function, but only one return() executes based on condition and by that control goes back to the calling point. In case of functions without return(); the control automatically gets back to the calling point after its scope.

8.3.3 *Function call*

Activating the function definition by passing the necessary argument values or references is called function call.

Syntax:

```
[variable =] functionname(arguments);

Ex:
int x;
x=xyz(10,20); /* function call by passing arguments */
dis( ); /* function call without arguments */
```

8.4 Types of variables or scope of variables

There are two types of variables that one can distinguish in 'C' programming with user-defined functions, they are:

local variables
global variables

8.4.1 *Local Variables*

Any variables, which are declared and used within the user-defined function, are called as local variables.

In local variables again there are 4 types, they are:

1. automatic
2. static
3. register
4. extern

8.4.1.1 Automatic Local Variables

Any variable declared within the function body is called automatic local variable or simply local variable. Their lifetime is till the lifetime of the function in which they are declared and they are private to that function. One can declare the variables with same names in different functions of the same program.

8.4.1.2 Static Variables

These are also local variables but they retain their values in between function calls, that means even though they are defined locally they act as global variables for their lifetime. That is their value remains unchanged outside the scope of the function in which they are declared. Their lifetime is till the life of entire program. Static variables must be initialized at the time of declaration. The general syntax is:

static type-name variable-name=value;

The following program explains the difference between automatic local variables & static variables.

```
void main ()
{
void dis (void); /* * function without arguments, without
        return values* */
void dis1()void);     /* function without arguments, without
        return value* */
int i;
for(i=1; i<=10;++i)
{
dis(); /* * calling both functions one by one 10 times* */
dis1();
}
}
void dis() /* function which uses automatic variables */
{
int i=1;
printf("%d\t",i);
i++;
}
void dis1  ()     /* * function which uses static variable */
{
static int i = 1 ; /* declaring and initializing static
        variable */
printf ("%d\n",i);
i++;
}
```

Output of this program is:

```
1   1
1   2
1   3
1   4
1   5
1   6
1   7
1   8
1   9
1   10
```

As the output shows, the static variable initializes only once when the function is executed for the first time. After that it retains its value in between function calls until the end of program execution. But local (automatic) variables are declared as and when the function containing them is executed and they retain their scope until the end of function execution.

8.4.1.3 Register Variables

If you put key word register while declaring local variables then their values are stored in processor registers(register memory) instead of computer memory. As we know accessing values from registers is faster than that of memory, the processing time of programs with register variables is usually faster than those of other variables.

The general syntax for declaring register variables is

register type-name variables-name;

Ex: register int k;

If there are not enough registers to store values, then compiler ignores the key-word register and they act as local variables automatically. Register variables can never be declared global.

8.4.1.4 Extern Variables

These are the variables defined in one program and can be used in another program. Whenever we include other program file into the present program file and if we want to use the memory allocated to the variable in the other file instead of declaring one more variable, we can declare that variable as extern variable.

The general syntax is

extern type-name variable-name;

8.4.2 *Global Variables*

These are the variables, which are declared outside of any function. Their lifetime is the lifetime of entire program. Whatever the changes made in one function will affect in the other function also if that function performs operations on the same global variables. These variables are also called as public variables, which means that they are available to all the functions in the program.

8.5 Arrays As Function Arguments

While passing array as an argument you must pass array name and size of the array. For example:

int a[100];

If n numbers are stored in array a (0<=n<100) and the function name is xx() then while calling you must give the argument as follows.

xx(a, n);

Where a is the array name and n is the number of elements stored in the array.

The following program explains how to pass an array as an argument to the function. This program finds 10th smallest in an array of n elements.

```
#include <stdio.h>
void main ()
{
int  small (int [],int);
int  a[100],n, i, smallest, large;
printf ("enter n\n");
scanf ("%d", &n);
for (i =1 ; i<= n; ++ i)
scanf ("%d", &a[i]);
```

```
large=a[1];
for (i=1;i<=n;++i)
if (large<a[i])
large=a[i];
for(i=1; i<=10;++i)
{
smallest = small(a, n );
for (j =1; i < = n ; == j)
if (a(j) = = smallest)
a[j] = large;
}
printf("10 th smallest = %d", smallest);
getch ( ) ;
}
/* * end of main * */
/* * function for finding the smallest **/
int small (int a[] , int x )
{
int s = a [1] , k ;
for (k=1; k<=x;++k)
if (s>a[k])
s=a[k];
return( s);
}
```

NOTE: for passing character array, as an argument to the function there is no necessity of passing the size of the array. Only mentioning the array name is enough, by that the compiler itself knows the size by the use of null character, which is stored at the end of the string.

8.6 Call By Value & Call By Reference

8.6.1 Call By Value

If we are calling the function just by passing values of arguments then, only the copy of the value of variable or arguments is passed. Whatever may be the change that takes place inside the body of the function for these arguments will not affect in calling function.

```
Ex: void  dis (int , int );  /* prototype. */
main( )
{                                  /* function definition */
int  a=10, b=5;                    void dis(int x int y)
dis(a,b);                          {
                                   x=x+5;
printf("%d\t%d\n",a,b);            y=x+y;
}                                  }
Prints 10, 5
```

8.6.2 Call By Reference

In this case we are actually passing the address of the variable(the actual reference) where value is stored. By passing the address(reference) the changes made in the called function will reflect the same in the calling function also.

```
Ex: void dis (int *, int *);  /* function prototype */
main ()
{
int a =20,b=25;
printf( "%d  %d\n",a,b); /* prints 20,25; /*
dis(&a,&b); /* function call */
printf("%d  %d\n",a,b); /* prints 30,55 because the values changed in the function
          will affect  the values of a & b; */
getch();
}
void dis(int *x, int y) / fn definition */
{
x* = * x +10;
y=*y+*x;
}
```

This program uses a function for adding 2 float values. The values are taken from the key board in the main function and passed as arguments to the function where they will be added and result will be returned back to the main program.

```
/* program name: fun1.c  */
/*  Simple function to add two numbers */
#include<stdio.h>
#include<conio.h>

float add(float,float);  /*  declaration, specifies add is a
      function, it takes two arguments of type float and gives
       a float value */
void main()
{
float a,b,c;
clrscr();
printf("\n enter two numbers\n");
scanf("%f%f",&a,&b);
c=add(a,b);  /*  function call, passes the values of a and b to
     function definition */
printf("\n sum of %.3f and %.3f = %.3f\n",a,b,c);
 /*  rounds up the values upto 3 digit precision */
getch();
}
```

```
/* Function definition */
float add(float x, float y)
{
return(x+y);
}
```

Output
enter two numbers
10.2 20.459
sum of 10.200 and 20.459 = 30.659

The following program finds the factorial of a number using function.

```
 /*  program name: fun2.c  */
 /* Simple function for finding factorial of an integer value
     */
#include<stdio.h>
#include<conio.h>
long fact(int ); /* declaration, specifies fact is a function,
     it takes an arguments of type int and gives a long
     integer value */
void main()
{
int n;
long f;
clrscr();
printf("\n enter a number\n");
scanf("%d",&n);
f=fact(n);   /*  function call, passes the value of n to
      function definition and returned value is assigned to
      variable f */
printf("\n factorial of %d = %ld\n",n,f);
getch();
}
/* Function definition */
long fact(int x)
{
long f=1;
int i;
for(i=1;i<=x;++i)
f=f*i;
return(f); /*  returns the value of factorial to main()   */
}
```

```
Output
enter a number
4
factorial of 4 = 24
```

This program takes the integer value input n and prints all the numbers from 1 to n along with their factorials in different columns.

```
/*   program name: fun3.c   */
/*  Simple function for finding factorial of an integer value
    */
#include<stdio.h>
#include<conio.h>
long fact(int );  /*  declaration, specifies fact is a cfunction,
        it takes an arguments of type int and gives a long
        integer value */
void main()
{
int n,i;
long f;
clrscr();
printf("\n enter a number\n");
scanf("%d",&n);
for(i=1;i<=n;++i)
{
f=fact(i);    /*   function call, passes the value of i to
        function definition and returned value is assigned to
        variable f */
printf("\n factorial of %d = %12ld",i,f);
}
getch();
}
/* Function definition */
long fact(int x)
{
long f=1;
int i;
for(i=1;i<=x;++i)
f=f*i;
return(f);
}
```

```
Output
enter a number
4
factorial of 1 =  1
factorial of 2 =  2
factorial of 3 =  6
factorial of 4 =        24
```

The above program can only find the factorial of a number up to long integer value of factorial(i.e. upto factorial of 15 which is within the range of long integer). When the number exceeds 15 we will get wrong results. To avoid this we need to modify the above program as given below. With this program we can find the factorial of numbers up to 186. The program displays the result in the general float format.

```
/* program name: fun4.c   */
/* simple function for finding factorial of an integer  value
     */
#include<stdio.h>
#include<conio.h>
double fact(int );    /*   declaration, specifies fact is a
        function, it takes an arguments of type int and gives a
        long integer value */
void main()
{
int n,i;
double f;
clrscr();
printf("\n enter a number\n");
scanf("%d",&n);
for(i=1;i<=n;++i)
{
f=fact(i);    /*  function call, passes the value of i to
        function definition and returned value is assigned to
        variable f */
printf("\n factorial of %d = %12g",i,f);
}
getch();
}
 /* Function definition */
double fact(int x)
{
double f=1;
int i;
for(i=1;i<=x;++i)
f=f*i;
return(f);
}
```

Output

```
enter a number
4
factorial of 1 = 1
factorial of 2 = 2
factorial of 3 = 6
factorial of 4 = 24
```

Now consider the function for checking whether the given number is prime or not.

```
  /*  program name:  fun5.c    */
  /* Function for checking given number is prime or not */
#include<stdio.h>
#include<conio.h>
int prime(int );  /*  declaration */
void main()
{
int n,i;
clrscr();
printf("\n enter a number\n");
scanf("%d",&n);
i=prime(n);
if(i==0)
printf("\n given number %d is prime\n",n);
else
printf("\n given number %d is not prime\n",n);
getch();
}
  /* Function definition */
int prime(int x)
{
int i,t=0; /* t is taken as flag and changes its value when
       the number is not prime */
for(i=2;i<=x/2;++i)
if(x%i==0)  /* when divide the remainder becomes zero */
{
t=1; /*  changing the flag on division */
break; /*  terminates the loop  */
}
return(t);  /*  returns 0 if prime or 1 when not prime */
}
```

Output
enter a number
4
given number 4 is not prime

The above program can be modified to get all the prime numbers in between the numbers m and n.

```
  /*   program name:  fun6.c    */
  /*   Function for checking given number is prime or not */
  /*   It prints all primes between m & n where m < n   */
```

```
#include<stdio.h>
#include<conio.h>
int prime(int );  /*  declaration */
void main()
{
int m,n,i;
clrscr();
printf("\n enter m and n \n");
scanf("%d%d",&m,&n);
printf("\n prime numbers between %d and %d are\n",m,n);
for(i=m;i<=n;++i)
if(prime(i)==0)  /*   calling  the  function  as  a  relational
        expression  */
printf("%8d",i);
getch();
}
 /* Function definition */
int prime(int x)
{
int i,t=0; /*  t is taken as flag  */
for(i=2;i<=x/2;++i)
if(x%i==0)  /*  when divide the remainder becomes zero */
{
t=1; /*  changing the flag on division */
break; /*  terminates the loop  */
}
return(t);  /*  returns 0 if prime or 1 when not prime */
}
```

Output
enter m and n
10 50
the prime numbers between 10 and 50 are
11 13 17 19 23 29 31 37 41 43 47

In the above program we have given m=10 and n=50. The program works without any problem. If we give m=50 and n=10 we will not get any output and it will not display any message saying that the first input number should be smaller. The following program does the same and will ask to input the values for m and n correctly and will continue until we give the proper input.

```
/*  program name: fun7.c  */
/*  Function for checking given number is prime or not */
/*  It prints all primes between m & n where m < n  */
/*  It checks the validity of the input m should be less than
    or equal to n  */
```

```
#include<stdio.h>
#include<conio.h>
int prime(int );  /*  declaration  */
void main()
{
int m,n,i;
clrscr();
do
{
printf("\n enter m and n \n");
scanf("%d%d",&m,&n);
if(m>n)
printf("the value of m should be less than or equal to n \n");
}while(m>n);  /*  when m is greater than n it again goes to the
      loop to input another number */
printf("\n prime numbers between %d and %d are\n",m,n);
for(i=m;i<=n;++i)
if(prime(i)==0)  /*   calling  the  function  as  a  relational
      expression  */
printf("%8d",i);
getch();
}
 /* Function definition */
int prime(int x)
{
int i,t=0; /*  t is taken as flag  */
for(i=2;i<=x/2;++i)
if(x%i==0)  /*  when divide the remainder becomes zero */
{
t=1; /*  changing the flag on division */
break; /*  terminates the loop  */
}
return(t);  /*  returns 0 if prime or 1 when not prime */
}
```

Output
enter m and n
50 10
the value of m should be less than or equal to n
enter m and n
10 50
the prime numbers between 10 and 50 are

11	13	17	19	23	29	31	37	41	43	47

The following program takes the list of numbers and prints all the primes from that list.

```
/*  program name: fun8.c  */
/*  Function for checking given number is prime or not */
/*  It prints all primes from a given list of n numbers  */
#include<stdio.h>
#include<conio.h>
int prime(int ); /*  declaration */
void main()
{
int a[100],n,i;
clrscr();
printf("\n enter  n \n");
scanf("%d",&n);
printf("\n enter %d integer values\n",n);
for(i=0;i<n;++i)
scanf("%d",&a[i]);
printf("\n prime numbers form the given list are\n");
for(i=0;i<n;++i)
if(prime(a[i])==0)
printf("%8d",a[i]);
getch();
}
/* Function definition */
int prime(int x)
{
int i,t=0; /*  t is taken as flag  */
for(i=2;i<=x/2;++i)
if(x%i==0)  /*  when divide the remainder becomes zero */
{
t=1; /*  changing the flag on division */
break; /*  terminates the loop  */
}
return(t);  /*  returns 0 if prime or 1 when not prime */
}
```

Output

```
enter n
10
enter 10 integer values
2 30 13 56 47 29 18 45 52 61
prime numbers from the given list are
2       13      47      29      61
```

The following program does the same as above but takes an array of numbers as an argument and the function does not return any value but prints the result in the function itself.

```
  /*  program name: fun9.c  */
  /*  Array as function argument  */
  /*  Function for checking given number is prime or not */
  /*  Passes entire array to the function and will not return
       anything, the result is displayed in the function itself
       */
#include<stdio.h>
#include<conio.h>
void prime(int [],int);  /*  declaration, specifies prime is a
      function, it takes two arguments one is of int array and
      another simple int  */
void main()
{
int a[100],n, i;
clrscr();
printf("\n enter  n \n");
scanf("%d", &n);
printf("\n enter %d integer values\n", n);
for(i=0;i<n; ++i)
scanf("%d", &a[i]);
printf("\n prime numbers form the given list are\n");
prime(a,n); /*  calling the function by passing entire array
      and number of actual elements in the array  */
getch();
}
 /* Function definition */
void prime(int x[],int n)
{
int i, j, t=0;
for(j=0;j<n; ++j)
{
t=0;
for(i=2;i<=x[j]/2;++i)
if(x[j]%i==0)
{
t=1; /*  changing the flag on division */
break; /*  terminates the loop  */
}
if(t==0)
printf("%8d",x[j]);
}
}
```

```
Output
enter n
10
enter 10  integer values
2 30 13 56 47 29 18 45 52 61
prime numbers from the given list are
2        13        47        29        61
```

GCD of two numbers can be defined as the greatest number, which divides those two numbers. For this we find all the factors of individual numbers and consider the common factors. The greatest common factor is the GCD of those two numbers.

The following program uses a function for finding the GCD of two numbers.

```
/*  program name: fun10.c  */
/*  Function for finding GCD of two numbers */
#include<stdio.h>
#include<conio.h>
int gcd(int,int);  /*  declaration  */
void main()
{
int m,n,r;
clrscr();
printf("\n enter m, n \n");
scanf("%d%d",&m,&n);
r=gcd(m,n);
printf("\n GCD of %d and %d = %d\n",m,n,r);
getch();
}
/* Function definition */
int gcd(int x,int y)
{
int r;
while(y!=0)
{
r=x%y;
x=y;
y=r;
}
return(x);  /*  when y becomes zero x contains GCD  */
}
```

```
Output
enter m,n
24 28
GCD of 24 and 28 = 4
```

The above program is modified to get the GCD of list of 'n' numbers.

```
/*  program name: fun11.c  */
/*  Function for finding gcd of two numbers */
/*  Program finds gcd of a list of n numbers  */
#include<stdio.h>
#include<conio.h>
int gcd(int,int);
void main()
{
int n,i,r, a[100];
clrscr();
printf("\n enter n \n");
scanf("%d",&n);
printf("\nenter %d numbers\n",n);
for(i=0;i<n;++i)
scanf("%d",&a[i]);
r=gcd(a[0],a[1]);  /*  calling the function by passing first
      two values of list  */
for(i=2;i<n;++i)
r=gcd(r,a[i]);  /*  calling the function by passing previous
      result and next number of the array  */
printf("\n GCD of given list of numbers = %d\n",r);
getch();
}

/* Function definition */
int gcd(int x,int y)
{
int r;
while(y!=0)
{
r=x%y;
x=y;
y=r;
}
return(x);  /*  when y becomes zero x contains GCD  */
}
```

Output
enter n
6
enter 6 numbers
24 40 48 28 64 88
GCD of given list of numbers = 4

In all of the above program we have used only single user defined function. We can use any number of user defined functions according to our requirements. The following program uses two functions, one for finding GCD of two numbers and other for finding the LCM of two numbers. The LCM function calls GCD function while calculating LCM. In such cases the function declaration must be either global or declared in the respective function in which it is called.

```
/*  program name: fun12.c  */
/* Function for finding LCM of two numbers */
/*  It uses function for finding GCD of two numbers */
#include<stdio.h>
#include<conio.h>
int lcm(int,int);
int gcd(int,int);
void main()
{
int m,n,r;
clrscr();
printf("\n enter m, n \n");
scanf("%d%d",&m,&n);
r=lcm(m,n);  /*  calling the function  */
printf("\n LCM of %d and %d = %d\n",m,n,r);
getch();
}
/* Function definition for lcm() */
int lcm(int x,int y)
{
int r;
r=x*y/gcd(x,y); /*  calculating lcm by calling gcd()
function  */
return(r);
}
/* Function definition */
int gcd(int x,int y)
{
int r;
while(y!=0)
{
r=x%y;
x=y;
y=r;
}
return(x);  /*  when y becomes zero x contains GCD  */
}
```

Output
enter m,n
10 25
LCM of 10 and 25 = 50

The following program finds GCD and LCM of given two numbers.

```
 /*  program name: fun13.c   */
 /* Function for finding LCM of two numbers */
 /*  It uses  function for finding GCD of two numbers */
#include<stdio.h>
#include<conio.h>
int lcm(int,int);
int gcd(int,int);
void main()
{
int m,n,r;
clrscr();
printf("\n enter m, n \n");
scanf("%d%d",&m,&n);
r=lcm(m,n);
printf("\n LCM of %d and %d = %d\n",m,n,r);
r=gcd(m,n);
printf("\n GCD of %d and %d = %d\n",m,n,r);
getch();
}

 /* Function definition for lcm() */
int lcm(int x,int y)
{
int r;
r=x*y/gcd(x,y);
return(r);
}
 /* Function definition */
int gcd(int x,int y)
{
int r;
while(y!=0)
{
r=x%y;
x=y;
y=r;
}
```

```
return(x);  /*  when y becomes zero x contains GCD  */
}
```

Output
enter m,n
10 25
LCM of 10 and 25 = 50
GCD of 10 and 25 = 5

This program finds the LCM of list of 'n' numbers.

```
/*  program name: fun14.c  */
/*  Function for finding lcm of two numbers */
/*  Program finds lcm of a list of n numbers  */
/*  It uses function for finding gcd of two numbers  */
#include<stdio.h>
#include<conio.h>
long lcm(int,int);
int gcd(int,int);
void main()
{
int n,i, a[100];
long r;
clrscr();
printf("\n enter n \n");
scanf("%d",&n);
printf("\nenter %d numbers\n",n);
for(i=0;i<n;++i)
scanf("%d",&a[i]);

r=lcm(a[0],a[1]);
for(i=2;i<n;++i)
r=lcm(r,a[i]);
printf("\n LCM of given list of numbers = %ld\n",r);
getch();
}

 /* Function definition for lcm() */
long lcm(int x,int y)
{
long r;
r=x*y/gcd(x,y);
return r;
}
```

```
/* Function definition */
int gcd(int x,int y)
{
int r;
while(y!=0)
{
r=x%y;
x=y;
y=r;
}
return(x);   /*  when y becomes zero x contains GCD  */
}
```

Output
enter n
6
enter 6 numbers
2 4 6 8 10 12
LCM of given list of numbers = 120

Let us write a program to print the Fibonacci series. Fibonacci series is a sequence of numbers starting with 0 and 1 and whose subsequent terms are given by adding the two previous terms. In this program we are using a function just for adding the two numbers.

```
/*  program name: fun15.c   */
/*  Function for printing fibonacci series  for first n terms
    */
#include<stdio.h>
#include<conio.h>
long fib(long,long);
void main()
{
int n,i;
long f0,f1,f;

clrscr();
printf("\n enter n \n");
scanf("%d",&n);
f0=0;
f1=1;  /*  initializing first two terms  */
printf("\nThe first %d fibonacci terms are\n",n);
for(i=0;i<n;++i)
{
f=fib(f0,f1); /*  calling the function by value */
printf(" %9ld",f0);
```

```
f0=f1;
f1=f;
}
getch();
}

 /* Function definition for fib() */
long fib(long x,long  y)
{
return(x+y);
}
```

Output
enter n
6
The first 6 fibonacci terms are
0 1 1 2 3 5

The following program does the same task as above but by using call by reference technique.

```
 /*  program name: fun16.c  */
 /*  Function for printing fibonacci series  for first n terms
       */
  /* Call by reference */
#include<stdio.h>
#include<conio.h>
void fib(long*,long*);
void main()
{
int n,i;
long f0,f1,f;

clrscr();
printf("\n enter n \n");
scanf("%d",&n);
f0=0;
f1=1;  /*  initializing first two terms  */
printf("\nThe first %d fibonacci terms are\n",n);
for(i=0;i<n;++i)
{
printf(" %9ld",f0);
fib(&f0,&f1); /*  calling by reference */
}
```

```
getch();
}

 /* Function definition for fib() */
void fib(long *x,long *y)
{
long f;
f=*x+*y;
*x=*y;
*y=f;
}
```

Output
enter n
8
The first 8 fibonacci terms are
0 1 1 2 3 5 8 13

Let us write a program, which interchanges the contents of two variables using a function. For this we need to use reference variables or global variables. Because any changes made by the function in local variables will not be reflected in the calling function. Following two programs shows the difference between 'call by value' and 'call by reference'.

```
 /*  program name: fun17.c  */
 /*  Function for swaping of two numbers */
 /* Call by value */
#include<stdio.h>
#include<conio.h>
void swap(int,int);
void main()
{
int n,m;

clrscr();
printf("\n enter m,n \n");
scanf("%d%d",&m,&n);
printf("\n given numbers before swaping  are %d and %d\n",m,n);
swap(m,n);
printf("\n given numbers after swaping in main program  are %d
     and %d\n",m,n);
getch();
}
```

```
/* Function definition for swap() */
void swap(int m,int n)
{
int r;
r=m; /*  swapping of numbers  */
m=n;
n=r;
printf("\n given numbers after swapping  in function are %d
     and %d\n",m,n);
}
```

Output
enter m,n
12 24
given numbers before swaping are 12 and 24
given numbers after swapping in function are 24 and 12
given numbers after swaping in main program are 12 and 24

The problem in the above output is because of the use of local variables and call by value. This problem is solved in the next program by call by reference.

```
/*   program name: fun18.c    */
/* Function for swapping of two numbers */
/* Call by reference */
#include<stdio.h>
#include<conio.h>
void swap(int*,int*);
void main()
{
int n,m;
clrscr();
printf("\n enter m,n \n");
scanf("%d%d",&m,&n);
printf("\n given numbers before swapping  are %d and %d\n",m,n);
swap(&m,&n); /*  calling by reference */
printf("\n given numbers after swapping in main program are %d
     and %d\n",m,n);
getch();
}

/* Function definition for swap() */
void swap(int *m,int *n)
{
int r;
```

```
r=*m; /*  swaping of numbers    */
*m=*n;
*n=r;
printf("\n given numbers after swapping  in function are %d
      and %d\n",*m,*n);
}
```

> **Output**
> enter m,n
> 12 24
> given numbers before swaping are 12 and 24
> given numbers after swapping in function are 24 and 12
> given numbers after swaping in main program are 24 and 12

In the above programs while calling a function with the help of reference parameters we have used pointers. This is because only with the help of pointer variables we can specify the same address for actual as well as formal parameters (actual parameters are the arguments used in the function call statements and formal parameters are the arguments used in function definition for receiving the arguments passed). The names of actual and formal parameters may be same or different but when they are using the same memory address then any changes that are made in either of the functions (calling function or called function) will be available for other functions.

Unlike the ordinary variables when passed as an argument to the called function where they create a separate copy of the parameters, the arrays or strings actually pass the base address, which is a reference. This is nothing but call by reference that we have discussed earlier.

In the following program the main() function passes two dimensional array as an argument to the matread() function and matprint() function. Changes done in the matread() are available for the matprint() even they will not return any value. Because each and every function refer to the same memory address of the arrays.

```
 /*  program name: fun19.c   */
 /*  Function for reading a matrix */
 /*  Function for printing the matrix    */
#include<stdio.h>
#include<conio.h>
void matread(int[10][10],int,int);
void matprint(int[10][10],int,int);
void main()
{
int n,m; /*  order of the matrix */
int a[10][10];
clrscr();
printf("\n enter order of the matrix m and n \n");
scanf("%d%d",&m,&n);
```

```
printf("\n enter matrix elements\n");
matread(a,m,n); /*  calling the function  */
printf(" given matrix is \n\n");
matprint(a,m,n); /*  calling the function  */
getch();
}

 /* Function definition for matread() */
void matread(int x[10][10],int m,int n)
{
int i,j;
for(i=0;i<m;++i)
for(j=0;j<n;++j)
scanf("%d",&x[i][j]);
}

 /* Function definition for matprint() */
void matprint(int x[10][10],int m,int n)
{
int i,j;
for(i=0;i<m;++i)
{
for(j=0;j<n;++j)
printf("%8d",x[i][j]);
printf("\n");
}
}
```

Output

```
enter order of matrix m and n
3 3
enter matrix elements
1 2 3 4 5 6 7 8 9
given matrix is
1       2       3
4       5       6
7       8       9
```

The following program adds two matrices of order m and n. It makes use of three functions one for reading matrix, which is called twice to read two matrices through the reference variable. Second function is used for printing the matrix, which is called three times for printing two input matrices and the resultant matrix. The third function called only once, which adds the two inputted matrices and stores the result in the resultant matrix.

```
/*  program name: fun20.c  */
/*  Function for reading a matrix */
/*  Function for printing the matrix  */
/*  Function for adding matrix  */
/*  Program adds two matrices */
#include<stdio.h>
#include<conio.h>
void matread(int[10][10],int,int);
void matprint(int[10][10],int,int);
void matadd(int[10][10],int[10][10],int[10][10],int, int);
void main()
{
int n,m; /*  order of the matrix */
int a[10][10],b[10][10],c[10][10];
clrscr();
printf("\n enter order of the matrix m and n \n");
scanf("%d%d",&m,&n);
printf("\n enter elements for matrix a \n");
matread(a,m,n); /*  calling the function  */
printf("\n enter elements for matrix b \n");
matread(b,m,n); /*  calling the function  */

printf(" given a matrix is \n\n");
matprint(a,m,n); /*  calling the function  */
printf(" given b matrix is \n\n");
matprint(b,m,n); /*  calling the function  */
matadd(a,b,c,m,n); /*  calling add function by passing all
    three matrices, the result is stored in matrix c  */
printf(" the resultant c matrix is \n\n");
matprint(c,m,n); /*  calling the function  */
getch();
}

 /* Function definition for matread() */
void matread(int x[10][10],int m,int n)
{
int i,j;
for(i=0;i<m;++i)
for(j=0;j<n;++j)
scanf("%d",&x[i][j]);
}
 /* Function definition for matprint() */
void matprint(int x[10][10],int m,int n)
{
int i,j;
```

```
for(i=0;i<m;++i)
{
for(j=0;j<n;++j)
printf("%8d",x[i][j]);
printf("\n");
}
}
 /* Function definition for matadd() */
void matadd(x, y, z, m,n)
int x[10][10],y[10][10],z[10][10],m,n;
{
int i,j;
for(i=0;i<m;++i)
for(j=0;j<n;++j)
z[i][j]=x[i][j]+y[i][j];
}
```

```
Output
enter order of matrix m and n
3 3

enter elements for matrix a

1 2 3 4 5 6 7 8 9
enter elements for matrix b

9 8 7 6 5 4 3 2 1
given a matrix is

1       2       3
4       5       6
7       8       9
given b matrix is

9       8       7
6       5       4
3       2       1
the resultant c matrix is

10      10      10
10      10      10
10      10      10
```

The following program multiplies two matrices of order m and n. It makes use of three functions one for reading matrix, which is called twice to read two matrices through the reference variable. Second function is used for printing the matrix, which is called three times for printing two input matrices and the resultant matrix. The third function just called once which multiplies the two inputted matrices and stores the result in the resultant matrix.

```
 /*  program name: fun21.c   */
 /*  Function for reading a matrix */
 /*  Function for printing the matrix   */
 /*  Function for multiplying two matrix  */
 /*  Program to multiply two matrices */
#include<stdio.h>
#include<conio.h>
void matread(int[10][10],int,int);
void matprint(int[10][10],int,int);
void matmul(int[10][10],int[10][10],int[10][10],int, int);
void main()
{
int n,m; /*  order of the matrix */
int a[10][10],b[10][10],c[10][10];
clrscr();
printf("\n enter order of the matrix m and n \n");
scanf("%d%d",&m,&n);
printf("\n enter elements for matrix a \n");
matread(a,m,n); /*  calling the function  */
printf("\n enter elements for matrix b \n");
matread(b,m,n); /*  calling the function  */

printf(" given a matrix is \n\n");
matprint(a,m,n); /*  calling the function  */
printf(" given b matrix is \n\n");
matprint(b,m,n); /*  calling the function  */
matmul(a,b,c,m,n); /*  calling matmul function by passing all
      three matrices, the result is stored in matrix c  */
printf(" the resultant c matrix is \n\n");
matprint(c,m,n); /*  calling the function  */
getch();
}

 /* Function definition for matread() */
void matread(int x[10][10],int m,int n)
{
int i,j;
for(i=0;i<m;++i)
for(j=0;j<n;++j)
```

```
scanf("%d",&x[i][j]);
}
 /* Function definition for matprint() */
void matprint(int x[10][10],int m,int n)
{
int i,j;
for(i=0;i<m;++i)
{
for(j=0;j<n;++j)
printf("%8d",x[i][j]);
printf("\n");
}
}
 /* Function definition for matmul() */
void matmul(x,y,z,m,n)
int x[10][10],y[10][10],z[10][10], m, n;
{
int i,j,k;
for(i=0;i<m;++i)
for(j=0;j<n;++j)
{
z[i][j]=0;
for(k=0;k<n;++k)
z[i][j]+=x[i][k]*y[k][j];
}
}
```

Output

```
enter order of matrix m and n
3 3

enter elements for matrix a

1 2 3 4 5 6 7 8 9
enter elements for matrix b

9 8 7 6 5 4 3 2 1
given a matrix is

1     2     3
4     5     6
7     8     9
given b matrix is

9     8     7
6     5     4
3     2     1
the resultant c matrix is

10    10    10
10    10    10
10    10    10
```

In the following few programs we will discuss about the strings and different operations on them such as finding length of a string, combining two strings (concatenation), comparing two strings, copying one string to another, reversing a string etc. For these common operations number of standard built-in functions are provided in 'string.h' header file. In the following program we are not using these built-in functions instead we will write the code for these functions. Note that passing strings as parameters are call by reference by default.

First we will see how to find the length of a string.

```
/*  program name: fun22.c  */
/*  Program for finding length of a string using
function */
#include<stdio.h>
#include<conio.h>
int stlen(char[]);
void main()
{
char s[100];
int n;
clrscr();
printf("\n enter a string \n");
gets(s);
printf("\n Given string is %s \n",s);
n=stlen(s);
printf("\n The length is %d\n",n);
getch();
}

/* Function definition for stlen() */
int stlen(char s[])
{
int n=0;
while(s[n]!='\0')
n++;
return n;
}
```

output
enter a string
Bangalore is a garden city
Given string is Bangalore is a garden city
The length is 26

String concatenation means combining two strings. Copying one string at the end of another string can do this. The following program illustrates string concatenation. It makes use of the user defined function concate(), which takes two strings as its parameters.

```
/*  program name: fun23.c  */
/*  Program for concatenation of two strings using function
    */
#include<stdio.h>
```

```
#include<conio.h>
void concate(char[],char[]);
void main()
{
char s1[100],s2[50];
clrscr();
printf("\n enter first string \n");
gets(s1);
printf("\n enter second string \n");
gets(s2);
printf("\n The first string is %s\n",s1);
printf("\n The second string is %s\n",s2);
concate(s1,s2);   /* calling function, the resultant string
    stores in s1 */
printf("\n The resultant string is %s\n",s1);
getch();
}
 /* Function definition for concate() */
void concate(char s1[],char s2[])
{
int n=0,m=0;
while(s1[n]!='\0')
n++;
printf("\n length of first string is %d",n);
while(s2[m]!='\0')
{
s1[n]=s2[m];
n++;
m++;
}
printf("\n length of second string is %d",m);
s1[n]='\0';  /* marking the end of resultant string  */
}
```

output
enter first string
programming
enter second string
skills
The first string is programming
The second string is skills
length of first string is 11
length of first string is 6
The resultant string is programmingskills

The following program includes a function that compares two strings. Comparing two strings means, checking for the equality of individual characters in the order from beginning (lexicographical order). When first characters of both the strings are same alphabetically (their ASCII values must be equal), then only we proceed to check the second character and so on. When we get unequal characters then we come to the conclusion that the two strings are not equal. They are equal only when we reach the end of both the strings without any differences in the ASCII values of the corresponding characters of both the strings. In the following program we make use of the library function 'strcmpi()'for comparing the strings. It returns '0' if both the strings are equal or a positive value if first string is greater than the second string lexicographically or a negative value if first string is less than the second string lexicographically. This library function ignores the case of the characters (upper case and lower case are considered same).

```
 /*  program name: fun24.c */
 /*  Program for comparing two string using function */
 /*  It makes use of standard library function for comparing
     */
#include<stdio.h>
#include<conio.h>
#include<string.h>
int stcomp(char[],char[]);
void main()
{
char s1[50],s2[50];
int n;
clrscr();
printf("\n enter first string \n");
gets(s1);
printf("\n enter second string \n");
gets(s2);
printf("\n The first string is %s\n",s1);
printf("\n The second string is %s\n",s2);
n=stcomp(s1,s2);  /*  calling function  */
if(n==0)
printf("\n The given strings are equal\n");
else
if(n>0)
printf("\n The first string is greater than second
string\n");
else
printf("\n The first string is smaller than second string\n");
getch();
}

 /* Function definition for stcomp() */
int stcomp(char s1[],char s2[])
```

```
{
return(strcmpi(s1,s2));
}
```

Output 1
enter first string
programming
enter second string
skills
The first string is programming
The second string is skills
The first string is smaller than second string

Output 2
enter first string
India is great
enter second string
INDIA is Great
The first string is India is great
The second string is INDIA is Great
The strings are equal

The following program is a modified version of the above program, which does not make use of the library function instead it uses a user defined function for comparing two strings. Here the function definition is given in such a way that it takes into consideration the case of the characters.

```
/*  program name: fun25.c  */
/*  Program for comparing two string using function */
/*  It will not make use of standard library function for
    comparing  */
#include<stdio.h>
#include<conio.h>
int stcomp(char[],char[]);
void main()
{
char s1[50],s2[50];
int n;
clrscr();
printf("\n enter first string \n");
gets(s1);
printf("\n enter second string \n");
gets(s2);
printf("\n The first string is %s\n",s1);
```

```
printf("\n The second string is %s\n",s2);
n=stcomp(s1,s2);  /*  calling function  */
if(n==0)
printf("\n The given strings are equal\n");
else
if(n>0)
printf("\n The first string is greater than second string\n");
else
printf("\n The first string is smaller than second string\n");
getch();
}

 /* Function definition for stcomp() */
int stcomp(char s1[],char s2[])
{
int n=0;
while(s1[n]!='\0' || s2[n]!='\0')
{
if(s1[n]<s2[n])
return(-1);
else
if(s1[n]>s2[n])
return(1);
n++;
}
return(0);
}
```

Output 1
enter first string
reddy
enter second string
keshav
The first string is reddy
The second string is keshav
The first string is greater than second string

Output 2
enter first string
India is great
enter second string
INDIA is Great
The first string is India is great
The second string is INDIA is Great
The first string is greater than second string

The following program copies contents of one string to another string with the help of user defined functions (stcpy()). The main () function passes two parameters (by reference)to the 'stcpy()' where the first parameter contains the string which is to be copied to the second parameter.

```
/*  program name: fun26.c   */
/*  Program for copying one string to another string using
    function. It will not make use of standard library
    function for string copy  */
#include<stdio.h>
#include<conio.h>
void stcpy(char[],char[]);
void main()
{
char s1[50],s2[50];
clrscr();
printf("\n enter a string \n");
gets(s1);
printf("\n The given string is %s\n",s1);
stcpy(s1,s2);  /* calling function, result  stored in s2  */
printf("\n The copied string is %s\n",s2);
getch();
}

 /* Function definition for stcpy() */
void  stcpy(char s1[],char s2[])
{
int n=0;
while(s1[n]!='\0')
{
s2[n]=s1[n];
n++;
}
s2[n]='\0';
}
```

Output
enter a string
computer skills
The given string is computer skills
The copied string is computer skills

The following program reverses the given string with the use of user defined function 'strev()'.

```
/*  program name: fun27.c   */
/*  Program for reversing a string using function */
/*  It will not make use of standard library function for
    string reversing  */
#include<stdio.h>
#include<conio.h>
void strev(char[],char[]);
```

```
void main()
{
char s1[50],s2[50];
     clrscr();
     printf("\n enter a string \n");
     gets(s1);
     printf("\n The given string is %s\n",s1);
     strev(s1,s2);  /*  calling function and result is stored in s2
          */
     printf("\n The reversed string is %s\n",s2);
     getch();
     }

      /* Function definition for strev() */
     void  strev(char s1[],char s2[])
     {
     int n=0,i=0;
     while(s1[n]!='\0')
     n++;
     for(--n;n>=0;--n)
     {
     s2[i]=s1[n];
     i++;
     }
     s2[i]='\0';
     }
```

Output
enter a string
computer skills
The given string is computer skills
The reversed string is slliks retupmoc

Let us try to combine all string operations we discussed above in one program with the menu options for each. The user is allowed to choose any of the string operations from the menu options.

```
      /* program name: fun28.c  */
      /* A menu driven program for string length, string copy,
         string concate, string compare and reverse of string
         using functions */
      /* It will not make use of standard library functions  */
     #include<stdio.h>
     #include<conio.h>
     int stlen(char []);
     void concate(char [],char []);
     int stcomp(char[] ,char[]);
```

```
void  stcpy(char [],char []);
void strev(char[],char[]);

void main()
{
char s1[50],s2[50];
int ch,n;
do
{
clrscr();
printf("\n String operations \n\t 1
   Length\n\t2concate\n\t3 Compare\n\t4 Copy\n\t5
   Reverse\n\t6 exit\n\t enter choice\n");
scanf("%d",&ch);
fflush(stdin);
switch(ch)
{
case 1:
   printf("\n Enter a string \n");
   gets(s1);
   n=stlen(s1);
   printf("\n string = %s\nlength = %d\n",s1,n);
   break;
case 2:
   printf("\n enter first string \n");
   gets(s1);
   printf("\n enter second string \n");
   gets(s2);
   printf("\n The first string is %s\n",s1);
   printf("\n The second string is %s\n",s2);
   concate(s1,s2);
   printf("\n The resultant string is %s\n",s1);
   break;
case 3:
   printf("\n enter first string \n");
   gets(s1);
   printf("\n enter second string \n");
   gets(s2);
   printf("\n The first string is %s\n",s1);
   printf("\n The second string is %s\n",s2);
   n=stcomp(s1,s2);  /*  calling function   */
   if(n==0)
   printf("\n The given strings are equal\n");
   else
   if(n>0)
```

```
        printf("\n The first string is greater than second string\n");
        else
        printf("\n The first string is smaller than second string\n");
        break;
     case 4:
        printf("\n enter a string \n");
        gets(s1);
        printf("\n The given string is %s\n",s1);
        stcpy(s1,s2);
        printf("\n The copied string is %s\n",s2);
        break;
     case 5:
        printf("\n enter a string \n");
        gets(s1);
        printf("\n The given string is %s\n",s1);
        strev(s1,s2);
        printf("\n The reversed string is %s\n",s2);
        break;
     case 6: break;
     default: printf("\n wrong choice re-enter\n");
     }
     printf("\n press any key to continue..\n");
     getch();
     }while(ch!=6);
     }

      /* Function definition for stlen() */
     int stlen(char s[])
     {
     int n=0;
     while(s[n]!='\0')
     n++;
     return n;
     }
      /* Function definition for concate() */
     void concate(char s1[],char s2[])
     {
     int n=0,m=0;
     while(s1[n]!='\0')
     n++;
     printf("\n length of first string is %d",n);
     while(s2[m]!='\0')
     {
     s1[n]=s2[m];
     n++;
     m++;
```

```
}
printf("\n length of second string is %d",m);
s1[n]='\0';  /*  marking the end of resultant string  */
}
 /* Function definition for stcomp() */
int stcomp(char s1[],char s2[])
{
int n=0;
while(s1[n]!='\0' || s2[n]!='\0')
{
if(s1[n]<s2[n])
return(-1);
else
if(s1[n]>s2[n])
return(1);
n++;
}
return(0);
}
 /* Function definition for stcpy() */
void  stcpy(char s1[],char s2[])
{
int n=0;
while(s1[n]!='\0')
{
s2[n]=s1[n];
n++;
}
s2[n]='\0';
}

 /* Function definition for strev() */
void  strev(char s1[],char s2[])
{
int n=0,i=0;
while(s1[n]!='\0')
n++;
for(--n;n>=0;--n)
{
s2[i]=s1[n];
i++;
}
s2[i]='\0';
}
```

The output of this program is left as an exercise for the reader.

8.7 Recursion

Recursive function is a function, which calls itself. Certain expressions can be easily implemented by recursion.

Examples:

1. n! = n*(n-1) !
   =n*(n-1)*(n-2) !

So factorial of a number is defined in terms of factorial of a number itself.

2. a*b =a+a*(b-1)
   =a+a+a*(b-2)
   =a+a+a+...+a*(b-(b+1))

Recursion makes use of stacks to store the values internally.

Examples:

1. Recursive function for factorial.

```
long fact(int n)
{
if (n==1)
return(1);
else
return(n*fact(n-1));
}
```

2. Recursive function for multiplying two numbers.

```
long mul(int a,int b)
{
if(b==1)
return(a);
else
return(a+mul(a,b-1));
}
```

To make the above concept clear let us consider the following examples.
This program finds the factorial of the number recursively.

```
 /*  program name: fun29.c  */
 /*  recursive function to find factorial */
#include<stdio.h>
#include<conio.h>
long fact(int);
void main()
{
int n;
```

```
long f;
clrscr();
printf("\n enter n\n");
scanf("%d",&n);
f=fact(n);
printf("\n factorial of %d = %ld\n",n,f);
getch();
}
long fact(int x)
{
if(x<=1)
return(1);
else
return(x*fact(x-1));
}
```

```
output
enter n
10

factorial of 10 = 3628800
```

The expression x^y is defined recursively as $x * x^{y-1}$. The following program implements this with the help of recursive function.

```
 /*  program name: fun30.c  */
 /*  recursive function to find x to the power of y */
#include<stdio.h>
#include<conio.h>
long xtopy(int,int);
void main()
{
int x,y;
long f;
clrscr();
printf("\n enter x,y\n");
scanf("%d%d",&x,&y);
f=xtopy(x,y);
printf("\n %d to the power of %d = %ld\n",x,y,f);
getch();
}
long xtopy(int x,int y)
{
if(y==0)
return(1);
```

```
else
if(y==1)
return x;
else
return(x*xtopy(x,y-1));
}
```

```
output

enter x,y
5 6

5 to the power of 6 = 15625
```

This program uses the recursive function for multiplying two numbers.

```
  /*  program name: fun31.c  */
  /*  recursive function to find product of two numbers */
#include<stdio.h>
#include<conio.h>
long mult(int,int);
void main()
{
int x,y;
long f;
clrscr();
printf("\n enter x,y\n");
scanf("%d%d",&x,&y);
f=mult(x,y);
printf("\n product of %d and %d = %ld\n",x,y,f);
getch();
}
long mult(int x,int y)
{
if(y==0)
return(0);
else
if(y==1)
return x;
else
return(x+mult(x,y-1));
}
```

```
output

enter x,y
8 10

product of 8 and 10 = 80
```

This program prints the first 'n' Fibonacci terms. The Fibonacci series is recursively defined as fib(fi,fi+1)=fib(fi+1,fi+fi+1). That means the successive terms will be the sum of previous two terms.

```
 /*  program name: fun32.c  */
 /*  recursive function to print fibonacci series */
#include<stdio.h>
#include<conio.h>
void fib(int,int,int);
void main()
{
int n,f0,f1;
f0=0;
f1=1;
clrscr();
printf("\n enter n\n");
scanf("%d",&n);
fib(f0,f1,n);
getch();
}
void fib(int x,int y,int n)
{
int f;
if(n!=0)
{
printf("%9d",x);
f=y+x;
x=y;
y=f;
fib(x,y,n-1);
}
}
```

output

```
enter n
20
    0    1    1    2    3    5    8   13   21   34   55   89  144  233  377  610
  987 1597 2584 4181
```

The GCD of two numbers can be recursively found as shown in the following program.

```
 /*  program name: fun33.c  */
 /*  recursive function to find gcd of two numbers */
#include<stdio.h>
```

```
#include<conio.h>
int gcd(int,int);
void main()
{
int n,m,g;
clrscr();
printf("\n enter n, m\n");
scanf("%d%d",&n,&m);
g=gcd(n,m);
printf("\n GCD of %d and %d = %d\n",n,m,g);
getch();
}
int gcd(int x,int y)
{
int r;
if(x==0)
return(y);
else
{
r=y%x;
y=x;
x=r;
return(gcd(x,y));
}
}
```

```
output

 enter n, m
48
90

 GCD of 48 and 90 = 6
```

The following program finds the sum of first n natural numbers using recursive function.

```
/*  program name: fun34.c  */
/*  Program for finding sum of series s=1+2+3....+n using
    recursion  */

#include<stdio.h>
#include<conio.h>
long sum(unsigned int);
void main()
{
unsigned int i,n;
long s;
```

```
clrscr();
printf("enter n\n");
scanf("%u",&n);
s=sum(n);

printf("sum of series = %ld\n",s);
getch();
}
 /*  recursive function for finding sum of series */
long sum(unsigned int x)
{
if(x==0)
return(0);
else
return(x+ sum(x-1));
}
```

Output
enter n
50
sum of series = 1275

Now we will consider different variety of programs, which we have already discussed in previous sections. Here we are separating certain parts of the program and make them as functions, which eases the programmers in the task of understanding, debugging and It may reduce the processing time and memory utilization of the computer. In the following program factorial is calculated with the help of a function.

```
 /*  program name: fun35.c  */
 /*  program to find  'e' the power of x */
 /*  function to find factorial of a number */
#include<stdio.h>
#include<conio.h>
#include<math.h>
double fact(int);
void main()
{
int n,i;
float ex=0,x;
clrscr();
printf("\n enter n, and x\n");
scanf("%d%f",&n,&x);
for(i=0;i<=n;++i)
ex=ex+pow(x,i)/fact(i);
printf("\n ex calculated up to %d terms = %f\n",n,ex);
```

```
getch();
}
 /*  function definition  */
double fact(int x)
{
if(x<=1)
return(1);
else
return ( x*fact(x-1));
}
```

```
output

enter n, and x
50
5

ex calculated up to 50 terms = 148.413177
```

This program takes angle in degrees and number of iterative steps as input. It converts angle in degrees into radians then finds the value of the sine series upto the specified number of terms.

```
/*  program name: fun36.c  */
/*  program to find sin(x) */
/*  function to find factorial of a number */
#include<stdio.h>
#include<conio.h>
#include<math.h>
double fact(int);
void main()
{
int n,i,t=1;
float sinx=0,x;
clrscr();
printf("\n enter n, and x\n");
scanf("%d%f",&n,&x);
x=x*3.142/180;
for(i=1;i<=n;i=i+2)
{
sinx+=pow(x,i)/fact(i)*t;
t=-t;
}
printf("\n  sin  of  %f  radian  calculated  up  to  %d  terms  =
       %f\n",x,n,sinx);
getch();
}
```

```
/*  function for factorial  */
double fact(int x)
{
if(x<=1)
return(1);
else
return ( x*fact(x-1));
}
```

output

enter n, and x
40
60

sin of 1.047333 radian calculated up to 40 terms = 0.866093

This program takes angle in degrees and number of steps as input. It converts angle in degrees into radians then finds the value of the cosine series upto the specified number of terms.

```
/*  program name: fun37.c  */
/*  program to find cos(x) */
/*  function to find factorial of a number */
#include<stdio.h>
#include<conio.h>
#include<math.h>
double fact(int);
void main()
{
int n,i,t=1;
float cosx=0,x;
clrscr();
printf("\n enter n, and x\n");
scanf("%d%f",&n,&x);
x=x*3.142/180;
for(i=0;i<=n;i=i+2)
{
cosx+=pow(x,i)/fact(i)*t;
t=-t;
}
printf("\n cos of %f radian calculated up to %d terms =
      %f\n",x,n,cosx);
getch();
}
```

```
/*  function definition  */
double fact(int x)
{
if(x<=1)
return(1);
else
return ( x*fact(x-1));
}
```

output

enter n, and x
49 60

cos of 1.047333 radian calculated up to 49 terms = 0.499882

8.8 Structures As Function Arguments

It is possible to pass structure as an argument to the function, as well as return a structure from the function. In the function definition and function prototype you must declare the type of the structure i.e., the name of the structure template.

```
/*  program name: fun38.c  */
/*  program to illustrate passing structure to function */
/*  this program considers employee information */
#include<stdio.h>
#include<conio.h>
struct emp
{
int eno;
char name[20],addr[20];
};
void sample(struct emp);
void main()
{
struct emp e;
clrscr();
printf("\n enter eno name and address\n");
scanf("%d%s%s",&e.eno,e.name,e.addr);
sample(e);
getch();
}
void sample(struct emp x)
{
```

```
printf("\n emp number =%d",x.eno);
printf("\n emp name =%s",x.name);
printf("\n emp address =%s",x.addr);
}
```

```
output

enter eno name and address
123
keshav
bangalore

emp number =123
emp name =keshav
emp address =bangalore
```

This program implements a function, which returns a structure.

Note: Arrays cannot be returned from the function. But a structure containing array as its member can be returned. Array of structures cannot be returned.

```
/*  program name: fun39.c        */
/*  program to illustrate returning a structure from a function
    */
/*  this program considers employee information */
#include<stdio.h>
#include<conio.h>
struct emp
{
int eno;
char name[20],addr[20];
};
struct emp sample();
void main()
{
struct emp x;
x=sample();
printf("\n emp number =%d",x.eno);
printf("\n emp name =%s",x.name);
printf("\n emp address =%s",x.addr);
getch();
} /*  end of main()  */

 /*  function definition  */
struct emp sample()
{
```

```
struct emp e;
clrscr();
printf("\n enter eno name and address\n");
scanf("%d%s%s",&e.eno,e.name,e.addr);
return e;
}
```

```
output

enter eno name and address
342
rayudu
bombay

emp number =342
emp name =rayudu
emp address =bombay
```

Programs on number conversions

In our daily life we use decimal number system. In decimal number system we have ten digits from 0 to 9, so the base is 10. Similarly we have other number systems such as binary, octal, hexadecimal etc. Computer makes use of binary number system for computation. In binary system we have only two digits 0 and 1. To get the clear concept of different number systems it is essential to know their base and the number of digits used. In the following few programs let us try to inter convert different number systems.

Now consider converting a decimal number into binary number system. As we all know binary number system has base two, for converting decimal to binary we need to divide the decimal number successively by 2 and write the reminders in reverse order. For example, to convert the decimal number 22 to binary we have to follow the following steps.

1. Divide 22 by 2 we get the remainder 0 and quotient 11.
2. Now divide 11 by 2 we get the remainder 1 and quotient 5.
3. Divide 5 by 2 we get the remainder 1 and quotient 2.
4. Divide 2 by 2 we get the remainder 0 and quotient 1.
5. Divide 1 by 2 we get remainder 1 and quotient 0.

We stop dividing the quotient by 2 when it becomes 0. Now we write all the remainders in the reverse order(from step 5 to 1)we get the binary number 10110, which is the binary equivalent of decimal number 22.

How do we go about implementing this task in a program? We start normally by taking input and passing this to the function. In the body of the function we can take help of an integer array to store the remainders each time we divide the number and after each division number is replaced by the quotient. This will continue till the quotient becomes zero and all remainders are stored in the array. For displaying the binary number we just display the array in reverse order. The following program implements this.

```
/*  program name: fun40.c  */
/*  program to convert a decimal number into binary using
    function */
#include<stdio.h>
#include<conio.h>
void bin(int);
void main()
{
int n;
clrscr();
printf("\n enter a decimal integer\n");
scanf("%d",&n);
bin(n);
getch();
}
void bin(int n)
{
int a[30],i=0;
while(n!=0)
{
a[i]=n%2;
n=n/2;
i++;
}
printf("\n binary number is ");
for(--i;i>=0;--i)
printf("%d",a[i]);
}
```

output

enter a decimal integer
342

binary number is 101010110

Like decimal and binary number systems we have octal number system which has base 8 and makes use of the digits 0 to 7. For converting a decimal number into octal we need to divide the decimal number by eight successively by replacing the number with quotient and writing the remainders in the reverse order. For example, to convert the decimal number 150 to octal we have to follow the following steps.

1) **Divide 150 by 8 to get the remainder 6 and quotient 18.**
2) **Now divide 18 by 8 we get the remainder 2 and quotient 2.**
3) **Divide 2 by 8 we get the remainder 2 and quotient 0.**

We stop dividing the quotient by 8 when it becomes 0. Now we write all the remainders in the reverse order (from step 3 to 1) we get the octal number 226, which is the octal equivalent of decimal number 150.

Here we use the same technique as we used in the above program for implementing this concept in a program.

```
/*  program name: fun41.c  */
/*  program to convert a decimal number to octal using
    function */
```

```
#include<stdio.h>
#include<conio.h>
void octal(int);
void main()
{
int n;
clrscr();
printf("\n enter a decimal integer\n");
scanf("%d",&n);
octal(n);
getch();
}
void octal(int n)
{
int a[30],i=0;
while(n!=0)
{
a[i]=n%8;
n=n/8;
i++;
}
printf("\n octal number is ");
for(--i;i>=0;--i)
printf("%d",a[i]);
}
```

output

enter a decimal integer
123

octal number is 173

Hexadecimal number system is of base 16 and makes use of sixteen digits (0 to 9 and alphabets A to F). 'A' is equivalent to 10,'B' is equivalent to 11 and so on up to 'F' equals 15. If we divide a decimal number by 16 the possible remainders will be any one number in the range 0 to 15. We can use the same technique as that of converting decimal to octal or decimal to binary and write all the remainders in the reverse order to get the hexadecimal equivalent of the given decimal number.

Note: the remainders 10 to 15 are denoted by the corresponding hexadecimal digits from A to F.

The following program converts decimal number to hexadecimal number.

```
/*  program name: fun42.c  */
/* program to convert a decimal number to hexadecimal using
     function */
#include<stdio.h>
#include<conio.h>
void hex(int);
```

```
void main()
{
int n;
clrscr();
printf("\n enter a decimal integer\n");
scanf("%d",&n);
hex(n);
getch();
}
void hex(int n)
{
char a[30];
int i=0;
while(n!=0)
{
switch(n%16)
{
case 0:  a[i]='0';
         break;
case 1:  a[i]='1';
         break;
case 2:  a[i]='2';
         break;
case 3:  a[i]='3';
         break;
case 4:  a[i]='4';
         break;
case 5:  a[i]='5';
         break;
case 6:  a[i]='6';
         break;
case 7:  a[i]='7';
         break;
case 8:  a[i]='8';
         break;
case 9:  a[i]='9';
         break;
case 10: a[i]='A';
         break;
case 11: a[i]='B';
         break;
case 12: a[i]='C';
         break;
case 13: a[i]='D';
         break;
```

```
case 14: a[i]='E';
     break;
case 15: a[i]='F';
     break;
}
n=n/16;
i++;
}
printf("\n hexadecimal number is ");
for(--i;i>=0;--i)
printf("%c",a[i]);
}
```

output

enter a decimal integer
1234

hexadecimal number is 4D2

For converting octal number to decimal number we need to multiply instead of division. Here we first separate each digit of the octal number and each digit is multiplied with 8 to the power of digit's position from least significant digit (LSB) and all are added. For example, converting octal number $(123)_8$ into decimal we calculate $1*8^2+2*8^1+3*8^0=64+16+3=83$. The octal number can be taken from the keyboard using scanf() function with the format "%o". While entering the octal number care should be taken to see that all the digits of a number should be in the range 0 to 7.

The following program converts octal number to decimal number.

```
 /*  program name: fun43.c  */
 /*  program to convert a octal number to decimal using
     function */
#include<stdio.h>
#include<conio.h>
#include<math.h>
void decimal(int);
void main()
{
int n;
clrscr();
printf("\n enter an octal integer\n");
scanf("%o",&n); /*  for taking input of an octal number. */
decimal(n);
getch();
}
void decimal(int n)
{
```

```
int d=0,i=0;
while(n!=0)
{
d=d+pow(8,i)*(n%8); /* each time the last digit is multiplied
      with 8to the power of its position from LSB */
n=n/8;
i++;
}
printf("\n decimal number is %d",d);
}
```

```
output

enter an octal integer
134

decimal number is 92
```

To convert octal number to binary, just replace each octal digit with its three digit binary equivalent. For example, octal number 123 is converted to binary by writing 001010011(1=001,2=010,3=011). Here the trailing (first two)zeros can be removed as it will not affect the result(1010011). However we are implementing the program using a different logic explained below.

We have already seen how to convert decimal number to binary and octal number to decimal. So to convert an octal number to binary first we convert given octal number to decimal and the obtained decimal number can be converted to binary. In the following program we make use of two functions one for converting octal to decimal (bin()) and another to convert decimal to binary(bin1()).

```
/*  program name: fun44.c  */
/* program to convert a octal number to binary using function
    */
#include<stdio.h>
#include<conio.h>
#include<math.h>
void bin(int);
void bin1(int);
void main()
{
int n;
clrscr();
printf("\n enter an octal integer\n");
scanf("%o",&n);
bin(n);
getch();
}
```

```
 /*  function for converting octal to decimal  */
void bin(int n)
{
int d=0,i=0;
while(n!=0)
{
d=d+pow(8,i)*(n%8);
n=n/8;
i++;
}
bin1(d);
}
 /*  function for converting decimal to binary  */
void bin1(int n)
{
int a[30],i=0;
while(n!=0)
{
a[i]=n%2;
n=n/2;
i++;
}
printf("\n binary number is ");
for(--i;i>=0;--i)
printf("%d",a[i]);
}
```

```
output

enter an octal integer
132

binary number is 1011010
```

Conversion of octal number to hexadecimal is very simple manually. We need to convert individual digits of an octal number into three digit equivalent binary format and regrouping the results into four binary digits each from left to right. Now for each four digit group we write equivalent hexadecimal digits which becomes the hexadecimal equivalent of given octal number. However we are not implementing this technique. We use our own technique which converts octal to decimal and then decimal to hexadecimal (the functions for which we have already implemented in the above programs).

```
 /*  program name: fun45.c  */
 /*  program to convert a octal number to hexadecimal using
     function */
#include<stdio.h>
#include<conio.h>
```

```
#include<math.h>
void hex(int);
void hex1(int);
void main()
{
int n;
clrscr();
printf("\n enter an octal integer\n");
scanf("%o",&n);
hex(n);
getch();
}
 /* function to convert octal to decimal */
void hex(int n)
{
int d=0,i=0;
while(n!=0)
{
d=d+pow(8,i)*(n%8);
n=n/8;
i++;
}
hex1(d);
}
 /* function to convert decimal to hexadecimal */
void hex1(int n)
{
char a[30];
int i=0;
while(n!=0)
{
switch(n%16)
{
case 0:  a[i]='0';
     break;
case 1:  a[i]='1';
     break;
case 2:  a[i]='2';
     break;
case 3:  a[i]='3';
     break;
case 4:  a[i]='4';
     break;
case 5:  a[i]='5';
     break;
```

```
case 6:  a[i]='6';
    break;
case 7:  a[i]='7';
    break;
case 8:  a[i]='8';
    break;
case 9:  a[i]='9';
    break;
case 10: a[i]='A';
    break;
case 11: a[i]='B';
    break;
case 12: a[i]='C';
    break;
case 13: a[i]='D';
    break;
case 14: a[i]='E';
    break;
case 15: a[i]='F';
    break;
}
n=n/16;
i++;
}
printf("\n hexadecimal number is ");
for(--i;i>=0;--i)
printf("%c",a[i]);
}
```

output

enter an octal integer
541

hexadecimal number is 161

The hexadecimal number can be converted to its equivalent decimal number by multiplying each hexadecimal digit with 16 to the power of its position from left to right and adding all these intermediate results. For example consider the hexadecimal number $(2DA)_{16}$, we can write $2*16^2+13*16^1+10*16^0=2*256+13*16+10*1=512+208+10=(730)_{10}$ (because D=13 and A=10).

The hexadecimal number can be inputted from the keyboard by using the format "%x" in the scanf() statement. However when the user enters wrong input it will not respond and gives wrong results. The following program takes hexadecimal number as a string and checks for its validity before converting it to decimal. In case user enters wrong input with suitable message it demands for correct input.

```
/*  program name: fun46.c  */
/*  program to convert a hexadecimal number to decimal using
     function */
#include<stdio.h>
#include<conio.h>
#include<math.h>
#include<string.h>
void dec(char []);
void main()
{
int t,i=0;
char h[20];
clrscr();
do
{
t=0;
printf("\n enter a hexadecimal integer\n");
scanf("%s",h);
for(i=0;i<strlen(h);++i)
{
if(!(h[i]>='0'&& h[i]<='9' || h[i]>='a' && h[i]<='f' ||
   h[i]>='A' && h[i]<='F'))
{
t=1;
printf("\n enterd number is wrong re-enter...\n");
}
}
}while(t==1);

dec(h);
getch();
}
void dec(char h[])
{
long d=0;
int i,n;
n=strlen(h);
for(i=n-1;i>=0;--i)
{
switch(h[i])
{
case '0': d=d+pow(16,n-i-1)*0;
     break;
case '1': d=d+pow(16,n-i-1)*1;
     break;
```

```
case '2': d=d+pow(16,n-i-1)*2;
     break;
case '3': d=d+pow(16,n-i-1)*3;
     break;
case '4': d=d+pow(16,n-i-1)*4;
     break;
case '5': d=d+pow(16,n-i-1)*5;
     break;
case '6': d=d+pow(16,n-i-1)*6;
     break;
case '7': d=d+pow(16,n-i-1)*7;
     break;
case '8': d=d+pow(16,n-i-1)*8;
     break;
case '9':d=d+pow(16,n-i-1)*9;
     break;

case 'a':
case 'A':d=d+pow(16,n-i-1)*10;
     break;
case 'b':
case 'B':d=d+pow(16,n-i-1)*11;
     break;
case 'c':
case 'C':d=d+pow(16,n-i-1)*12;
     break;
case 'd':
case 'D':d=d+pow(16,n-i-1)*13;
     break;
case 'e':
case 'E':d=d+pow(16,n-i-1)*14;
     break;
case 'f':
case 'F':d=d+pow(16,n-i-1)*15;
     break;
}
}
printf("\n decimal number = %ld\n",d);
}
```

output

enter a hexadecimal integer
325

decimal number = 805

Converting hexadecimal number to an octal number involves the following steps.

1. Convert each digit of the hexadecimal number into four digit equivalent binary number.
2. Regroup the binary number into three digits each from left to right (LSB to MSB).
3. For each group of three binary digits write the equivalent octal digit.

For example consider the hexadecimal number $(A564F)_{16}$, this can be written in binary as 1010 0101 0110 0100 1111. Now regroup the binary digits three bits each from left to right. We get 010 100 101 011 001 001 111(extra 0 is added in the beginning to make group of three digits each which will not affect the result). Now we can write octal equivalent to each group to get octal equivalent of the given hexadecimal number $(2453117)_8$. However we are not implementing this logic in the following program instead we are using a different logic which converts hexadecimal to decimal as explained in the previous program and then decimal number is converted to octal as we have already discussed.

```
 /*  program name: fun47.c  */
 /*  program to convert a hexadecimal number to octal using
      function */
#include<stdio.h>
#include<conio.h>
#include<math.h>
#include<string.h>
void oct(char []);
void oct1(long);

void main()
{
int t,i=0;
char h[20];
clrscr();
do
{
t=0;
printf("\n enter a hexadecimal integer\n");
scanf("%s",h);
for(i=0;i<strlen(h);++i)
{
if(!(h[i]>='0'&& h[i]<='9' || h[i]>='a' && h[i]<='f' ||
   h[i]>='A' && h[i]<='F'))
{
t=1;
printf("\n enterd number is wrong re-enter...\n");
}
}
}while(t==1);

oct(h);
getch();
```

```
}
void oct(char h[])
{
long d=0;
int i,n;
n=strlen(h);
for(i=n-1;i>=0;--i)
{
switch(h[i])
{
case '0': d=d+pow(16,n-i-1)*0;
      break;
case '1': d=d+pow(16,n-i-1)*1;
      break;
case '2': d=d+pow(16,n-i-1)*2;
      break;
case '3': d=d+pow(16,n-i-1)*3;
      break;
case '4': d=d+pow(16,n-i-1)*4;
      break;
case '5': d=d+pow(16,n-i-1)*5;
      break;
case '6': d=d+pow(16,n-i-1)*6;
      break;
case '7': d=d+pow(16,n-i-1)*7;
      break;
case '8': d=d+pow(16,n-i-1)*8;
      break;
case '9':d=d+pow(16,n-i-1)*9;
      break;

case 'a':
case 'A':d=d+pow(16,n-i-1)*10;
      break;
case 'b':
case 'B':d=d+pow(16,n-i-1)*11;
      break;
case 'c':
case 'C':d=d+pow(16,n-i-1)*12;
      break;
case 'd':
case 'D':d=d+pow(16,n-i-1)*13;
      break;
case 'e':
case 'E':d=d+pow(16,n-i-1)*14;
      break;
```

```
case 'f':
case 'F':d=d+pow(16,n-i-1)*15;
     break;
}
}
oct1(d);
}
void oct1(long n)
{
int a[30],i=0;
while(n!=0)
{
a[i]=n%8;
n=n/8;
i++;
}
printf("\n octal number is ");
for(--i;i>=0;--i)
printf("%d",a[i]);
}
```

```
output

enter a hexadecimal integer
5AB4

octal number is 55264
```

In the following program we are converting the given hexadecimal number to binary through intermediate decimal conversion. That means hexadecimal is converted to decimal and then decimal is converted to binary.

```
/*  program name: fun48.c   */
/*  program to convert a hexadecimal number to binary  using
     function */
#include<stdio.h>
#include<conio.h>
#include<math.h>
#include<string.h>
void bin(char []);
void bin1(long);

void main()
{
int t,i=0;
char h[20];
clrscr();
```

```
do
{
t=0;
printf("\n enter a hexadecimal integer\n");
scanf("%s",h);
for(i=0;i<strlen(h);++i)
{
if(!(h[i]>='0'&& h[i]<='9' || h[i]>='a' && h[i]<='f' ||
   h[i]>='A' && h[i]<='F'))
{
t=1;
printf("\n enterd number is wrong re-enter...\n");
}
}
}while(t==1);

bin(h);
getch();
}
void bin(char h[])
{
long d=0;
int i,n;
n=strlen(h);
for(i=n-1;i>=0;--i)
{
switch(h[i])
{
case '0': d=d+pow(16,n-i-1)*0;
     break;
case '1': d=d+pow(16,n-i-1)*1;
     break;
case '2': d=d+pow(16,n-i-1)*2;
     break;
case '3': d=d+pow(16,n-i-1)*3;
     break;
case '4': d=d+pow(16,n-i-1)*4;
     break;
case '5': d=d+pow(16,n-i-1)*5;
     break;
case '6': d=d+pow(16,n-i-1)*6;
     break;
case '7': d=d+pow(16,n-i-1)*7;
     break;
case '8': d=d+pow(16,n-i-1)*8;
     break;
```

```
case '9':d=d+pow(16,n-i-1)*9;
     break;

case 'a':
case 'A':d=d+pow(16,n-i-1)*10;
     break;
case 'b':
case 'B':d=d+pow(16,n-i-1)*11;
     break;
case 'c':
case 'C':d=d+pow(16,n-i-1)*12;
     break;
case 'd':
case 'D':d=d+pow(16,n-i-1)*13;
     break;
case 'e':
case 'E':d=d+pow(16,n-i-1)*14;
     break;
case 'f':
case 'F':d=d+pow(16,n-i-1)*15;
     break;
}
}
bin1(d);
}
void bin1(long n)
{
int a[30],i=0;
while(n!=0)
{
a[i]=n%2;
n=n/2;
i++;
}
printf("\n binary number is ");
for(--i;i>=0;--i)
printf("%d",a[i]);
}
```

output

enter a hexadecimal integer
AC34

binary number is 1010110000110100

Like decimal to binary conversion we can convert binary to decimal. For this we have to consider individual digits of the binary number and multiply them with 2 to the power of respective position starting from LSB and add them altogether to get equivalent decimal number.

```
 /*  program name: fun49.c  */
 /*  program to convert a binary to number to decimal using
     function */
#include<stdio.h>
#include<conio.h>
#include<math.h>
#include<string.h>
void dec(char []);
void main()
{
int t,i=0;
char h[20];
clrscr();
do
{
t=0;
printf("\n enter a binary integer\n");
scanf("%s",h);
for(i=0;i<strlen(h);++i)
{
if(!(h[i]>='0'&& h[i]<='1'))
{
t=1;
printf("\n entered number is wrong re-enter...\n");
}
}
}while(t==1);

dec(h);
getch();
}
 /*  function definition  */
void dec(char h[])
{
long d=0;
int i,n;
n=strlen(h);
for(i=n-1;i>=0;--i)
{
switch(h[i])
{
```

```
case '0': d=d+pow(2,n-i-1)*0;
    break;
case '1': d=d+pow(2,n-i-1)*1;
    break;
}
}
printf("\n decimal number = %ld\n",d);
}
```

```
output

enter a binary integer
100011101

decimal number = 285
```

In all of the above number conversion programs we have considered only integer numbers. In the following few programs we convert float values. First we consider the conversion of float decimal to hexadecimal. For this we need to handle integer part and fraction part separately. We have already discussed how to convert integer parts. For converting the fractional parts we have to multiply each fractional digits with 10 to the power of negative of its position counting from decimal point. In case of integer numbers we are counting the position starting from 0 but for fraction it starts from 1. For example the decimal number $(234.68)_{10}$ can be converted to hexadecimal as $2*10^2+3*10^1+4*10^0+6*10^{-1}+8*10^{-2}$, which is equivalent to $(EA.AE140)_{16}$.

The following program illustrates this.

```
/*  program name: fun50.c  */
/* decimal to hexadecimal conversion by inputting a float
   value. */
#include<stdio.h>
#include<conio.h>
void main()
  {
  float n;
  int a[20];
  long b,c;
  int i=0;
  clrscr();
  printf("enter the values\n");
  scanf("%f",&n);
  b=n;

while(b!=0)
{
```

```
a[i]=b%16;
    if(a[i]>=10 )

    switch(a[i])
    {
    case 10:a[i]='a';break ;
    case 11:a[i]='b';break ;
    case 12:a[i]='c';break ;
    case 13:a[i]='d';break ;
    case 14:a[i]='e';break ;
    case 15:a[i]='f';break ;
}
i++;
b=b/16;
}
for(--i;i>=0;--i)
{
if(a[i]<=9)
printf("%d",a[i]);
else
printf("%c",a[i]);
}
printf(".");
    b=n;
    n=n-b;

for(i=1;i<=5;++i)
{
n=n*16;
    b=n;
            switch(b)
    {
    case 10:printf("a");break ;
    case 11:printf("b");break ;
    case 12:printf("c");break ;
    case 13:printf("d");break ;
    case 14:printf("e");break ;
    case 15:printf("f");break ;
    default: printf("%d",b);
            }
            n=n-b;
            }
getch();
}
```

Output
enter the values
234.68
ea.ae140

In the following program we consider the conversion of float hexadecimal to decimal. For this we need to handle integer part and fractional part separately. We have already discussed how to convert integer parts. For converting the fractional parts we have to multiply each fractional digits with 16 to the power of negative of its position counting from decimal point. In case of integer numbers we are counting the position starting from 0 but for fraction it starts from 1. For example the hexadecimal number $(20A.12)_{16}$ can be converted to decimal as follows.

1. The integer part and the fractional part will be separated.
2. Integer part 20A can be written as $2*16^2+0*16^1+10*16^0= 2*256+0*16+10*1 = 512+0+10 = (522)_{10}$.
3. For fractional part .12 we can write $1*16^{-1}+2*16^{-2}= 1/16+2/256= =(0.0703125)_{10}$.
4. Now write the results of steps 2 and 3 separating them by decimal point to get the decimal equivalent of given hexadecimal number i.e. 522.0703125.

The following program illustrates this.

```
 /*  program name: fun51.c  */
 /*  hexadecimal to decimal with float value */
#include<stdio.h>
#include<conio.h>
#include<string.h>
#include<math.h>
  void main()
   {
   char a[20];
   int i=0,n,t=0,k,p;
   double x=0;
   clrscr();
   printf("enter the hexadecimal number\n");
   scanf("%s",a);
   for(i=0;i<strlen(a);++i)
   {
   if(!((a[i]>='0') && (a[i]<='9')))
   if(!((a[i]>='a') &&(a[i]<='f')))
   if(a[i]!='.')
   {
   printf("given number is not hexadecimal\n");
   t=1;
   break;
   }
   }
   if(t==0)
   {
   i=0;
   while(a[i]!='.')
   i++;
   k=0;
```

```
for(--i;i>=0;--i)
{
 switch(a[i])
 {
 case '0': p=0; break;
 case '1': p=1; break;
 case '2': p=2; break;
 case '3': p=3; break;

 case '4': p=4; break;
 case '5': p=5; break;
 case '6': p=6; break;
 case '7': p=7; break;
 case '8': p=8; break;
 case '9': p=9; break;
 case 'a': p=10; break;
 case 'b': p=11; break;
 case 'c': p=12; break;
 case 'd': p=13; break;
 case 'e': p=14; break;
 case 'f': p=15; break;
 }
 x=x+pow(16,k)*p;
 k++;
 }
 i=0;
while(a[i]!='.')
i++;
k=1;
for(++i;i<strlen(a);++i)
{
 switch(a[i])
 {
 case '0': p=0; break;
 case '1': p=1; break;
 case '2': p=2; break;
 case '3': p=3; break;

 case '4': p=4; break;
 case '5': p=5; break;
 case '6': p=6; break;
 case '7': p=7; break;
 case '8': p=8; break;
 case '9': p=9; break;
 case 'a': p=10; break;
```

```
case 'b': p=11; break;
case 'c': p=12; break;
case 'd': p=13; break;
case 'e': p=14; break;
case 'f': p=15; break;
}
x=x+pow(16,-k)*p;
k++;
}
printf("\n decimal = %lf\n",x);
}
getch();
}
```

Output
enter the hexadecimal number
abc.123

decimal = 2748.071045

In the following program we are finding the position of occurrence of each digit in an integer number. It also finds frequency of occurrence of each digit. A function is used to do this, which takes three parameters. The first parameter is the given number, second parameter is particular digit and the third parameter is a total number of digits in the given number. This function is called 10 times repeatedly, as there are 10 possible digits in a decimal integer (0 to 9). Each time we are passing different digit from 0 to 9 and it returns how many times that digit is present. In the function itself we are displaying the position of occurrence of each digit whenever it is present. Here the number of digits parameter (3rd parameter to the function) is essential because the digit positions has to be calculated from left to right.

```
/*  program name: fun52.c  */
/*  position of occurrence of each digit in a number */
#include<stdio.h>
#include<conio.h>

int digitpos(int,int,int);

void main()
{
int n,m,i,t,d=0;
clrscr();
    printf("\n enter n \n");
    scanf("%d",&n);
    m=n;
    while(m!=0)
    {
    d++;
```

```
        m=m/10;
        }
        for(i=0;i<=9;++i)
        {
        t=digitpos(n,i,d);
        printf("\n digit %d present %d times",i,t);
       }
        getch();
}
int digitpos(int x,int y,int z)
{
int t=0,i=0;
while(x!=0)
{
if(x%10==y)
{
printf("\n digit %d present at %d position ",y,z-i);
t++;
}
i++;
x=x/10;
}
return(t);
}
```

Output

enter n
23112

digit 0 present 0 times
digit 1 present at 4 position
digit 1 present at 3 position
digit 1 present 2 times
digit 2 present at 5 position
digit 2 present at 1 position
digit 2 present 2 times
digit 3 present at 2 position
digit 3 present 1 times
digit 4 present 0 times
digit 5 present 0 times
digit 6 present 0 times
digit 7 present 0 times
digit 8 present 0 times
digit 9 present 0 times

Note: In all of the above programs we have seen that the function is declared before the main() function and defined after main(). This function declaration can be omitted when the function is defined before main(). Usually when the functions are too small it is better to write the direct definition of such functions in the starting of the program. This makes the program easily understandable and reduces the processor time, which is needed to search the definition. However when the functions are too big it is better to mention their declaration before the main() and define the function after main(). It is not a rule but it is a best practice. In the following few programs we have defined the small functions before the main () function.

Programs on solving numerical methods

Bisection Method

The following program finds the real root of polynomial equation f(x)=0 by the successive bisection method. In this method two initial values (x0 and x1) are given in such a way that f(x0)*f(x1) must be negative. This is necessary because our root should be in between x0 and x1. In a polynomial of degree 'n' we have n different roots but through this iterative method we can find only one real root. After taking the input their average should be considered for the next iteration whose value by sign matches with x0 or x1 and suitably replace x0 or x1 with that average. This should continue until reaching the required precision. The program displays all the intermediate results of x0, x1, x(average) and f(x). Finally it displays the root of the given equation.

```
/*  program name: fun53.c  */
/*  program to solve polynomial equation using bisection
method */
#include<stdio.h>
#include<conio.h>
float bisect(float x) /* function definition before
main() */
{
return(x*x-9);
}
void main()
{
float x0,x1,x,fx;
int t;
clrscr();
do
{
t=0;
printf("\n enter initial values x1 and x2\n");
scanf("%f%f",&x0,&x1);
if(bisect(x0)*bisect(x1)>0)
{
printf("\n initial values are wrong re-enter\n");
t=1;
}
}while(t==1);
printf("x0x1xf(x0)f(x1)\n");
x=(x0+x1)/2;
fx=bisect(x);
while(fx>0.0001)
```

```
{
printf("%.4f  %.4f  %.4f  %.4f  %.4f \n", x0, x1, x,
bisect(x0), bisect(x1));
if(bisect(x)*bisect(x0)>0)
x0=x;
else
x1=x;
x=(x0+x1)/2;
fx=bisect(x);
if(fx<0)
fx=-fx;
}
printf("\n the root of the equation = %f", x);
getch();
}
```

Output

enter initial values x1 and x2
1 8

x0	x1	x	f(x0)	f(x1)
1.0000	8.0000	4.5000	-8.0000	55.0000
1.0000	4.5000	2.7500	-8.0000	11.2500
2.7500	4.5000	3.6250	-1.4375	11.2500
2.7500	3.6250	3.1875	-1.4375	4.1406
2.7500	3.1875	2.9688	-1.4375	1.1602
2.9688	3.1875	3.0781	-0.1865	1.1602
2.9688	3.0781	3.0234	-0.1865	0.4749
2.9688	3.0234	2.9961	-0.1865	0.1412
2.9961	3.0234	3.0098	-0.0234	0.1412
2.9961	3.0098	3.0029	-0.0234	0.0587
2.9961	3.0029	2.9995	-0.0234	0.0176
2.9995	3.0029	3.0012	-0.0029	0.0176
2.9995	3.0012	3.0004	-0.0029	0.0073
2.9995	3.0004	2.9999	-0.0029	0.0022
2.9999	3.0004	3.0002	-0.0004	0.0022
2.9999	3.0002	3.0000	-0.0004	0.0009

the root of the equation = 2.999992

Secant Method

The following program finds the real root of polynomial equation f(x)=0 by the 'secant method'. In this method two initial values(x0 and x1) are given in such a way that f(x0)*f(x1) must be negative. This is necessary because our root should be in between x0 and x1. In a polynomial of degree 'n' we have n different roots but through this iterative method we can find only one real root. The successive values will be calculated with the help of the equation

x=(x0*f(x1)-x1*f(x0))/(x1-x0).

After calculating x it should be considered for the next iteration whose sign matches with x0 or x1 and suitably replace x0 or x1 with that average. This should continue until reaching the required precision. The program displays all the intermediate results of x0, x1, x and f(x). Finally it displays the root of the give equation. The rate of convergence to the root is faster in this method compared to the method of successive bisection.

```
 /*  program name: fun54.c   */
 /*  program to solve polynomial equation using secant
method */
#include<stdio.h>
#include<conio.h>
float secant(float x)
{
return(x*x-9);
}
void main()
{
float x0,x1,x,fx;
int t;
clrscr();
do
{
t=0;
printf("\n enter initial values x1 and x2\n");
scanf("%f%f",&x0,&x1);
if(secant(x0)*secant(x1)>0)
{
printf("\n initial values are wrong re-enter\n");
t=1;
}
}while(t==1);
printf("x0x1xf(x0)f(x1)\n");
x=(x0*secant(x1)-x1*secant(x0))/(secant(x1)-secant(x0));
fx=secant(x);
if(fx<0)
fx=-fx;

while(fx>0.0001)
{
printf("%.4f  %.4f  %.4f  %.4f   %.4f\n", x0,x1,x,
secant(x0), secant(x1));
if(secant(x)*secant(x0)>0)
```

```
        x0=x;
        else
        x1=x;
        x=(x0*secant(x1)-x1*secant(x0))/(secant(x1)-secant(x0));
        fx=secant(x);
        if(fx<0)
        fx=-fx;
        }
        printf("\n the root of the equation = %f",x);
        getch();
        }
```

Output

enter initial values x1 and x2
2 7

x0	x1	x	f(x0)	f(x1)
2.0000	7.0000	2.5556	-5.0000	40.0000
2.5556	7.0000	2.8140	-2.4691	40.0000
2.8140	7.0000	2.9242	-1.0817	40.0000
2.9242	7.0000	2.9694	-0.4492	40.0000
2.9694	7.0000	2.9877	-0.1824	40.0000
2.9877	7.0000	2.9951	-0.0734	40.0000
2.9951	7.0000	2.9980	-0.0294	40.0000
2.9980	7.0000	2.9992	-0.0118	40.0000
2.9992	7.0000	2.9997	-0.0047	40.0000
2.9997	7.0000	2.9999	-0.0019	40.0000
2.9999	7.0000	2.9999	-0.0008	40.0000
2.9999	7.0000	3.0000	-0.0003	40.0000

the root of the equation = 2.999992

Newton Rapson Method

The following program finds the real root of polynomial equation f(x)=0 by the 'Newton Rapson Method'. In this method only one initial value(x0) is given. In this iterative method the successive values are calculated with the help of the equation

$x = x0 - f(x0)/f'(x0)$.

Here f' is the first derivative of the given polynomial equation. After calculating x it should be considered for the next iteration. This should continue until reaching the required precision. The program displays all the intermediate results of x0, x and f(x). Finally it displays the root of the give equation. The rate of convergence to the solution in this method is faster than the above two methods.

```
/*  program name: fun55.c  */
/* program to solve polynomial equation using Newton Rapson
   method */
#include<stdio.h>
```

```
#include<conio.h>
float fx(float x)
{
return(x*x-9);
}
float fx1(float x)
{
return(2*x);
}

void main()
{
float x0,x,f;
clrscr();
printf("\n enter initial value\n");
scanf("%f",&x0);

printf("x0xf(x0)f(x)\n");
x=x0-fx(x0)/fx1(x0);
f=fx(x);
if(f<0)
f=-f;

while(f>0.0001)
{
printf("%.4f   %.4f  %.4f   %.4f\n",x0,x,fx(x0),fx(x));
x=x0-fx(x0)/fx1(x0);
x0=x;
f=fx(x0);
if(f<0)
f=-f;
}
printf("\n the root of the equation = %f",x);
getch();
}
```

Output

```
enter initial value
9
x0      x       f(x0)   f(x)
9.0000  5.0000  72.0000 16.0000
5.0000  5.0000  16.0000 16.0000
3.4000  3.4000  2.5600  2.5600
3.0235  3.0235  0.1417  0.1417
3.0001  3.0001  0.0005  0.0005

the root of the equation = 3.000000
```

Gauss Siedel Method

The following program solves the system of simultaneous equations through the 'Gauss Siedel' iterative method. It makes use of two dimensional array which stores coefficients of each equation in different rows and the single dimensional array which stores the result.

```
/*  program name: fun56.c  */
/*  program to solve a set of simultaneous equations using
Gauss seidel method */
#include<stdio.h>
#include<conio.h>
void matread(float a[10][10],int n)
{
int i,j;
printf("enter coefficients of equations\n");for(i=0;i<n;++i)
for(j=0;j<=n;++j)
scanf("%f",&a[i][j]);
}

void main()
{
float a[10][10],x[10],sum,e,big,t,re;
int n,i,j,k,n1;
clrscr();
printf("\n enter number of equations\n");
scanf("%d",&n);
matread(a,n);
printf("\n enter accuracy, and number of iteration to
carry out\n");
scanf("%f%d",&e,&n1);
for(i=0;i<n;++i)
x[i]=0;
for(k=1;k<=n1;++k)
{
big=0;
for(i=0;i<n;++i)
{
sum=0;
for(j=0;j<n;++j)
if(i!=j)
sum=sum+a[i][j]*x[j];
t=(a[i][n]-sum)/a[i][i];
re=(x[i]-t)/t;
if(re<0)
re=-re;
if(re>big)
```

```
big=re;
x[i]=t;
}
if(big<=e)
{
printf("convergent solution\n");
for(i=0;i<n;++i)
printf("%.5f\t",x[i]);
break;
}
}
if(k>n)
{
printf("\n does not converge in %d steps\n",n1);
printf(" solution\n");
for(i=0;i<n;++i)
printf("%.5f\t",x[i]);
}
getch();
}
```

Output

```
enter number of equations
2
enter coefficients of equations
2 1 5
1 0 2

enter accuracy, and number of iteration to carry out
0.0001
30
convergent solution
2.99994 -0.99994
does not converge in 30 steps
solution
2.99994 -0.99994
```

8.9 Macros

Macros are the type of preprocessor statements and used as functions for small tasks. When we are using the user defined functions, time consumption is more. This is because when a function is called,

1. the program control has to keep track of the present location of its code(calling point) which needs some amount of time say t1.
2. it has to search the definition of the calling function and it takes time for this say t2.
3. it has to transfer the control of program execution to the function definition which requires time say t3.

4. it has to execute the body of the function which requires the time say t4.
5. after completion of the execution of the function the control has to transfer from body of the function to the calling point which takes the time say t5.
6. it has to get back the address stored in the first step to resume its execution from that point which takes time say t6.

Among the six different time slots given above only one is used for executing the function and remaining for additional tasks around it. It is essential to reduce this time in order to make the program execution faster. The 'macros' help in this regard.

When a macro is called(like function call), the program control will not be transferred to the macro code definition instead the definition of the macro code will be brought to the calling point and executed at that point only. So it needs searching of the macro, transferring the copy of macro code to the calling point and executing it. Only three steps in case of macros as compared to 6 steps in functions.

The main disadvantage of a macro is that each time when we call a macro the copy of the macro definition comes to the calling point and after its execution it remains in that point only. When a macro is called several times, several copies will be extracted which results in wastage of computer memory(macro expansion). So it is advised to write the macros when their definition is too small(usually one line) and the number of calls is less. Otherwise it is better to go for user defined functions.

To define a macro we have to use the preprocessor statement #define. The macrc may or may not take parameters but type of parameters and return value type should not be mentioned. Consider the following statement that defines the macro for adding two numbers and returns their result.

#define add(a,b) a+b

Note that macros does not terminate with semicolon. They may have semicolons used in between the statements when there are multiple statements in a macro.

The following program illustrates the use of macros by considering the macro for finding the largest and second largest of three numbers.

```
/*  program name: fun57.c  */
/*  largest and second largest using macro  */
#include<stdio.h>
#include<conio.h>
#define max(a,b)  (a>b)? a : b

void main()
{
int x,y,z,sl,l;
clrscr();
printf("enter the values\n");
scanf("%d%d%d",&x,&y,&z);
l=max(x,y);
if(z>l)
{
sl=l;
```

```
l=z;
}
else
{
if(l==x)
sl=max(y,z);
else
sl=max(x,z);
}
printf("largest = %d\n second largest = %d\n",l,sl);
getch();
}
```

Output	Output
enter the valuves 43 54 34 largest = 54 second largest = 43	enter the valuves 12 43 212 largest = 212 second largest = 43

The following program illustrates a macro without parameter which is used to display a message on the screen.

```
/* program name: fun58.c  */
/*  Macro to display message  */
#include<stdio.h>
#include<conio.h>
#define out printf("Welcome to C the world of C
programming")
void main()
{
clrscr();
out; /* macro call */
getch();
}
```

Output
Welcome to C the world of C programming

The following program uses the macro to calculate the discriminent of a quadratic equation for calculating the roots.

```
/*  program name: fun59.c  */
/*  Quadratic equation roots using macro  */
#include<stdio.h>
#include<conio.h>
#include<math.h>
#define des(a,b,c) b*b-4*a*c

void main()
{
  float x1,x2,d;
  int a,b,c;
  clrscr();
  printf("\n enter a,b,c\n");
  scanf("%d%d%d",&a,&b,&c);
  if(a==0)
  printf("\n not a quadratic equation\n");
  else
  {
  d=des(a,b,c);
  if(d==0)
  {
  printf("\n roots are equal\n");
  x1=-b/(2.0*a);
  x2=-b/(2.0*a);
  printf(" x1= %f\n x2=%f\n",x1,x2);
  }
  else
  if(d>0)
  {
  printf("\n roots are distinct\n");
  x1=(-b+sqrt(d))/(2.0*a);
  x2=(-b-sqrt(d))/(2.0*a);
  printf(" x1= %f\n x2=%f\n",x1,x2);
  }
  else
  {
  printf("\n roots are imaginary\n");
  x1=-b/(2.0*a);
  x2=sqrt(-d)/(2.0*a);
printf(" real part= %f\n imaginary part= %f\n", x1, x2);
  }
}
getch();
}
```

Output	Output
enter a,b,c 2 3 1 roots are distinct x1= -0.500000 x2=-1.000000	enter a,b,c 3 1 2 roots are imaginary real part= -0.166667 imaginary part=0.799305

The following program makes use of pointers for passing the parameters to the function by reference. The memory allotted for the reference variables in different functions remains same by sharing the common memory location. The changes that takes place in one function are reflected in other functions also.

```
 /*  program name: fun60.c  */
 /*  reading and printing a list of n numbers using
pointers  */
 /*  searching a number in the list using binary search  */
 /*  make use of function for sorting and searching  */
void sort(int*,int);
void search(int *,int,int);

#include<stdio.h>
#include<conio.h>
void main()
{
int *a,i=0,n,x;
clrscr();
printf("\n enter n\n");
scanf("%d",&n);
printf("\n enter %d numbers\n",n);
for(i=0;i<n;++i)
scanf("%d",(a+i));
printf("\n enter a number to search\n");
scanf("%d",&x);
printf("\n given numbers are\n");
for(i=0;i<n;++i)
printf("%6d",*(a+i));
sort(a,n);  /*  calling a function by passing reference  */
printf("\n given numbers after arranging are\n");
for(i=0;i<n;++i)
printf("%6d",*(a+i));
search(a,n,x);  /*  calling search function */
```

```
getch();
}
  /*  function for sorting using bubble sort  */
void sort(int *a,int n)
{
int i,j,t;
for(i=0;i<(n-1);++i)
for(j=0;j<(n-1);++j)
if(*(a+j)>*(a+j+1))
{
t=*(a+j);
*(a+j)=*(a+j+1);
*(a+j+1)=t;
}
}

void search(int *a, int n, int x)
{
int low=0, high=n-1,mid;while(low<=high)
{
mid=(low+high)/2;
if(*(a+mid)==x)
{
printf("\n search is success at position %d\n",mid+1);
break;
}
else
if(*(a+mid)<x)
low=mid+1;
else
high=mid-1;
}
if(low>high)
printf("\n unsuccessful search\n");
}
```

Output

```
enter n
5

enter 5 numbers
32 54 322 1 22

enter a number to search
3

given numbers are
  32  54  322   1  22
given numbers after arranging are
   1  22  32  54  322
unsuccessful search
```

Suppose n is the total number of events and r is the number of events occurred at a time then the possibilities of different events to occur is given by permutations i.e., nPr= n!/(n-r)!. This needs finding the factorial twice, one for n and other for n-r. The following program uses the factorial function to find factorial recursively.

```
 /*  program name: fun61.c  */
 /*  Program for npr permutations   */
#include<stdio.h>
#include<conio.h>
long fact(int);
void main()
{
int n,r;
clrscr();
printf(" enter n and r \n");
scanf("%d%d",&n,&r);
printf("\npermutations = %d",fact(n)/fact(n-r));
getch();
}
 /*  recursive function for factorial   */
long fact(int n)
{
if(n<=1)
return(1);
else
return(n*fact(n-1));
}
```

Output
enter n and r
5 3

permutations = 60

Suppose n is the total number of events and r is the number of events occurred at a time then the possibilities of different events to occur is given by combinations i.e., nCr= n!/((n-r)!*r!. It avoids the possible duplicates as compared to permutations. This needs finding the factorial thrice, one for n, second for n-r and third for r. The following program uses the factorial function to find factorial recursively.

```
 /*  program name: fun62.c  */
 /*  Program for nCr combinations   */
#include<stdio.h>
#include<conio.h>
long fact(int);
void main()
{
int n,r;
clrscr();
printf(" enter n and r \n");
```

```
scanf("%d%d",&n,&r);
printf("\ncombinations = %d",fact(n)/(fact(n-r)*fact(r) ));
getch();
}
 /*  recursive function for factorial  */
long fact(int n)
{
if(n<=1)
return(1);
else
return(n*fact(n-1));
}
```

Output
enter n and r
5
3

combinations = 10

The following is a multiple function program. It finds the area and volumes of different geometrical shapes. Just to get the awareness of multiple functions we have included this program. It illustrates the functions with arguments and return values, with arguments but without return values, without arguments but with return values and without arguments and return values.

```
 /*  program name: fun63.c  */
 /*  program to illustrate use of multiple functions  */
 /*  Finds area and volumes of geometrical shapes  */
#include<stdio.h>
#include<conio.h>
float circle(int);
void rectangle(int,int);
float spheare();
void cylinder();
# define pi 3.142
void main()
{
int r,a,b,ch;
float area,vol;
do
{
clrscr();
printf("\n\n\n\n\t\t Area or Volumes\n");
printf("\t\t 1 Area of Circle\n");
printf("\t\t 2 Area of Rectangle \n");
printf("\t\t 3 Volume of Spheare\n");
printf("\t\t 4 Volume of Cylinder\n");
printf("\t\t 5 exit\n");
printf("\n\t Enter Your Choice\n");
scanf("%d",&ch);
```

```
switch(ch)
{
case 1:
printf("\n enter radius \n");
scanf("%d",&r);
area=circle(r);
printf("\n Area of circle with radius %d = %.4f\n",r,area);
break;
case 2:
printf("\n enter sides  \n");
scanf("%d%d",&a,&b);
rectangle(a,b);
break;
case 3:
vol=spheare();
printf("\n Volume of spheare  = %.4f\n",vol);
break;
case 4:
cylinder();
break;

case 5: break;
default:
printf("\n wrong choice .... \n");
}
getch();
}while(ch!=4);
}

 /*  function for area of circle  */
 /*  both arguments and return value  */
float circle(int r)
{
float a;
a=pi*r*r;
return(a);
}
 /*  function for area of rectangle  */
 /*  takes arguments but no return value   */
void rectangle(int a,int b)
{
long area;
area=a*b;
printf("\n  Area  of  Rectangle  with  sides  %d  and  %d  =
        %ld",a,b,area);
}
```

```
 /*  function for volume of spheare   */
 /*  returns value but no parameters  */
float spheare()
{
float vol;
int r;
printf("\n enter radius\n");
scanf("%d",&r);
vol=pi*4/3*r*r*r;
return(vol);
}

 /*  function for volume of Cylinder  */
 /*  no returns value and no parameters   */
void cylinder()
{
float vol;
int r,h;
printf("\n enter radius and height\n");
scanf("%d%d",&r,&h);
vol=pi*r*r*h;
printf("\n volume of Cylinder with radius %d and height %d =
      %f",r,h;vol);
}
```

Stack is the data structure in which elements are inserted and deleted from only one end. The insertion operation is called as push and deletion is called as pop. During insertion when the number of elements exceeds the limit then such a condition is called as overflow condition and when the stack is empty and we are trying to delete an element from the stack, then such a condition is called as underflow. The following is the menu driven program to handle stack operations. It make use of functions for push, pop and display operations. The elements are stored and retrieved from the array.

```
 /*  program name: fun64.c  */
 /*  Program for handling stacks  */
 /*  performs push, pop and display contents of stack using
      functions  */
 /*  uses arrays */
 /*  menu driven */
#include<stdio.h>
#include<conio.h>
void push(int [],int,int);
int pop(int [],int);
void display(int[],int);
#define max 10
```

```
void main()
{
int n,ch,a[20],x,top=0;
do
{
clrscr();
printf("\n\n\n\n\t\t STACK OPERATIONS\n");
printf("\t\t 1 PUSH\n");
printf("\t\t 2 POP \n");
printf("\t\t 3 DISPLAY\n");
printf("\t\t 4 exit\n");
printf("\n\t Enter Your Choice\n");
scanf("%d",&ch);
switch(ch)
{
case 1:
if(top>=max)
printf("\n stack overflows on push\n");
else
{
printf("\n enter the number to insert\n");
scanf("%d",&x);
top++;
push(a,top,x);
}
break;
case 2:
if(top<=0)
printf("\n stack underflows on pop\n");
else
{
x=pop(a,top);
printf("\n deleted element is %d\n",x);
top--;
}
break;
case 3:
if(top<=0)
printf("\n stack is empty\n");
else
display(a,top);
break;
case 4: break;
default:
printf("\n wrong choice .... \n");
```

```
}
getch();
}while(ch!=4);
}

 /*  function for push */
void push(int a[],int t,int x)
{
a[t]=x;
printf("\n pushed the element successfully\n");
}

 /*  function for pop */
int pop(int a[],int t)
{
int x;
x=a[t];
printf("\n poped the element successfully\n");
return(x);
}
 /*  function for display()  */
void display(int a[],int t)
{
int i;
printf("\n the contents of the stack are\n");
for(i=1;i<=t;++i)
printf("%6d",a[i]);
}
```

Queue is the data structure in which elements are inserted at one end called Rear end and deleted from other end called Front end. During insertion when the number of elements exceeds the limit then such a condition is called as overflow condition and when the queue is empty and we are trying to delete an element from the queue, then such a condition is called as underflow. The following is the menu driven program to handle queue operations. It makes use of functions for insertion, deletion and display operations. The elements are stored and retrieved from the array.

```
 /*  program name: fun65.c  */
 /*  program for handling queues  */
 /*  performs insert, delete  and displays contents of queue,
       using functions  */
 /*  uses arrays */
 /*  menu driven */
#include<stdio.h>
#include<conio.h>
void insert(int [],int,int);
```

```
int dele(int [],int);
void display(int[],int);
#define max 10
void main()
{
int n,ch,a[20],x,rear=0,front=0,i;
do
{
  clrscr();
  printf("\n\n\n\n\t\t QUEUE OPERATIONS\n");
  printf("\t\t 1 INSERT\n");
  printf("\t\t 2 DELETE \n");
  printf("\t\t 3 DISPLAY\n");
  printf("\t\t 4 exit\n");
  printf("\n\t Enter Your Choice\n");
  scanf("%d",&ch);
 switch(ch)
 {
 case 1:
   if(rear>=max)
   printf("\n Queue is full and overflows on insertion\n");
   else
   {
   printf("\n enter the number to insert\n");
   scanf("%d",&x);
   rear++;
   insert(a,rear,x);
   if(front==0)
   front=1;
   }
   break;
 case 2:
   if(front<=0)
   printf("\n queue is empty and underflows on deletion\n");
   else
   {
   x=dele(a,front);
   printf("\n deleted element is %d\n",x);
   for(i=2;i<=rear;++i)
   a[i-1]=a[i];
   rear--;
   if(rear==0)
   front=0;
   }
   break;
```

```
case 3:
  if(front<=0)
  printf("\n queue is empty\n");
  else
  display(a,rear);
  break;
case 4: break;
default:
  printf("\n wrong choice .... \n");
}
getch();
}while(ch!=4);
}

 /*  function for insert */
void insert(int a[],int r,int x)
{
  a[r]=x;
  printf("\n Inserted the element successfully\n");
}
 /*  function for delete */
int dele(int a[],int f)
{
  int x;
  x=a[f];
  printf("\n deleted the element successfully\n");
  return(x);
}
 /*  function for display()  */
void display(int a[],int r)
{
  int i;
  printf("\n the contents of the queue are\n");
  printf("Front =>");
  for(i=1;i<=r;++i)
  printf("%6d",a[i]);
  printf(" <= Rear\n");
}
```

This is a simple program that uses recursion. The sum of two positive integers is given recursively as adding 1 to first number and subtracting 1 from second number until the second number becomes zero. The function can be recursively called by passing new parameters where first parameter is increased by one and second parameter is decreased by one. The following program implements this recursive function.

```
/* Program name : fun66.c */
/* Program to add 2 non negative integers */
/* using recursive function */
#include<stdio.h>
#include<conio.h>
unsigned sum(unsigned,unsigned );
void main()
{
unsigned int a,b,s;
clrscr();
printf(" enter two numbers a and b \n");
scanf("%u%u",&a,&b);
s=sum(a,b);
printf("\nsum of %u and %u = %u",a,b,s);
getch();
}
/* recursive function for addition */
unsigned int sum(unsigned a, unsigned b)
{
if(b==0)
return a;
else
return(sum(++a,--b));
}
```

Output
enter two numbers a and b
20 30

sum of 20 and 30 = 50

The following program solves the problem of 'Tower of Honai' recursively. It keeps on calling the function recursively until all the disks are processed. Here we are displaying 'L' to indicate left disk, 'R' to indicate right disk and 'C' to indicate center disk. What are all the replacements takes place will be shown on the screen.

```
/* Program name : fun67.c */
/* Program for tower of Honai */
/* Using recursive function */
#include<stdio.h>
#include<conio.h>
void tower(int, char, char, char);
void main()
{
int n;
```

```
char l='L',c ='C',r ='R';
clrscr();
printf(" enter number of disks \n");
scanf("%d",&n);
printf("\n tower of honai problem with %d disks\n",n);
tower(n,l,c,r);
getch();
}
/* recursive function for tower of honai */
void tower(int n,char l,char c, char r)
{
if(n!=0)
{
            /*move n-1 disks from starting to the intermediate
      needle */
tower(n-1,l,r,c);
/*move disk n from start to destination */
printf("Move disk %d from %c to %c\n",n,l,r);
/*move n-1 disks from intermediate needle to destination
needle*/
tower(n-1,c,l,r);
}
}
```

Output
enter number of disks
3
tower of honai problem with 3 disks
Move disk 1 from L to R
Move disk 2 from L to C
Move disk 1 from R to C
Move disk 3 from L to R
Move disk 1 from C to L
Move disk 2 from C to R
Move disk 1 from L to R

The recursive procedure can be applied to binary search also. We have already discussed about working procedure of binary search in previous chapter. Each time, when we are considering the new list, its starting and ending positions will be sent as parameters to the function recursively. The program will stop on successful search or when the low becomes greater than high. In this program we are first arranging the numbers using function, before applying the binary search algorithm.

```
/* Program name : fun68.c */
/* Program to search a number in a list */
/* using recursion */
```

```
/* Binary search method */
/* Arranges the given list and then searches */
#include<stdio.h>
#include<conio.h>
int bsearch(int[],int, int, int);
void arrange(int[],int);
void main()
{
int n,i;
int a[100],x,t;
clrscr();
printf("\n enter n \n");
scanf("%d",&n);
printf("enter %d numbers\n",n);
for(i=1;i<=n;++i)
scanf("%d",&a[i]);
printf("\n enter number to search\n");
scanf("%d",&x);
printf("given list\n");
for(i=1;i<=n;++i)
printf("%8d",a[i]);
arrange(a,n);/* arranging the list in ascending order*/
t=bsearch(a,1,n,x);/* returns position on success or 0 on
failure*/
printf("\nordered list\n");
for(i=1;i<=n;++i)
printf("%8d",a[i]);
if(t==0)
printf("\n element %d not present in the list\n",x);
else
printf("\n element %d is present at position %d in the
list\n",x,t);
getch();
}
/* function for sorting using bubble sort*/
void arrange(int a[],int n)
{
int i,j,t;
for(i=1;i<n;++i)
for(j=1;j<n;++j)
if(a[j]>a[j+1])
{
t=a[j];
a[j]=a[j+1];
a[j+1]=t;
```

```
}
}
/* recursive function for binary search*/
int bsearch(int a[], int l, int h, int x)
{
int m;
if(l>h)
return(0); /* unsuccessful */
else
{
m=(l+h)/2;
if(a[m]==x)
return m;
else
if(a[m]<x)
return(bsearch(a,m+1,h,x));
else
return(bsearch(a,l,m-1,x));
}
}
```

Output

```
enter n
5
enter 5 numbers
43 6 32 54 64

enter number to search
54
given list
   43    6    32    54    64
ordered list
    6   32    43    54    64
element 54 is present at position 4 in the list
```

9

Files

9.1 Introduction

Files are of the most useful concepts in programming. Infact it is with the help of files computers are used in data processing. Since the number of inputs that can be given through the keyboard is limited because of obvious reasons. So it is desirable to store them somewhere (in the computer memory itself) and make the computer to take the input from that place. This is the concept of files (of course, files need not always contain only data but also the programs). The other inherent advantage is that the output can also be in another file - which in turn can be accessed or used by other programs.

Quite often, it becomes necessary to manipulate large amounts of data, which cannot be typed manually through the keyboard. It may also be possible that the output of one program becomes an input to the other. In such cases, the data are simply stored in files. Files are what they mean in normal English – they just hold data. Each file is given a name. Instead of asking for the input from the keyboard, the program simply opens the files and reads them. Similarly one can ask the program to write it into a file. Obviously this will be a much faster & more accurate method. If the output of one program is to become the input to the other, one program will write into the file and the other will read from it. Such files can also be copied into auxiliary storage Medias like floppies or CDs and transported.

Files are of at most important while dealing with large amount of data. Now let us discuss how do we go about creating a file. Each file is given a name. File names should be maximum 8 characters primary name and 3 characters secondary name. The primary name is compulsory where as secondary name is optional. To do any file operation in C programming, we need a 'file pointer'. File pointer is a pointer to the structure whose definition is given below.

```
struct {
      short             level;
      unsigned          flags;
      char              fd;
      unsigned char     hold;
```

```
short             bsize;
unsigned char *buffer, *curp;
unsigned          istemp;
short             token;
   };
```

All these members are utilized by the C compiler while doing internal operations on files. We have to assign a file to the file pointer at the time of opening the file. The general syntax for declaring the file pointer is,

FILE * pointername;
For example
FILE *f;

Once the file pointer is defined we can open the file with the help of fopen() function which takes two arguments, namely, name of the file to open and mode of the file. Depending on what operation is done on the program, the file has to be "opened". You cannot operate on the file until it is opened. A file can be opened for one of the three basic operations – to read data from it, to write data into it or to attach additional data to it. These modes are called read, write and append modes respectively indicated by the letters r, w and a. The opened files are assigned to a file pointer as shown below.

filepointer=fopen("filename","mode");
For example f=fopen("student.dat","r");

Basically there are two types of file opening modes, text and binary. When the file is opened in text mode the data will be stored and processed in the text format only. When it is opened in the binary mode the data storage and processing will be in the binary format. In each of these two types there exists three main modes namely read, write and append. In text mode they will be given as r, w and a where as in binary format they will be given as rb, wb and ab.

When a file is opened in read mode the file pointer contains the address of the starting character in the file on successful opening. When file open fails the file pointer contains NULL. There are certain reasons where file opening fails viz. when the specified file does not exist or specified path does not exist or the file name given is wrong.

So it is essential to check the file pointer value after opening the file to confirm it. Let us take a look at the following example:

```
# include<stdio.h>
FILE *f;
f = fopen("student.dat", 'r');
if (f==NULL)
printf("File does not open");
```

This statement opens the file called student.dat and assigns its pointer to f. Once the file is opened successfully we are free to do I/O operations on files.

9.2 I/O Operations on Files

The main functions we have in C to do input operations on files are given below.

1. c=fgetc(f); - it reads a single character from the present file pointer location(where f is pointing) and assigns it to character variable c.
2. fscanf(f, "format", &variablename(,s)); - it reads formatted data from the file and stores in the specified variable. The type of variable should match the corresponding format(like for int-%d, for float-%f etc.). We can have more than one variable. In such cases they should be separated by commas and their corresponding formats should be mentioned in the format string.
3. fgets(f,s); - reads a string s from the present file pointer position f.
4. n=getw(f); - gets an integer(one word length) from the present file pointer position.
5. fread((char *)&strvar,sizeof(strvar),1,f); - it reads the entire structure(as a record)into the structure variable. The members of the structure may be of different data types so that type casting(char *)is essential.

For output operations on files we have the following library functions.

1. fputc(f,c); - it writes the contents of a character variable c into the current file pointer position f.
2. fputs(f,s); - it writes the contents of a string variable s into the current file pointer position f.
3. fprintf(f,"format",variablename(,s)); - it writes the formatted output into the file.
4. putw(f,n); - puts an integer n to the current file pointer position f.
5. fwrite((char *)&strvar,sizeof(strvar),1,f); - it writes the contents of the structure(strvar) into the file at the current pointer position.

Each existing file will be marked with an EOF(end of file) in the end to mark the end of the file and this is useful while reading the file. While writing, the EOF is automatically attached to the file. Once all operations of the file are over, it should be closed using a fclose(filepointer); statement. A program successfully terminates only if all of it's files are closed properly.

9.3 Traversing through file

We can traverse through the file for searching the records or modifying the records etc. To traverse, we have to take the file pointer to the specified data area inside the file. fseek()function can be used for this purpose. The syntax for this function is,

fseek(filepointer, numberofbytes, SEEK_XXX);

where the numberofbytes must be an integer and it indicates how many bytes to move from specified location given by SEEK_XXX. Here XXX can take any one of the three options namely,

1. SET – to indicate from the beginning of the file,
2. END – to indicate from the end of the file and
3. CUR – to indicate from the current location of the file pointer.

The number of bytes must be zero or any positive number when SEEK_SET is used, zero or negative number when SEEK_END is used and positive or negative number when SEEK_CUR is used. When the numberofbytes is having negative value file pointer goes backward and when it is positive file pointer goes forward. For example

fseek(f,10,SEEK_SET); - takes the file pointer to the 10th byte from the beginning.

fseek(f,-sizeof(strvar),SEEK_END); - takes the file pointer to the beginning of the last record in the file. The record is given by the structure strvar.

ftell(f); - returns the number of bytes in the file from beginning to the current file pointer position. To get the total number of bytes in the file we need to move the file pointer to the end of the file before using this function.

To delete a file through the C program the function
remove ("filename"); is used and to change the name of the file, the function
rename("oldfilename","newfilename"); is used.

Now let us see different programs to make the above concepts clear.

9.4 Programs

This program takes the file name dynamically by the user and opens it and after confirming the successful opening closes the file. If file does not open successfully it gives suitable error message.

```
/* Program name: file1.c */
/* opening and closing a data file*/
#include<stdio.h>
#include<conio.h>
  void main()
  {
    FILE *f;
    char fname[`'];
    clrscr();
    printf("\n enter a file to open\n");
    scanf("%s",fname);
    f=fopen(fname,"r");
    if(f!=NULL)
    {
     printf("file is successfully opened\n now program will
       closes it\n");
    fclose(f);
    }
    else
    printf("file name does not exit\n ");
getch();
}
```

Output1

enter a file to open
student.doc
file name does not exit

Output2

enter a file to open
bookfl0.cpp
file is successfully opened
now program will closes it

This program takes the file name dynamically and opens the file. It reads the data character by character from the file with the help of fgetc() function and displays on the screen with suitable delay. The delay is given with the help of delay() function just to display the output slowly on the screen. Before reading the contents of the file we have to count the number of bytes in the file which can be done with the help of the function ftell().

```
/* Program name: file2.c */
/* opening and closing a data file*/
/* display the contents of the file character by character */
/* uses delay() to give the delay while displaying */
#include<stdio.h>
#include<conio.h>
#include<dos.h> /* for delay () function */
  void main()
  {
   FILE *f;
   char fname[` `],c;
   int n,i;
   clrscr();
   printf("\n enter a file to open\n");
   scanf("%s",fname);
   f=fopen(fname,"r");
   if(f!=NULL)
   {
   printf("the contents of the file\n");
   fseek(f,0,SEEK_END);/* takes the file control to the end
     */
   n=ftell(f);/* gives number of bytes in the file */
   fseek(f,0,SEEK_SET);/* takes the control to the beginning
     */
   for(i=1;i<=n;++i)
   {
   c=fgetc(f); /* gets a single character from the current
     file
pointer position and file pointer advances to
next character*/
   printf("%c",c);
   delay(50); /* gives a delay of 50 milli seconds after each
character display */
   }
   fclose(f);
   }
   else
   printf("file name does not exit\n ");
getch();
}
```

Output

```
enter a file to open
file1.c
the contents of the file
/* opening and closing a data file*/
#include<stdio.h>
#include<conio.h>
void main()
 {
 FILE *f;
 char fname[' '];
 clrscr();
 printf("\n enter a file to open\n");
 scanf("%s",fname);
 f=fopen(fname,"r");
 if(f!=NULL)
 {
 printf("file is successfully opened\n now program will closes it\n");
 fclose(f);
 }
 else
 printf("file name does not exit\n ");
getch();
}
```

The following program creates the new file after taking the data from the keyboard and when user stops giving input it displays the content of the file on the screen. For creating the file we need to open the file in either write mode or append mode. After creating a file we should close it and open it back in the reading mode to get the input from the file.

```
/* Program name: file3.c */
/* creates a new file*/
/* takes input from keyboard and writes to the file */
/* display the contents of the file character by character */
/* uses delay() to give the delay while displaying */
#include<stdio.h>
#include<conio.h>
#include<ctype.h>
#include<dos.h> /* for delay() function */
  void main()
   {
    FILE *f;
    char fname[` `],c;
    int n,i;
    clrscr();
```

```
printf("\n enter a file to open\n");
scanf("%s",fname);
f=fopen(fname,"w"); /* opens the file in writing mode*/
if(f!=NULL)
{
printf("input the characters\n");
do
{
fflush(stdin);
while((c=getchar())!='\n')
fputc(c,f);/*writes each character to the file*/
printf("\n you like to continue (y/Y)?");
fflush(stdin);
c=getchar();
}while(toupper(c)=='Y');
fclose(f);/* closes the files after completing creation*/
f=fopen(fname,"r");/* opens file for reading the data*/
fseek(f,0,SEEK_END);/* takes the file control to the end */
n=ftell(f);/* gives number of bytes in the file */
fseek(f,0,SEEK_SET);/* takes the control to the beginning
    */
for(i=1;i<=n;++i)
{
c=fgetc(f);
printf("%c",c);
delay(50);
}
fclose(f);/*closes the file after completing reading*/
}
else
printf("file name does not exit\n ");
getch();
}
```

Output

enter a file to open
keshav
input the characters
Monitor is a standard output device.

you like to continue (y/Y)?y
Keyboard is a standard input device.

you like to continue (y/Y)?n
Monitor is a standard output device. Keyboard is a standard input device.

The following program illustrates the use of getw() and putw() functions used to read a word(an int) from the file and write a word to the file respectively. This program opens the file for writing the data and keeps on taking the integer inputs from the user until user wishes to terminate. When user stops giving input then program closes the file and reopens for reading. It reads the file one word at a time by using getw() function and displays on the screen.

```
/* Program name: file4.c */
/* program to illustrate getw() and putw() for files */
#include<stdio.h>
#include<conio.h>
void main()
{
FILE *f;
int n,n1,i;
char ch,fname[' '];
clrscr();
printf("\n enter file name\n");
scanf("%s",fname);
f=fopen(fname,"a");
if(f==NULL)
{
printf(" file open failed\n");
}
else
{
do
{
printf("enter a number\n");
scanf("%d",&n);
putw(n,f);
printf("more data Y/N? : ");
fflush(stdin);
ch=getchar();
}while(ch=='Y' || ch=='y');
fclose(f);
f=fopen(fname,"r");
fseek(f,0,SEEK_END);
n1=ftell(f)/2;/* number of words */
fseek(f,0,SEEK_SET);
for(i=1;i<=n1;++i)
{
n=getw(f);
printf("%5d",n);
}
```

```
fclose(f);
}
getch();
}
```

Output

```
enter file name
xyz.dat
enter a number
21
more data Y/N? : y
enter a number
5
more data Y/N? : y
enter a number
54
more data Y/N? : y
enter a number
43
more data Y/N? : n
  21  5  54  43
```

Some times it is essential to combine the data from different files into one. The following program combines (merges) two files. For this first we need to open one file in append mode to which we have to add the data from the other file. Then the file pointer of this file should be taken to the end of the file. The second file from which we have to add the data to the first file has to be opened in the read mode. Data can be read from the second file and written into the first file.

```
/* Program name: file5.c */
/* program to merge two files */
#include<stdio.h>
#include<conio.h>
#include<dos.h>
void main()
{
FILE *f,*f1;
int n,i;
char ch,fname1['`'],fname2['`'],s;
clrscr();
printf("\n enter two file names\n");
scanf("%s%s",fname1,fname2);
f=fopen(fname1,"w");
f1=fopen(fname2,"w");
/* data for first file */
do
{
printf("enter string\n");
```

```
fflush(stdin);
while((s=getchar())!='\n')
fputc(s,f);
printf("more data Y/N? : ");
fflush(stdin);
ch=getchar();
}while(ch=='Y' || ch=='y');
fclose(f);
/* data for second file */
printf("\n enter data for second file\n");
do
{
printf("enter string\n");
fflush(stdin);
while((s=getchar())!='\n')
fputc(s,f1);
printf("more data Y/N? : ");
fflush(stdin);
ch=getchar();}while(ch=='Y' || ch=='y');
fclose(f1);

f=fopen(fname1,"a");
fseek(f,0,SEEK_END);/*takes file pointer to the end of the
        file*/
f1=fopen(fname2,"r");
fseek(f1,0,SEEK_END);
n=ftell(f1);
fseek(f1,0,SEEK_SET);
for(i=1;i<=n;++i) /* merging file2 in file1 */
{
ch=fgetc(f1);
fputc(ch,f);
}
fclose(f);
fclose(f1);
/* display data from merged file */
printf("\n data from file is\n");
f=fopen(fname1,"r");
fseek(f,0,SEEK_END);
n=ftell(f);
fseek(f,0,SEEK_SET);
for(i=1;i<=n;++i) /* reading and printing */
{
ch=fgetc(f);
printf("%c",ch);
```

```
delay(10);
}
fclose(f);
getch();
}
```

Output

```
enter two file names
abc
xyz
enter string
erwerwerwerwerwe
more data Y/N? : y
enter string
ewrwerwe
more data Y/N? : n

enter data for second file
enter string
dfsdfsdfsdfsdfsdfsd sdfsdfs
more data Y/N? : y
enter string
fsdfsdfsdfs
more data Y/N? : n

data from file is
erwerwerwerwerweewrwerwedfsdfsdfsdfsdfsdfsd sdfsdfsfsdfsdfsdfs
```

This program illustrates the use of fread() and fwrite() functions by creating the student file and displaying it on the screen. After creating a file, the number of records in a file can be found using ftell()/sezeof(strvar);. Before using this statement in the program, we need to ensure that the file pointer is pointing to the end of the file.

```
/* Program name: file6.c */
/* student information */
/* takes data for n students*/
/* displays the data with format*/
#include<stdio.h>
#include<conio.h>
struct student
{
int rno,age;
```

```
        char name[20],addr[30];
        }s;

          void main()
           {
            FILE *f;
            int i,n;

            char fname[' '];
            clrscr();
            printf("\n enter file name to store student data\n");
            scanf("%s",fname);

            f=fopen(fname,"a");/* opens file in append mode*/
            if(f!=NULL)
            {
            fseek(f,0,SEEK_END);/* takes the file pointer to the end
              of file*/
            printf("\n enter n");/* number of record to write*/
            scanf("%d",&n);

           printf("\n  enter  rno  name  address  and  age  for  %d
              students\n",n);
            for(i=1;i<=n;++i)
            {
            scanf("%d%s%s%d",&s.rno,s.name,s.addr,&s.age);
            fwrite((char*)&s,sizeof(s),1,f);/* write the record into
              file*/
            }
            fclose(f);
            f=fopen(fname,"r");/* opens for reading and display*/
            fseek(f,0,SEEK_END);
            n=ftell(f)/sizeof(s);/* gets number of records*/
            fseek(f,0,SEEK_SET);
            printf("\n\t\t students information\n");
           printf("\n rno            name               address        age\n");
          printf("===================================================\n");
            for(i=1;i<=n;++i)
            {
            fread((char *)&s,sizeof(s),1,f);
          /* reads a record from file and stores in structure variable
              s*/
            printf("%5d%15s%20s%5d\n",s.rno,s.name,s.addr,s.age);
            }
```

```
printf("==================================================\n");
 fclose(f);
 }
 else
 printf("\n file does not open\n");
 getch();
 }
```

Output

enter file name to store student data
stud.dat

enter n4

enter rno name address and age for 4 students
123 keshav bangalore 23
124 rayudu nellore 24
125 dawn kochin 25
126 charly chennai 30

students information

rno	name	address	age
123	keshav	bangalore	23
124	rayudu	nellore	24
125	dawn	kochin	25
126	charly	chennai	30

This program is similar to the above program and it finds the average age of all the students and the name of the highest scored student.

```
/* Program name: file7.c */
/* student marks and age using file*/
/* average age of all the students*/
/* name of highest scorer*/
#include<stdio.h>
#include<conio.h>
#include<math.h>
struct student
```

```
{
int rno,marks,age;
char name[20];
}s,s1;

  void main()
   {
    FILE *f;
    char fname[' '];
    int i,small=0,n;
    float avg=0;
    clrscr();
    printf("\n enter file name\n");
    scanf("%s",fname);
    f=fopen(fname,"w");
    fseek(f,0,SEEK_END);
    printf("\n enter n");
    scanf("%d",&n);
       printf("\n enter rno name age and marks for %d
   students\n",n);
    for(i=1;i<=n;++i)
    {
    scanf("%d%s%d%d",&s.rno,s.name,&s.age,&s.marks);
    fwrite((char*)&s,sizeof(s),1,f);
    }
    fclose(f);
    f=fopen(fname,"r");
    fseek(f,0,SEEK_END);
    n=ftell(f)/sizeof(s);
    fseek(f,0,SEEK_SET);
    printf("\n students information\n");
    printf("\n rno           name      age   marks\n");

    for(i=1;i<=n;++i)
    {
    fread((char *)&s,sizeof(s),1,f);
    printf("%5d%15s%5d%5d\n",s.rno,s.name,s.age,s.marks);
    avg=avg+s.age;
    if(small<s.marks)
    {
    small=s.marks;
    s1=s;
    }
    }
```

```
avg=avg/n;
printf("\n avg age of all students = %f\n",avg);
printf("highest scored student name = %20s\n",s1.name);
getch();
}
```

Output

```
enter the file name
gf

enter n3

enter rno name age and marks for 3 students
32 tom 32 54
33 jerry 24 70
12 jack 28 69

students information

rno    name   age  marks
 32     tom    32   54
 33    jerry   24   70
 12    jack    28   69

avg age of all students = 28.000000
highest scored student name =          jerry
```

This program takes the student information like name, roll no., marks and calculates the grade.

```
/* Program name: file8.c */
/*Program for student file */
/* name marks grade*/

#include<string.h>
#include<stdio.h>
#include<conio.h>
void main()
{
struct student
{
char name[20];
```

```
   int permark;
   char grade[20];
   }s;

   int i,n;
   FILE *fp;
   clrscr();
   printf("enter how many students\n");
   scanf("%d",&n);
   fp=fopen("student.dat","a");
   for(i=1;i<=n;++i)
   {
   printf("enter name permarks\n");
   scanf("%s%d",s.name,&s.permark);
   if(s.permark>=70)
   strcpy(s.grade, "distinction");
   if((s.permark>=60)&&(s.permark<70))
   strcpy(s.grade,"first class");

    if((s.permark>=50)&&(s.permark<60))
   strcpy(s.grade,"second class");
    if((s.permark>=35)&&(s.permark<50))
   strcpy(s.grade,"pass class");
    if(s.permark<35)
   strcpy(s.grade,"fails");
  fwrite((char*)&s, sizeof(s),1,fp);
  }
  fclose(fp);
  fopen("student.dat","r");
  fseek(fp,0,SEEK_END);
  n=ftell(fp)/sizeof(s);
  fseek(fp,0,SEEK_SET);
  printf("\n students information\n");
  printf("                NAME   MARKS                GRADE\n");

  for(i=1;i<=n;++i)
  {
  fread((char*)&s,sizeof(s),1,fp);
  printf("%20s%8d%20s\n",s.name,s.permark,s.grade);
  }
  fclose(fp);
  getch();
  }
```

Output
enter how many students
2
enter name permarks
jahangir 78
enter name permarks
rehman 35

students information

NAME	MARKS	GRADE
jahangir	78	distinction
rehman	35	pass class

This program reads a text file and counts the number of characters, words and lines present in the file. The number of characters will be found using the function ftell() after moving the file pointer to the end. The number of words and lines will be calculated by checking the space and enter key(\n) characters present in the file.

```
/* Program name: file9.c */
/* Program for counting the no. Of characters, words, lines
in a text file */
#include<stdio.h>
#include<conio.h>
 void main()
 {
FILE *fp;
long lc=0,cc=0,wc=0,n,i;
char c,fname[' '];
 clrscr();
printf("\nenter file name\n");
scanf("%s",fname);
 fp=fopen(fname,"r");
 fseek(fp,0,SEEK_END);
 n=ftell(fp);
 fseek(fp,0,SEEK_SET);
 for(i=0;i<n;++i)
 {
 c=fgetc(fp);
 if(c==' ')
 wc++;
 else
 if(c=='\n')
 lc++;
```

```
else
cc++;
}
fclose(fp);
printf("no.of lines = %ld\n no. of words = %ld\nno. of
     characters = %ld\n",lc,wc,cc);
getch();
}
```

Output

enter file name
file2.c
no.of lines = 45
no. of words = 267
no. of characters = 1196

Now let us discuss the program which is frequently used for handling the employee information. This program is menu driven and allows the users to choose the options for adding the new employee record, deleting the record, modifying the record and displaying either particular or all the records from the employee database. In C language there is no specific statements or library functions to delete a record from the file or to modify the contents of the file. To delete a record we need to open the existing file in the read mode and a temporary file in write mode. Read the contents of the existing file one record at a time and write it into the temporary file. When the condition to delete a record is satisfied then, that record will not be written to the temporary file. After all the records are over the existing file will be removed from the disk and temporary file will be renamed as exiting file. Similarly to modify the record of the file the same procedure is applied but when the condition to modify record satisfies the contents of that record will be changed suitably before writing to the temporary file. The following program illustrates all these operations on the employee database.

```
/* Program name: file10.c */
/* employee information */
/* menu driven */
/* performs adding records, deleting records, modification
   of records, displays a particular record and displays
   all records with format*/
/* uses user defined function for each menu option */
#include<stdio.h>
#include<conio.h>
void add();
void delet();
void modify();
void disperticular();
void disall();

struct emp
```

```
        {
        int eno,age;
        char name[20],addr[30];
        }e;
        char fname['`']; /* for file name which is commonly used in
      different functions in this program*/

           void main()
            {

             int ch;
             printf("\n enter the file name\n");
             scanf("%s",fname);

             do
             {
             clrscr();
             printf("\n\t\t employee information\n");
             printf("\n\t1. Add new record");
             printf("\n\t2. Display an employ record");
             printf("\n\t3. Display all records");
             printf("\n\t4. Modify an employ record");
             printf("\n\t5. Delete an employ record");
             printf("\n\t6. Exit");
             printf("\n\t Enter your choice\n");
             scanf("%d",&ch);
             switch(ch)
             {
             case 1: add(); break;
             case 2: disperticular(); break;
             case 3: disall(); break;
             case 4:modify(); break;
             case 5: delet(); break;
             case 6: break;
             default: printf("\n wrong choice\n");
             }
             getch();
             }while(ch!=6);
             }
           /* function for adding a new record to the file*/
           void add()
             {
              FILE *f;
              int i,n;
              clrscr();
```

```
    f=fopen(fname,"a");/* opens file in append mode*/
    fseek(f,0,SEEK_END);
          printf("\n enter eno name address and age of an
                              employ\n");
    scanf("%d%s%s%d",&e.eno,e.name,e.addr,&e.age);
    fwrite((char*)&e,sizeof(e),1,f);
    fclose(f);
   }

  /* function for displaying a particular record from file
   */

void disperticular()
{
    FILE *f;
    int i,n,eno,t=0;
    printf("\n enter eno to display\n");
    scanf("%d",&eno);
    f=fopen(fname,"r");/* opens for reading and display*/
    fseek(f,0,SEEK_END);
    n=ftell(f)/sizeof(e);/* gets number of records*/
    fseek(f,0,SEEK_SET);
    for(i=1;i<=n;++i)
    {
    fread((char *)&e,sizeof(e),1,f);
    if(e.eno==eno) /* checks the condition */
    {
    printf("\n\t\t Employ Details\n");
          printf("\n eno          name                  address
                        age\n");
 printf("===================================================\n");
    printf("%5d%15s%20s%5d\n",e.eno,e.name,e.addr,e.age);
   t=1; /* changes flag variable t when record is present*/
 printf("===================================================\n");
    }
    }
    fclose(f);
    if(t==0)
    printf("\n employ does not exist\n");
}

  /* function for displaying all records from file */

void disall()
{
```

```
        FILE *f;
        int i,n;
        f=fopen(fname,"r");/* opens for reading and display*/
        fseek(f,0,SEEK_END);
        n=ftell(f)/sizeof(e);/* gets number of records*/
        fseek(f,0,SEEK_SET);
        printf("\n\t\t Employ Details\n");
              printf("\n eno              name                    address
                                  age\n");
      printf("================================================\n");

        for(i=1;i<=n;++i)
        {
        fread((char *)&e,sizeof(e),1,f);
        printf("%5d%15s%20s%5d\n",e.eno,e.name,e.addr,e.age);
        }
      printf("================================================\n");
        fclose(f);
    }

     /* function for modifying a particular record from file */

    void modify()
    {
        FILE *f,*f1;
        int i,n,eno,t=0;
        printf("\n enter eno to modify\n");
        scanf("%d",&eno);
        f=fopen(fname,"r");/* opens for reading and display*/
        fseek(f,0,SEEK_END);
        n=ftell(f)/sizeof(e);/* gets number of records*/
        fseek(f,0,SEEK_SET);
        f1=fopen("tmp","w");
        for(i=1;i<=n;++i)
        {
        fread((char *)&e,sizeof(e),1,f);
        if(e.eno==eno) /* checks the condition */
        {
        printf("\n\t\t Employ Details\n");
         printf("\n eno               name                    address
       age\n");
      printf("================================================\n");
         printf("%5d%15s%20s%5d\n",e.eno,e.name,e.addr,e.age);
       t=1; /* changes flag variable t when record is present*/
```

```
printf("==========================================\n");
  printf("enter new values\n");
        printf("\n enter eno name address and age of an
                    employ\n");
  scanf("%d%s%s%d",&e.eno,e.name,e.addr,&e.age);
  fwrite((char*)&e,sizeof(e),1,f1);
  }
  else
  fwrite((char*)&e,sizeof(e),1,f1);     }
  fclose(f);
  fclose(f1);
  remove(fname);
  rename("tmp",fname);
  if(t==0)
  printf("\n employ does not exist\n");
}

/* function for deleting a particular record from file */

void delet()
{
    FILE *f,*f1;
    int i,n,eno,t=0;
    printf("\n enter eno to delete\n");
    scanf("%d",&eno);
    f=fopen(fname,"r");/* opens for reading and display*/
    fseek(f,0,SEEK_END);
    n=ftell(f)/sizeof(e);/* gets number of records*/
    fseek(f,0,SEEK_SET);
    f1=fopen("tmp","w");
    for(i=1;i<=n;++i)
    {
    fread((char *)&e,sizeof(e),1,f);
    if(e.eno==eno) /* checks the condition */
    {
    printf("\n\t\t Employ Details\n");
          printf("\n eno        name                    address
                    age\n");
  printf("==========================================\n");
    printf("%5d%15s%20s%5d\n",e.eno,e.name,e.addr,e.age);
   t=1; /* changes flag variable t when record is present*/
  printf("==========================================\n");
    printf("\n record successfully deleted\n");
    }
    else
```

```
            fwrite((char*)&e,sizeof(e),1,f1);
            }
            fclose(f);
            fclose(f1);
            remove(fname);
            rename("tmp",fname);
            if(t==0)
            printf("\n employ does not exist\n");
        }
```

Output

```
        employee information

    1. Add new record
    2. Display an employ record
    3. Display all records
    4. Modify an employ record
    5. Delete an employ record
    6. Exit
     Enter your choice
1
enter eno name address and age of an employ
123 reddy bangalore 23

        employee information

    1. Add new record
    2. Display an employ record
    3. Display all records
    4. Modify an employ record
    5. Delete an employ record
    6. Exit
     Enter your choice
3

        Employ Details

Eno         name        address       age
==================================================
 12         eww         weewe          32
123         reddy       bangalore      23
213         sanketh     mumbai         32
==================================================
```

10

Special Programs

In this chapter we are considering certain programs, which needs more thinking to arrive the solution.

Let us consider the series 1 2 4 8 11 12 14 18 21 ...

To get the solution to this series we need to analyze it to find out the relationship between each term. The difference between first terms is 1 and next is 2 then it is 4 so it is increasing. But difference between 4th and 5th is 3 and that of 6th and 7th is 1 then for next it is 2 again 4. So maximum difference is 4. By this we can come to the conclusion that the difference is the modulus of 5 (%5) to its previous term. Let us start with 1, add 1%5 to 1 we will get 2, add 2%5 to 2 we will get 4, add 4%5 to 4 we will get 8, add 8%5 to 8 we will get 11 and so on. The following program implements this.

```
/* Program name : spl1.c */
/* Program to generate the series 1 2 4 8 11 12 14 18 21 ...
     upto n */
#include<stdio.h>
#include<conio.h>
void main()
{int i,n;
clrscr();
printf(" enter upper limit n\n");
scanf("%d",&n);
for(i=1;i<=n;i=i+i%5)
printf("%5d",i);
getch();
}
```

Output

enter upper limit n
50
1 2 4 8 11 12 14 18 21 22 24 28 31 32 34 38
41 42 44 48

The series 1 2 4 8 9 11 15 16 18 22...

Here we see the similar relationship between the terms as that of previous series. The difference is that after 8 we have 9 instead of 11 so the difference is one, which is modulus of 7 to the previous term. Now try out with first term as 1 and second term as 1 %7+1=2, third term 2%7+2=4, forth term 4%7+4=8, next term 8+8%7=9, then 9+9%7=11 and so on. By adding the modulus of 7 of previous term to previous term itself we will get the solution. The following program implements this.

```
/* Program name : spl2.c */
/* Program to generate the series 1  2  4  8  9 11  15 16 18
     22...upto n */
#include<stdio.h>
#include<conio.h>
void main()
{
int i,n;
clrscr();
printf(" enter upper limit n\n");
scanf("%d",&n);
for(i=1;i<=n;i=i+i%7)
printf("%5d",i);
getch();
}
```

```
Output
enter upper limit n
50
 1  2  4  8  9 11 15 16 18 22 23 25 29 30 32 36
37 39 43 44 46 50
```

Now the series 1 3 9 13 18 19... upto n, which is another similar but different in terms of relationship between each terms. The difference between first two terms is 2 but that of next two is 6, difference between 3rd and 4th is 4 and that of 4th and 5th is 5 again it is 1. So the difference is maximum 6 that means again the modulus of 7. To get 2nd term from 1st term whose difference is 2 there are two possibilities, first one multiply 1 by 2 and take its modulus with 7, second add 1 to itself and take modulus with 7. The first case fails for getting 3rd term but we will get by second option i.e., 3+3%7=6 and adding it to previous term i.e., 3 we will get 9 which is the 3rd term. Now (9+9)%7+9 =13 the 4th term and so on. The following program implements this logic.

```
/* Program name : spl3.c */
/*Program to generate series 1 3 9 13 18 19... upto n */
#include<stdio.h>
#include<conio.h>
```

```
void main()
{
int i,n;
clrscr();
printf(" enter upper limit n\n");
scanf("%d",&n);
for(i=1;i<=n;i=i+(i+i)%7)
printf("%5d",i);
getch();
}
```

```
Output
enter upper limit n
50
  1  3  9  13  18  19  22  24  30  34  39  40  43  45
```

Now we can look at the series 2 1 3 3 6 5 11 7 ... upto n. By clearly observing the series we can come to the conclusion that the given series can be divided into two series viz. 2 3 6 11 ... and 1 3 5 7.... The second series is straightforward and the difference between each term is 2. In the first series, the differences are not same but we can easily observe that starting from 2 we get the next term by adding the first term of second series i.e., 2+1 = 3 and adding 2nd term of second series to the second term of first series we will get 6 and so on. Look at the program given below to implement this.

```
/* Program name : spl4.c */
/*Program to generate series 2 1 3 3 6 5 11 7 ... upto n */
#include<stdio.h>
#include<conio.h>
void main()
{
int j,i,n;
clrscr();
printf(" enter upper limit n\n");
scanf("%d",&n);
j=2;
for(i=1;i<=n;i=i+2)
{
printf("%5d%5d",j,i);
j=j+i;
}
getch();
}
```

Output
enter upper limit n
50

```
    2    1    3    3    6    5   11    7   18    9   27   11   38   13   51   15
   66   17   83   19  102   21  123   23  146   25  171   27  198   29  227   31
  258   33  291   35  326   37  363   39  402   41  443   43  486   45  531   47
  578   49
```

Now we can look at the series 0 3 8 15 24 ....

Here clearly we can observe that there is constant change i.e., between first two terms it is 3 and between 2nd and 3rd terms it is 5 and between 3rd and 4th it is 7 and so on. So take a loop counter, which changes from 3, 5, 7 and so on and other variable with 0 as the starting value. Add this to loop counter value to get next terms values i.e., 0+3 =3, 3+5=8, 8+7=15, 15+9=24 and so on. The following program illustrates this.

```
/* Program name : spl5.c */
/* Program to generate the series 0 3 8 15 ... upto n */
#include<stdio.h>
#include<conio.h>
void main()
{
int j,i,n;
clrscr();
printf(" enter upper limit n\n");
scanf("%d",&n);
j=0;
for(i=3;i<=n;i=i+2)
{
printf("%5d",j);
j=j+i;
}
getch();
}
```

Output
enter upper limit n
50

```
    0    3    8   15   24   35   48   63   80   99  120  143  168
  195  224  255  288  323  360  399  440  483  528  575
```

Here is another series 1 4 10 22 46 94 ...

Finding the relation between such series is little difficult. The differences between terms are 3 6 12 24 48 ... this itself is a series starting with 3 and successive terms we will get by multiplying the term by 2 (3*2=6, 6*2=12, 12*2=24...). Now find the relation to get the required series with first term

as 1. Add 1 to 3 we will get 4 the 2nd term, adding 4 with 6(2nd term in the difference series) we will get 10 and so on. The following program implements this.

```
/* Program name : spl6.c */
/* Program to generate series 1 4 10 22 46 94 ... upto n */
#include<stdio.h>
#include<conio.h>
void main()
{
int j,i,n;
clrscr();
printf(" enter upper limit n\n");scanf("%d",&n);j=3;
for(i=1;i<=n;){printf("%5d",i);i=i+j;j=j*2;}getch();
}
```

Output
enter upper limit n
500
1 4 10 22 46 94 190 382

Here is an alternative logic for the above series i.e., 1 4 10 22 ...

The simple logic is, start with 1 the first term and to get next term adds the previous term to itself and a constant 2. That means 1+1+2=4, 4+4+2=10 and so on. The following program implements this logic.

```
/* Program name : spl7.c */
/* Program to generate series 1 4 10 22 46 94 ... upto n.
     alternative logic */
#include<stdio.h>
#include<conio.h>
void main(){int j,i,n;
clrscr();
printf(" enter upper limit n\n");
scanf("%d",&n);
for(i=1;i<=n;i=i+i+2)
printf("%5d",i);
getch();
}
```

Output
enter upper limit n
1000
1 4 10 22 46 94 190 382 766

The series 1 4 11 26 57 ...

It is similar to the above one. Here just what we need to do is add the term to itself and 2,3,4, and so on. I.e., 1, 1+1+2=4, 4+4+3=11, 11+11+4=26 and so on. The following program implements this logic.

```
/* Program name : spl8.c */
/*Program to generate series 1 4 11 26 57 120 ... upto n */
#include<stdio.h>
#include<conio.h>
void main()
{
int i,n;
long j;
clrscr();
printf(" enter upper limit n\n");
scanf("%d",&n);
j=0;
for(i=1;i<=n;i=i+1)
{
j=j+j+i;
printf("%15ld\t",j);
}
getch();
}
```

```
Output
enter upper limit n
20
      1        4       11       26       57      120      247      502
   1013     2036     4083     8178    16369    32752    65519   131054
 262125   524268  1048555  2097130
```

The series 1 3 8 19 42 ...

It is very much similar to the above series, we should start with one, add the term to itself and 1, 2, 3, 4 … to get the next successive terms. The following program implements this logic.

```
/* Program name : spl9.c */
/* Program to generate series 1 3 8 19 42 ... upto n */
    #include<stdio.h>
#include<conio.h>
void main()
{
int i,n;
long j;
clrscr();
printf(" enter upper limit n\n");
scanf("%d",&n);
j=1;
for(i=1;i<=n;i=i+1)
{
```

```
printf("%15ld\t",j);
j=j*2+i;
}
getch();
}
```

```
Output
enter upper limit n
30
        1          3          8         19         42
       89        184        375        758       1525
     3060       6131      12274      24561      49136
    98287     196590     393197     786412    1572843
  3145706    6291433   12582888   25165799   50331622
100663269  201326564  402653155  805306338 1610612705
```

The series 18 20 24 32 48… n terms.

The clear observation on the differences between the terms shows that the differences are 2 4 8 16… so start with 18 and keep on adding 2 and its multiple to get the next successive terms.

```
/* Program name : spl10.c */
/* Program to generate the series 18 20 24 32  ... upto n terms
     */
#include<stdio.h>
#include<conio.h>
void main()
{
int j,k,i,n;
clrscr();
printf(" enter upper limit n\n");
scanf("%d",&n);
j=2;
k=18;
for(i=1;i<=n;++i)
{
printf("%5d",k);
k=k+j;
j=j*2;
}
getch();
}
```

```
Output
enter upper limit n
10
   18     20     24     32     48
   80    144    272    528   1040
```

The series 4 7 12 21 38 71 ... upto n terms.

Here the 2nd term is just one less than the double of first term, and third term is 2 less than the double of 2nd term and so on. The following program implements this.

```
/* Program name : spl11.c */
/* Program to generate the series 4 7 12 21 38 71... upto n
      terms */
#include<stdio.h>
#include<conio.h>
void main()
{
int i,n;
long j;
clrscr();
printf(" enter upper limit n\n");
scanf("%d",&n);
j=4;
for(i=1;i<=n;++i)
{
printf("%10ld",j);
j=j*2-i;
}
getch();
}
```

Output
enter upper limit n
25

4	7	12	21	38
71	136	265	522	1035
2060	4109	8206	16399	32784
65553	131090	262163	524308	1048597
2097174	4194327	8388632	16777241	33554458

The series 2 3 6 11 18 27... upto n

The differences in between the terms is 1 3 5 7 9.... So start with 2 and add the terms of difference series we will get the required terms of the series.

```
/* Program name : spl12.c */
/* Program to generate series 2 3 6 11 18 27... upto n */
#include<stdio.h>
#include<conio.h>
void main()
{
```

```
int j,i,n;
clrscr();
printf(" enter upper limit n\n");
scanf("%d",&n);
j=2;
for(i=1;i<n*2;i=i+2)
{
printf("%8d",j);
j=j+i;
}
getch();
}
```

```
Output
enter upper limit n
20
       2       3       6      11      18      27      38
      51      66      83     102     123     146     171
     198     227     258     291     326     363
```

The above series can be solved with an alternative method, i.e., start with the series 0 1 2 3 … take their squares and add constant 2 to each term. The following program implements this.

```
/* Program name : spl13.c */
/* Program to generate the series 2 3 6 11 18 27... upto n
     terms, alternative solution */
#include<stdio.h>
#include<conio.h>
void main()
{
int i,n;
clrscr();
printf(" enter upper limit n\n");
scanf("%d",&n);
for(i=0;i<n;++i)
printf("%8d",i*i+2);
getch();
}
```

```
Output
enter upper limit n
25
       2       3       6      11      18      27
      38      51      66      83     102     123
     146     171     198     227     258     291
     326     363
```

It is a general problem. My Belgaum house phone number is a 5-digit number. The sum of 2nd and last digit is equal to the first digit of that number, the sum of 3rd digit and 4th digit is equal to the sum of rest of the digits and the difference of 3rd and 4th digit is equal to the sum of last two digits. The 2nd digit is a 6th digit from our decimal number system. What will be the phone number that satisfies these conditions?

Suppose a, b, c, d &e are five digits so that the phone number is abcde. The clear observation on the problem reveals the following clues.

1. The second digit b is 5 (Because it s 6th digit in our decimal number system, the digits are 0,1,...,9)
2. The sum of 2nd and last digit is equal to the first digit i.e., a=b+e.
3. The sum of 3rd and 4th digit is equal to the sum of rest of the digits, i.e., c+d=a+b+e.
4. The difference between 3rd and 4th digits equal to the sum of last two digits i.e., c-d=d+e.

By all these clues and using simple looping statements we can develop the program logic as follows.

```
/* Program name : spl14.c */
/* Phone number problem/
#include<stdio.h>
#include<conio.h>
void main()
{
int a,b,c,d,e;
clrscr();
printf("\n Phone number is : ");
for(a=1;a<=9;++a)
for(b=1;b<=9;++b)
for(c=1;c<=9;++c)
for(d=1;d<=9;++d)
for(e=1;e<=9;++e)
{
if(b==5 && a==(b+e) && (c+d)==(a+b+e) &&(c-b)==(d+e))
printf("%d%d%d%d%d",a,b,c,d,e);
}
getch();
}
```

Output

Phone number is : 65931

In the above program, we have used five looping statements each performing 10 iterations, which takes a total of 10^5 = 1,00,000 operations. Performing 1,00,000 iterations for a simple 5 digit number is not a feasible implementation of the problem. We can easily reduces the number of iterations by avoiding one loop for which the condition is straight forward, i.e., b=5. By avoiding just one loop we will reduce the number of operations from 1,00,000 to 10,000. The following program implements this.

```
/* Program name : spl15.c */
/* Phone number problem, optimized/
#include<stdio.h>
#include<conio.h>
void main()
{
int a,b,c,d,e;
clrscr();
printf("\n Phone number is : ");
b=5; /* constant and no need of loop for this */
for(a=1;a<=9;++a)
for(c=1;c<=9;++c)
for(d=1;d<=9;++d)
for(e=1;e<=9;++e)
{
if(b==5 && a==(b+e) && (c+d)==(a+b+e) &&(c-b)==(d+e))
printf(" %d%d%d%d%d",a,b,c,d,e);
}
getch();
}
```

The following program displays the digital clock on the screen. It gives the option for the user to set the starting time. When user enters the starting time the clock starts from that time otherwise the clock starts from 00:00:00 as the starting time. This program displays the time according to our digital clock only. The delay of 1000 Milli seconds is used in between each display. The function gotoxy() from conio.h is used to take the cursor to the specified line and column on the screen. In between each displays the clrscr() function is used to avoid the overwriting.

```
/* Program name : spl16.c */
/* Digital clock/
#include<stdio.h>
#include<dos.h>
#include<conio.h>
#include<ctype.h>
void main()
{
int a,b,c;
char ch;
clrscr();
printf("\n you like to set the time (y/n)? : ");
fflush(stdin);
scanf("%c",&ch);
if(toupper(ch)=='Y')
{
printf("\n starting time h m s\n");
```

```
scanf("%d%d%d",&a,&b,&c);
}
else
{
a=0;
b=0;
c=0;
}
while(!kbhit())
{
clrscr();
gotoxy(30,12);
printf("%d:%d:%d",a,b,c);
delay(1000);/* 1000 Millie second but depending on
processor speed we may need to reduce it */
c++;
if(c>59)
{
c=0;
b++;
if(b>59)
{
b=0;
a++;
if(a>23)
a=0;
}
}
}
getch();
}
```

Output

12:59:59

In the above program we were setting the time or it was taking it starting from 00:00:00 and if user entered wrong time, the program starts the clock from that time only without checking for its validity. The following is a bit modification. It takes the system time by using gettime() function and built-in time structure. Note that this program will not make use of delay function, which may leads to wrong timing based on the speed of the processor.

```
/* Program name : spl17.c */
/* Digital clock with system time/
/* Takes system time */
/* Delay function is not used */
#include<stdio.h>
#include<dos.h>
#include<conio.h>
```

```
void main()
{
struct time t;
while(!kbhit())
{
gettime(&t);
gotoxy(30,12);
printf("%3d :%3d :%3d",t.ti_hour,t.ti_min,t.ti_sec);
}
}
```

Let us take a general problem. I had been in Channai on my personnel works. I stayed in a big hotel, whose room number is three-digit number. All the rooms in that hotel are numbered serially from 1,2,3,... and my I took the room in such a way that sum of all the room numbers before my room is equal to sum of all the room numbers after my room in that hotel. Now the question is what is my room number and how many rooms are there in the hotel?

We can make the following observations from the problem.

1. My room number is three-digit number, so it must be in between 100 to 999.
2. Sum of all the room numbers from 1 to my room number (excluding my room number) is equal to sum of all room numbers after my room number in that hotel.

So we can start a loop from 100 to 999 and find the sum of all numbers from 1 to the present loop counter value. Now start finding the sum of the numbers after loop counter value till that sum is less than the previous sum. When the second sum will not be less than first sum then there are two possibilities. Either the second sum may be greater than the first sum or it may be equal to the first sum. When the second sum becomes equal to the first sum stop the loop and the loop counter value of the outer loop gives my room number and loop counter value of the inner second loop gives total rooms in the hotel. The following program implements this.

```
/* Program name : spl18.c */
/* Room number problem */
/* Using for () and while () loops */
#include<conio.h>
#include<stdio.h>
void main()
{
int i,j,k;
long s,s1;
clrscr();
for(i=100;i<=999;++i)/* room number is 3 digit number
        possibilities must be in-between 100 to 999*/
{
s=0;
for(j=1;j<i;++j)
s+=j; /* finds the sum of room numbers before My room */
s1=0;
```

```
j=i+1;
while(s1<s)
{
s1+=j; /* finds the sum of room numbers after My room */
j++;
}/* When comes out of loop there are two possibilities, s1
 may be equal to s or greater than s */
if(s==s1)/* when s1=s i gives My room number and j-1 gives
        total number of rooms/
{
printf("room number =%d\n sum=%ld\n total number of rooms
=%d\n",i,s,j-1);
}
}
getch();
}
```

Output
room number =204
sum=20706
total number of rooms =288

In the above program we have used total three loops, with two loops inside the outer loop. The first inner loop can be avoided by using the formula n*(n+1)/2 which finds sum of first n natural numbers. By using this we can avoid number of iterations, which makes the program more optimal. We also use a break; statement, so that as soon as we will get the solution we can stop further iterations. The following program implements this.

```
/* Program name : spl19.c */
/* Room number problem, optimized */
/* Using for () and while () loops */
#include<conio.h>
#include<stdio.h>
void main()
{
int i,j,k;
long s,s1;
clrscr();
for(i=100;i<=999;++i)/* room number is 3 digit number
possibilities must be in-between 100 to 999*/
{
s=(long)i*(i-1)/2;  /* finds the sum of room numbers before
My room */
s1=0;
j=i+1;
while(s1<s)
{
s1+=j; /* finds the sum of room numbers after My room */
```

```
j++;
}/* when comes out of loop there are two possibilities, s1
may be equal to s or greater than s */
if(s==s1)/* when s1=s i gives My room number and j-1 gives
    total number of rooms*/
{
printf("room number =%d\nsum=%ld\ntotal number of rooms
=%d\n",i,s,j-1);
break;
}
}
getch();
}
```

Output
room number =204
sum=20706
total number of rooms =288

This is again the same problem with bit modification. Here we are using functions for finding the sum so that the program logic becomes easy to understand and debug.

```
/* Program name : spl20.c */
/* Room number problem, using functions */
/* Using for () and while () loops */
#include<conio.h>
#include<stdio.h>
long sum(int);
int  sum1(int, long);
void main()
{
int i,j;
long s,s1;
clrscr();
for(i=100;i<=999;++i)/* room number is 3 digit number
possibilities must be in-between 100 to 999*/
{
s=sum(i-1);  /* finds sum of room numbers before my room */
j=sum1(i+1,s); /*finds sum of room numbers after My room */
if(j!=0)
{
printf("room number =%d\nsum=%ld\ntotal number of rooms
=%d\n",i,s,j);
}
}
getch();
}
/* Recursive function to find sum */
```

```
long sum(int x)
{
if(x==0)
return(0);
else
return(x+sum(x-1));
}
/* function for finding sum after my room number */

int sum1(int x, long s)
{
long sa=0;
int i=x;
while(sa<s)
{
sa+=i;
i++;
}
if(sa==s)
return(i-1);
else
return(0);
}
```

Output
room number =204
sum=20706
total number of rooms =288

An integer number is said to be an Adam's number if the number is squared and reversed then taken the square root, the resultant number will be reversed and if it becomes equal to the original number. To check whether the given integer number is Adam's number or not, we have to do the following steps.

1. Let n be the number
2. Let n1 will be square of n
3. Let r1 will be reverse of n1
4. Let n2 is the square root of r1
5. Let r2 is the reverse of n2
6. Check n=r2 when they are equal then n is an Adam's number.

The following program checks whether the given number is an Adam's number or not.

```
/* Program name : spl21.c */
/* Adam's Number Checking */
#include<stdio.h>
#include<conio.h>
#include<math.h>
void main()
{
long n;
```

```
long n1,n2;
clrscr();
printf("\nenter a number\n");
scanf("%ld",&n);
n1=n*n;
n2=0;
while(n1!=0)
{
n2=n2*10+n1%10;
n1=n1/10;
}
n1=sqrt(n2);
n2=0;
while(n1!=0)
{
n2=n2*10+n1%10;
n1=n1/10;
}

if(n2==n)
printf("\n %ld is Adam\'s number",n);
else
printf("\n not an Adam\'s number");
getch();
}
```

Output	Output
enter a number 14 not an Adam's number	enter a number 12 12 is Adam's number

This program finds all Adam's numbers from 1 to n, where n is the input from the keyboard.

```
/* Program name : spl22.c */
/* Adam's Number between 1 and n  */
#include<stdio.h>
#include<conio.h>
#include<math.h>
void main()
{

long n,i;
long n1,n2;
```

```
clrscr();
printf("\nenter a number\n");
scanf("%ld",&n);
for(i=1;i<=n;++i)
{
n1=i*i;
n2=0;
while(n1!=0)
{
n2=n2*10+n1%10;
n1=n1/10;
}
n1=sqrt(n2);
n2=0;
while(n1!=0)
{
n2=n2*10+n1%10;
n1=n1/10;
}

if(n2==i)
printf(" %9ld",i);
}
getch();
}
```

```
Output
enter a number
500
      1     2     3    11    12    13    21    22
     31   101   102   103   111   112   113   121
    122   201   202   211   212   221   301   311
```

Let us look at the different variety of programs. The programs involve positioning the text or numbers on the screen so as to get some pyramid or triangular shapes.

Consider the simple triangle of numbers.

```
1
1   2
1   2   3
1   2   3   4
```

For implementing this just we need to have nested loops in which outer loop changes number of times equal to the number of rows and inner loop starts each time from 1 and proceeds upto the value of outer loop counter.

```
/* Program name : spl23.c */
/* Triangle of numbers for a given number of rows */
#include<stdio.h>
#include<conio.h>
#include<math.h>
void main()
{

int n,i,j;
clrscr();
printf("\n enter upper limit\n");
scanf("%d",&n);
for(i=1;i<=n;++i)
{
for(j=1;j<=i;++j)
printf("%5d",j);
printf("\n");
}
getch();
}
```

Output

```
enter upper limit
10
 1
 1  2
 1  2  3
 1  2  3  4
 1  2  3  4  5
 1  2  3  4  5  6
 1  2  3  4  5  6  7
 1  2  3  4  5  6  7  8
 1  2  3  4  5  6  7  8  9
 1  2  3  4  5  6  7  8  9  10
```

Floyd gave the triangle of numbers as shown below.

```
1
2   3
4   5   6
7   8   9   10
```

Compared to the above pyramids this is little different. Here the numbers are changing continuously from 1, so we need a separate variable to get the terms. The following program implements this for the specified number of rows.

```
/* Program name : spl24.c */
/* Floyd triangle for specified number of rows */
#include<stdio.h>
#include<conio.h>
#include<math.h>
void main()
{
```

```
int n,i,j,k;
clrscr();
printf("\n enter number of rows\n");
scanf("%d",&n);
k=1;
for(i=1;i<=n;++i)
{
for(j=1;j<=i;++j)
{
printf("%4d",k);
k++;
}
printf("\n");
}
getch();
}
```

Output

```
enter number of rows
8
 1
 2  3
 4  5  6
 7  8  9 10
11 12 13 14 15
16 17 18 19 20 21
22 23 24 25 26 27 28
29 30 31 32 33 34 35 36
```

Pascal the mathematician gave his own triangle on numbers as shown below.

```
      1
    1 2
  1 2 3
1 2 3 4
```

This is also simple but needs positioning the numbers properly on the screen positions. The program that follows implements this for a specified number of rows.

```
/* Program name : spl25.c */
/* Pascal triangle for specified number of rows */
#include<stdio.h>
#include<conio.h>
#include<math.h>
void main()
{

int n,i,j,k,l1;
clrscr();
printf("\n enter number of rows\n");
scanf("%d",&n);
k=1,l1=1;
for(i=1;i<=n;++i)
{
for(j=1;j<=i;++j)
{
gotoxy(40-i*2+j*4,l1);
```

```
printf("%d",j);
}
l1++;
printf("\n");
}
getch();
}
```

```
Output
                          1
enter number of rows    1  2
8                      1  2  3
                     1  2  3  4
                   1  2  3  4  5
                 1  2  3  4  5  6
               1  2  3  4  5  6  7
             1  2  3  4  5  6  7  8
```

Consider the pyramid formed by numbers as given below.

```
      1
    3 2 3
  5 4 3 5 4
7 6 5 4 7 6 5
```

To generate such a pyramid, we need to use some technique to move the cursor to the specified location on the screen. The screen in text mode consists of 80 columns and 25 rows. The library function gotoxy(column, row); can be used to take the cursor. This also involves the logic to get the numbers of the pyramid as shown. In the first row has a single number and next successive rows are having two extra numbers. We also notice that the left hand side of the pyramid the numbers are increasing and right hand side decreasing from the left most element of the corresponding row. The following program implements this pyramid for the specified number of rows.

```
/* Program name : spl26.c */
/* Program to construct pyramid of numbers */
#include<stdio.h>
#include<conio.h>
void main()
{
int n,i,j,k,k1;
clrscr();
printf("\n enter n \n");
scanf("%d",&n);

for(i=1;i<=n;++i)
{
k1=i*3;
k=i;
for(j=1;j<=i;++j)
{
gotoxy(40-k1,i);
printf("%d",k);
```

```
k++;
k1-=3;
}
k=k-2;

for(j=1;j<i;++j)
{
gotoxy(40+k1,i);
printf("%d",k);
k--;
k1+=3;
}
}
getch();
}
```

Output

```
enter n
12
                                1
                              3 2 3
                            5 4 3 5 4
                          7 6 5 4 7 6 5
                        9 8 7 6 5 9 8 7 6
                     11 10 9 8 7 6 11 10 9 8 7
                  13 12 11 10 9 8 7 13 12 11 10 9 8
               15 14 13 12 11 10 9 8 15 14 13 12 11 10 9
            17 16 15 14 13 12 11 10 9 17 16 15 14 13 12 11 10
         19 18 17 16 15 14 13 12 11 10 19 18 17 16 15 14 13 12 11
      21 20 19 18 17 16 15 14 13 12 11 21 20 19 18 17 16 15 14 13 12
   23 22 21 20 19 18 17 16 15 14 13 12 23 22 21 20 19 18 17 16 15 14 13
```

The following is the little modification of previous program. Here the pyramid of numbers keeps on decreasing on both the sides of the middle element. The pyramid is given as

```
        1
      2 3 2
    3 4 5 4 3
  4 5 6 7 6 5 4
5 6 7 8 9 8 7 6 5
```

Note the difference of the pyramid compared to previous one. The middle elements are changing in steps of two. The program that follows implements this for a specified number of rows.

```
/* Program name : spl27.c */
/* Program to construct pyramid of numbers */
#include<stdio.h>
#include<conio.h>
```

```
void main()
{
int n,i,j,k,k1;
clrscr();
printf("\n enter n \n");
scanf("%d",&n);

for(i=1;i<=n;++i)
{
k1=0;
k=i;
for(j=1;j<=i;++j)
{
gotoxy(40-k1,i);
printf("%d",k);
k++;
k1+=3;
}
k--;
k1=3;
for(j=1;j<i;++j)
{
gotoxy(40+k1,i);
printf("%d",k);
k--;
k1+=3;
}
}
getch();
}
```

Output

```
enter n
12
                                        1
                                      2 3 2
                                    3 4 5 4 3
                                  4 5 6 7 6 5 4
                                5 6 7 8 9 8 7 6 5
                              6 7 8 9 10 11 10 9 8 7 6
                            7 8 9 10 11 12 13 12 11 10 9 8 7
                          8 9 10 11 12 13 14 15 14 13 12 11 10 9 8
                        9 10 11 12 13 14 15 16 17 16 15 14 13 12 11 10 9
                      10 11 12 13 14 15 16 17 18 19 18 17 16 15 14 13 12 11 10
                    11 12 13 14 15 16 17 18 19 20 21 20 19 18 17 16 15 14 13 12 11
                  12 13 14 15 16 17 18 19 20 21 22 23 22 21 20 19 18 17 16 15 14 13 12
```

The above two programs developed only half of the pyramids. No consider the following complete pyramid of numbers.

```
        1
     2  3  2
  3  4  5  4  3
     2  3  2
        1
```

This is similar to the just previous program pyramid but it is complete. The similar logic implements this in the following program.

```
/* Program name : spl28.c */
/* Program to construct complete pyramid of numbers */
#include<stdio.h>
#include<conio.h>
void main()
{
int n,i,j,k,k1,k2;
clrscr();
printf("\n enter n \n");
scanf("%d",&n);

for(i=1;i<=n;++i)
{
k1=i*3;
k=i;
for(j=1;j<=i;++j)
{
gotoxy(40-k1,i);
printf("%d",k);
k++;
k1-=3;
}
k=k-2;

for(j=1;j<i;++j)
{
gotoxy(40+k1,i);
printf("%d",k);
k--;
k1+=3;
}
}
k2=0;
for(i=n-1;i>=1;--i)
```

```
{
k1=i*3;
k=i;
k2++;
for(j=1;j<=i;++j)
{
gotoxy(40-k1,n+k2);
printf("%d",k);
k++;
k1-=3;
}
k=k-2;

for(j=1;j<i;++j)
{
gotoxy(40+k1,n+k2);
printf("%d",k);
k--;
k1+=3;
}
}
getch();
}
```

Output

```
enter n
8
                       1
                     2 3 2
                   3 4 5 4 3
                 4 5 6 7 6 5 4
               5 6 7 8 9 8 7 6 5
             6 7 8 9 10 11 10 9 8 7 6
           7 8 9 10 11 12 13 12 11 10 9 8 7
         8 9 10 11 12 13 14 15 14 13 12 11 10 9 8
           7 8 9 10 11 12 13 12 11 10 9 8 7
             6 7 8 9 10 11 10 9 8 7 6
               5 6 7 8 9 8 7 6 5
                 4 5 6 7 6 5 4
                   3 4 5 4 3
                     2 3 2
                       1
```

Now look at the program, which involves separation of digits. This program prints all the three digit numbers whose 2nd digit is equal to the sum of other two digits. Just a loop varying from 100 to 999 can do this. Here we need to take care that the loop counter value should not be affected during the operations in loop body.

```
/* Program name : spl29.c */
/* 3 digit numbers where second digit = first digit + third
digit  */
#include<stdio.h>
#include<conio.h>
#include<math.h>
```

```
void main()
{
int n1,n2,n3,i;
clrscr();
printf("\n all numbers whose middle digit is equal to sum
     of other two\n\n");
for(i=100;i<=999;++i)/* 3 digit numbers */
{
n1=i%10; /* first digit in n1 */
n2=(i/10)%10;/* second digit in n2 */
n3=(i/100)%10;/* third digit in n3 */
if(n1+n3==n2)
printf("%8d",i);
}
getch();
}
```

Output

all numbers whose middle digit is equal to sum of other two

110	121	132	143	154	165	176	187	198	220
231	242	253	264	275	286	297	330	341	352
363	374	385	396	440	451	462	473	484	495
550	561	572	583	594	660	671	682	693	770
781	792	880	891						

The following problem looks like simple, but it needs lot of thinking. This removes all the duplicate numbers from the given list. Removing the duplicates from the ordered list is easy because that needs just comparing the consecutive numbers for equality. When the list is not in order then we need to compare each and every element one by one with all other elements. Possibility of comparing the element with itself should be carefully handled. When we will get a duplicate, all the remaining elements from the list should be shifted backward and one should reduce from thetotal number of elements in the list. The program implements this.

```
/* Program name : spl30.c */
/* Program to delete duplicates from a list of numbers */
#include<stdio.h>
#include<conio.h>
void main()
{
int n,i,j,k,a[100];
clrscr();
printf("\n enter n \n");
```

```
scanf("%d",&n);
printf("enter %d numbers\n",n);
for(i=1;i<=n;++i)
scanf("%d",&a[i]);
printf("\n list before removing duplicates\n");
for(i=1;i<=n;++i)
printf("%8d",a[i]);
/* checking for duplicates one by one */
for(i=1;i<=n;++i)
{
for(j=1;j<=n;++j)
if(i!=j)
   if(a[i]==a[j])
      if(j!=n)
      {
      for(k=j;k<n;++k)
      a[k]=a[k+1];/*copies next elements */
      n--;/* one element is removed */
      }
}
printf("\n list after removing duplicates\n");
for(i=1;i<=n;++i)
printf("%8d",a[i]);
getch();
}
```

Output

enter n
8
enter 8 numbers
12 33 23 12 45 66 77 45

list before removing duplicates
12 33 23 12 45 66 77 45
list after removing duplicates
12 33 23 66 77 45

In this program we are searching for a number and if the number is present then it will be removed from the list. In case the number is not present in the list then the number will be inserted in the list in its proper position. The program assumes the data is already in the ascending order. The searching is done with simple linear search method. When the search number is present then we should delete it by copying all other elements of the list one backward from the successful position and reducing the total number of elements by one. When the search element is not present, then from the beginning of the list, we have to check the correct position to insert and then shift all remaining elements one forward to make the room for new element that needs insertion. Finally we should increase the total number of elements by one for the new list. The following program implements this.

```
/* Program name : spl31.c */
/* Program to search a number in an ordered list */
/* delete the number if it is present*/
/* Insert number in proper place if it is not present */
#include<stdio.h>
#include<conio.h>
void main()
{
int n,i,j;
int a[100],x,t=0;
clrscr();
printf("\n enter n \n");
scanf("%d",&n);
printf("enter %d numbers\n",n);
for(i=1;i<=n;++i)
scanf("%d",&a[i]);
printf("\n enter number to search\n");
scanf("%d",&x);
printf("given list\n");
for(i=1;i<=n;++i)
printf("%8d",a[i]);
/* searching using linear search and deletes if present*/
for(i=1;i<=n;++i)
if(a[i]==x)
{
printf("\n number %d is deleted successfully \n ",x);
t=1;
for(j=i+1;j<=n;++j)
a[j-1]=a[j];/*copying next successive numbers  */
n--;
break;
}
if(t==0)/* when not present */
for(i=1;i<=n;++i)
if(a[i]>x)
{
for(j=n;j>=i;--j)
a[j+1]=a[j];/* making the room by shifting the elements */
a[i]=x;
printf("\n element %d is inserted successfully \n ",x);
n++;
break;
```

```
}
if(t==0 && i>n) /* inserting at end */
{
printf("\n element %d is inserted successfully \n",x);
a[n+1]=x;
n++;
}
printf(" new list\n");
for(i=1;i<=n;++i)
printf("%8d",a[i]);

getch();
}
```

```
Output

enter n
5
enter 5 numbers
1 34 56 76 78

enter number to search
76
given list
    1   34   56   76   78
number 76 is deleted successfully
new list
    1   34   56   78
```

```
Output

enter n
5
enter 5 numbers
12 43 65 78 89

enter number to search
65
given list
   12   43   65   78   89
number 65 is deleted successfully
new list
   12   43   78   89
```

Insertion sort

This is a sorting technique, in which the elements of the list are placed in the proper place at the time of inputting the numbers. The first number of the list is taken into the array in first location. While inputting the second element into the array, we should check whether it is smaller than the first element or not. If it is smaller then first element should be shifted to second location in the array and this new element should be placed in the first location. While placing the third element we need to check whether the inserting element is smaller than first element, in that case both the present numbers will be shifted one position forward to make a room for it. in case the new element is smaller than the second but larger than the first, then room for it should be made after first location. When the new element is larger than other elements then it should be placed at the end of the list. This procedure should be applied during inserting the elements in the list. In case of descending order we need to follow just reverse procedure. The following program implements insertion sort and arranges the list in ascending order.

```
/* Program name : spl32.c */
/* program for insertion sort  */
#include<stdio.h>
#include<conio.h>
void main()
{
int n,i,j,a[50],x,k;
char ch;
clrscr();
i=0;
do
{
printf(" enter a number to insert\n");
scanf("%d",&x);
k=i-1;
while(x<a[k] && k>=0)
{
a[k+1]=a[k];
--k;
}
a[k+1]=x;
printf("new array\n");
for(j=0;j<=i;++j)
printf("%8d",a[j]);
printf("\nmore data Y/N? : ");
fflush(stdin);
ch=getchar();i++;
}while(ch=='Y' || ch=='y');
printf("\n final sorted array\n");
for(j=0;j<i;++j)
printf("%8d",a[j]);
getch();
}
```

Output

```
enter a number to insert
4
new array
   4
more data Y/N? : y
enter a number to insert
3
new array
   3    4
more data Y/N? : y
enter a number to insert
22
new array
   3    4   22
more data Y/N? : y
enter a number to insert
12
new array
   3    4   12   22
more data Y/N? : n

final sorted array
   3    4   12   22
```

Traversing the matrix means, processing all the elements of that matrix. Helical traversing means, processing all elements from beginning to the end one by one in such a way that,

1. First row should be processed completely.
2. Leaving the element in the first row (it is already processed) should process last column.
3. Process the last row by leaving the element in the last column (it is already processed)

4. Process first column by leaving elements in first and last row (they have already processed)
5. Now repeat from 2nd row, then last but one column, then last but one row and finally second column in such a way that there will not be duplicates.
6. Repeat this process until all the elements of the matrix are processed or traversed.

For example the matrix

1	2	3
4	5	6
3	4	5

```
Can be traversed as 1 2 3 6 5 4 3 4 5
The following program implements this.

/* Program name : spl33.c */
/* Program to traverse the given square matrix helically */
#include<stdio.h>
#include<conio.h>
void main()
{
int n,i,j;
int a[10][10];
clrscr();
printf("\n enter  n  order of a square matrix \n");
scanf("%d",&n);
printf(" enter matrix elements\n");
for(i=1;i<=n;++i)
for(j=1;j<=n;++j)
scanf("%d",&a[i][j]);
printf("given matrix is\n");
for(i=1;i<=n;++i)
{
for(j=1;j<=n;++j)
printf("%8d",a[i][j]);
printf("\n");
}
printf("traversed elements of matrix are\n");
i=1;
do
{
for(j=i;j<=n;++j)
printf("%8d",a[i][j]);
for(j=i+1;j<=n;++j)
printf("%8d",a[j][n]);
for(j=n-1;j>i-1;--j)
```

```
printf("%8d",a[n][j]);
for(j=n-1;j>i;--j)
printf("%8d",a[j][i]);
i++;
n--;
}while(n>0);
getch();
}
```

```
Output

 enter  n  order of a square matrix
2
 enter matrix elements
1234
given matrix is
     1    2
     3    4
traversed elements of matrix are
     1    2    4    3
```

Any matrix is said to be magic square if and only if sum of each row, sum of each column, sum of main and off diagonal must be equal and all the elements in the matrix must be distinct. For this it has to be a square matrix. The individual sum of all the rows should be taken and compared with each other for equality. The sum of each individual column must be taken and compared for equality, and so on.

In the following program first we are checking all the elements are distinct or not. Then we are finding the sum of main diagonal (trace of matrix). The trace is then compared with row sum of all the rows, column sum of all columns and finally the sum of off diagonal elements. The flag is used and changed suitably when there is no match.

```
/* Program name : spl34.c */
/* Program to check matrix for magic square */
/* rowsum=colsum=diagonal sum*/
/*elements in the matrix must be distinct*/
#include<stdio.h>
#include<conio.h>
void main()
{
int n,i,j;
int a[10][10],sr,sc,sd,soff,ii,jj,t;
clrscr();
printf("\n enter  n  order of a square matrix \n");
scanf("%d",&n);
printf(" enter matrix elements\n");
```

```
for(i=1;i<=n;++i)
for(j=1;j<=n;++j)
scanf("%d",&a[i][j]);
printf("given matrix is\n");
for(i=1;i<=n;++i)
{
for(j=1;j<=n;++j)
printf("%8d",a[i][j]);
printf("\n");
}
t=0; /* flag t is initialized to 0 */
/*checking for all the elements distinct*/
for(ii=1;ii<=n;++ii)
{
for(jj=1;jj<=n;++jj)
{
for(i=1;i<=n;++i)
for(j=1;j<=n;++j)
if((ii!=i) && (jj!=j) && (a[i][j]==a[ii][jj]))
t=1;/* flag changes*/
}
}
/* sum of main diagonal */
sd=0;
for(i=1;i<=n;++i)
sd+=a[i][i];
/* find sum of off diagonal */
soff=0;
for(i=1;i<=n;++i)
soff+=a[i][n+1-i];
if(sd!=soff)
t=1; /* flag changes */
/* compare each row sum with main diagonal sum */
for(i=1;i<=n;++i)
{
sr=0;
for(j=1;j<=n;++j)
sr+=a[i][j];
if(sr!=sd)
t=1;
}
/* compare each column sum with main diagonal sum */
for(i=1;i<=n;++i)
{
sc=0;
```

```
for(j=1;j<=n;++j)
sc+=a[j][i];
if(sc!=sd)
t=1;
}
if(t==0)
printf("given matrix is magic square\n");
else
printf("given matrix is not magic square\n");
getch();
}
```

Output 1	Output 2
enter n order of a square matrix 3 enter matrix elements 1 2 3 2 1 3 4 5 3 given matrix is 1 2 3 2 1 3 4 5 3 given matrix is not magic square	enter n order of a square matrix 3 enter matrix elements 5 4 9 10 6 2 3 8 7 given matrix is 5 4 9 10 6 2 3 8 7 given matrix is magic square

Now consider the similar and general problem. The problem is "there are three main gates for a village. In the first main gate there are 3 sub gates, in the second main gate there are 7 sub gates and in the third main gate there are 9 sub gates. A group of people come to the village in such a way that in the first main gate they pass in equal numbers through all sub gates. In the second and third main gates also they pass through sub gates equally. Now the question is how many peoples are there in the group."

For solving such program first we have to analyze the problem. The problem tells there are three main gates and 3, 7 and 9 sub gates in first, second and third main gates respectively. From the problem itself it is very much clear that the number of people must be equal to a number, which is divisible by 3, 7 and 9, so that number of peoples in each sub gates of all main gates will be equal. The following program finds the first solution where given condition satisfies.

Here we don't know where we can get the solution, so it is better to use while() loop instead of for() loop. We can start from 1 and keep on checking whether that is divisible by all the three numbers (3, 7 &9). We can keep one flag and when the flag value changes we can display the result and stop the process.

```
/* Program name: loop35.c */
/* Program to find first solution to the gate problem. */
/* This program utilizes while loop */
#include<stdio.h>
```

```
#include<conio.h>
void main()
{
int i=1,t=0;
clrscr();
while(t==0)
{
   if((i%3==0)&&(i%7==0)&&(i%9==0))
   {
      t=1;
      printf(" Number of persons = %d\n", i);
      printf(" Number of persons in each sub gates of first
                            main gate = %d\n", i/3);
      printf(" Number of persons in each sub gates of second
                            main gate = %d\n", i/7);
      printf(" Number of persons in each sub gates of third
                            main gate = %d\n", i/9);
   }
   i++;
} /* End of while*/
getch();
}
```

Output
Number of persons = 63
Number of persons in each sub gates of first main gate = 21
Number of persons in each sub gates of second main gate = 9
Number of persons in each sub gates of third main gate = 7

Now consider the following program. It is an alternative method to solve the above problem, which prints all possible solutions of number of peoples within the range 1 to 'n'. When range is given, we use for() loop to get the solution.

```
/* Program name: loop36.c */
/* Program to print all possible solutions of passing through
   the gate */
/* This program uses simple loop*/
/* No intermediate results */
#include<stdio.h>
#include<conio.h>
#include<math.h>
void main()
{
```

```
int n, i, j, k;
clrscr();
printf("\n Enter upper limit n \n");
scanf("%d", &n);
for(i=1;i<=n; ++i)
    {
    if((i%3==0)&&(i%7==0)&&(i%9==0))
    printf("%8d",i);
    }
getch();
}
```

Output
Enter the upper limit n
500
63 126 189 252 315 378 441

By making small change in the above program, we can print all intermediate results also, so that the output will be in more readable form.

```
/* Program name: loop37.c */
/* Program to print all possible solutions of passing through
     the gate */
/* This program uses simple loop*/
/* Displays results with number of passes in each gate */
#include<stdio.h>
#include<conio.h>
#include<math.h>
void main()
{
int n, i, j, k;
clrscr();
printf("\n Enter upper limit n \n");
scanf("%d", &n);
for(i=1;i<=n; ++i)
{
  if((i%3==0)&&(i%7==0)&&(i%9==0))
  printf("\n total = %5d 1st gate = %5d 2nd gate = %5d & 3rd
          gate = %5d",i,i/3,i/7,i/9);
}
getch();
}
```

```
Output
Enter upper limit n
500
total = 63     1st gate = 21     2nd gate = 9      3rd gate = 7
total = 126    1st gate = 42     2nd gate = 18     3rd gate = 14
total = 189    1st gate = 63     2nd gate = 27     3rd gate = 21
total = 252    1st gate = 84     2nd gate = 36     3rd gate = 28
total = 315    1st gate = 105    2nd gate = 45     3rd gate = 35
total = 378    1st gate = 126    2nd gate = 54     3rd gate = 42
total = 441    1st gate = 147    2nd gate = 63     3rd gate = 49
```

Here is another general problem, which is really interesting and helps to improve the thinking power and programming skills. The problem is simple, which states as follows.

> "In a village there was a family. There were three brothers in that family. Due to certain reasons they got divided. The three brothers had two common servants. There was a mango tree, the fruits given by which was to be shared by all the three. The two servants went and plucked all mangos from the tree. They kept the mangos there itself and went to elder brother and told 'mangos have been removed from the tree', and they went for taking food. The elder brother who was very sincere, came and saw the mangos. He divided the mangos into three equal parts. While dividing he got one mango extra, he gave that mango to one person who was near by. He took his part and went and told to the second brother that mangos have been removed from the tree and asked him to go and collect his share. The elder didn't tell him anything about that he had already divided mangos and had taken away his share.

By the time the second brother came there, the two groups of mangos(left after taking one group by eldest brother) were combined into one by servants, who went to the land after their food. The second brother is also sincere. He made the mangos into three equal parts, and he got one mango extra. He also gave that mango to the person near by. He took his part by leaving other two there itself. After keeping mangos in his house he went and told the youngest brother that mangos have been removed and asked him to go and collect his share. Like his eldest brother he also didn't tell him anything about that he had already divided mangoes and had taken away his share.

Before the arrival of third brother to the spot, the same servants saw the mangos into two groups and combined them into one. The youngest brother came to take mangos, he also saw one group and sincerely made three equal parts, during which again he got one extra mango. He also gave that extra mango to the person who was there. He took his part and went. When the two servants returning from the field, they again saw two groups of mangos, but this time the groups were too small. They thought those two groups were kept for them and they went with one group of mangos each."

Now the problem is how many mangos were there in the tree? How many mangos elder brother took? How many mangos second brother took? And how many mangos do youngest brother and two servants took? Three mangos were given to the unknown person.

After reading and understanding the problem clearly we have to think of logic to solve the problem. The first clue in this problem is each time the mangos is divided into three groups. The second clue is in each division there is an extra mango. Other things we need to consider is total mangos are taken into account for first division into three groups. For the second time two groups of first division are combined and made into three divisions. For the third time division, the two groups of second division are combined and made into three groups.

Suppose there are 'x' number of mangos in the tree, we have to think x%3 must be one. When the remainder after dividing x by 3 is one, the first brother takes y mangos where y=x/3. Now the remaining mangos are 2y (two groups). Now divide 2y by three and we should get one remainder. Say second brother takes z number of mangos, where z=2y/3. The remaining mangos are 2z. Now divide these 2z mangos into three and if we get one remainder, the youngest brother and two servants are taking 2z/3 mangos each. The following program gives the solution to this problem.

In the first program we are finding the first solution to the mango problem. And in the next two programs we are finding all-possible solutions of mango problem by taking a range for 'n' number of mangos in the tree.

```
/* Program name: loop38.c */
/* Program to print first possible solution to mango
    problem */
/* This program uses nested loop*/
#include<stdio.h>
#include<conio.h>
#include<math.h>
void main()
{
int i, j, k, t=0;
clrscr();
printf("\n Number of mangos in the tree\n");
i=1;
while(t==0)/* until getting the solution */
{
   if(i%3==1)
   {
   j=(i/3)*2; /* takes integer parts */
   if(j%3==1)
      {
      k=j/3*2;
      if(k%3==1)
            {
            t=1;
            printf("total =%d, first person = %d,
            second person = %d, third person and
            servants = %d\n",i,i/3,j/3,k/3);
            }
      }
   }
   i++;
}
```

```
getch();
}
```

Output
Number of mangos in the tree
Total =25, first person = 8, second person = 5, third person and servants = 3

The following program gives the possible solutions of the problem by considering the range for number of mangos.

```
/* Program name: loop39.c */
/*Program to print all possible solutions of mango problem
     from 1 to n*/
/* This program uses nested loop*/
#include<stdio.h>
#include<conio.h>
#include<math.h>
void main()
{
int n, i, j, k;
clrscr();
printf("\n Enter upper limit n \n");
scanf("%d", &n);
printf("\n Number of mangos in the tree\n", n);
for(i=1;i<=n; ++i)
{
   if(i%3==1)
   {
      j=(i/3)*2; /* takes integer parts */
      if(j%3==1)
      {
         k=j/3*2;
         if(k%3==1)
         printf("%8d",i);
      }
   }
}
getch();
}
```

Output
Enter upper limit n
1000
number of mangos in the tree

25	52	79	106	133	160	187	214	241	268
295	322	349	376	403	430	457	484	511	538
565	592	619	646	673	700	727	754	781	808
835	862	889	916	943	970	997			

We make small changes to the program to give the details of the outputs such as total mangos, mangos taken by first person, mangos taken by second person and mangos taken by third person and servants etc, which makes the result clear and easy to understand.

```
/* Program name: spl40.c */
/* Program to print all possible solutions of mango problem
      from 1 to n  */
/* This program uses nested loop*/
/* This program also gives intermediate results */
#include<stdio.h>
#include<conio.h>
#include<math.h>
void main()
{
int n, i, j, k;
clrscr();
printf("\n Enter upper limit n \n");
scanf("%d", &n);
printf("\n Number of mangos in the tree\n", n);
for(i=1;i<=n; ++i)
{
    if(i%3==1)
    {
    j=(i/3)*2; /* takes integer parts */
    if(j%3==1)
    {
        k=j/3*2;
        if(k%3==1)
        printf("\n Total=%4d 1st person=%4d 2nd
        person=%3d 3rd person & servants
        each=%d",i,i/3,j/3,k/3);
        }
    }
}
getch();
}
```

Output
Enter upper limit n
150
Number of mangos in the tree

Total = 25	1st person = 8	2nd person = 5	3rd person & servants each = 3
Total = 52	1st person = 17	2nd person = 11	3rd person & servants each = 7
Total = 79	1st person = 26	2nd person = 17	3rd person & servants each = 11
Total = 106	1st person = 35	2nd person = 23	3rd person & servants each = 15
Total = 133	1st person = 44	2nd person = 29	3rd person & servants each = 19

After solving the general problem, here is another general problem to improve the programming skill. The problem is simple again and interesting too. First we look at what the problem states.

"In a village there was a temple, in which three statues of Gods were installed. A priest does the pooja every day. There was a beautiful garden and a small well in that garden. Everyday the priest used to pluck the flowers only once form the garden and took bath in the well. Every time he took bath the number of flowers used to become double the actual number. He did pooja to the first statue with some of those flowers. With remaining flowers he took bath again and the flowers with him became double the number. With some of the second time doubled flowers he did pooja to the second statue. Now with remaining flowers again he took bath and the flowers again became double the number. He puts all the flowers to third statue. Now the question is "how many flowers the priest has to pick from the garden, so as to put equal flowers to all three statues and no flower left with him at end?"

By studying the problem we can notice following clues.

1) He plucks the flowers only once.
2) After each bath the flowers become double.
3) He takes bath three times.
4) He puts the flowers to first statue only after taking the bath first time, and still some flowers are left with him.
5) With the remaining flowers he takes bath second time and puts equal number of flowers to the second statue as that of first statue.
6) With remaining flower he takes bath third time and he puts flowers to third statue.
7) At the end no flowers left with him.

By all these observations it is easy to develop the logic to solve the problem.

Suppose he picks x flowers from the garden, after bath it becomes 2x. Suppose he puts y numbers of flowers to first statue, remaining flower with him is (2x-y). Now by taking bath second time the number of flowers will be z=(2x-y)*2. From these z flowers he puts y flowers to second statue (to maintain equality). Now the remaining flowers will be (z-y). Third time when he takes bath, the number of flowers with him will be (z-y)*2. He puts y number of flower to third statue. Now if (z-y)*2-y=0 then priest picked x number of flowers and each statue gets y number of flowers. The following program finds first solution to the problem.

```
/* Program name: spl41.c */
/* Program to print first solution to the flower problem */
/* This program uses nested loop*/
#include<stdio.h>
#include<conio.h>
#include<math.h>
void main()
{
int i, j, k, l, m, p, t=0;
clrscr();
printf("\n Numbers of flower picked first time are\n");
i=1;
while(t==0)
    {
```

```
m=2*i; /* after first bath it becomes double */
for(j=1;j<=m; ++j)
{
k=2*i-j; /* suppose j flowers for first god */
l=2*k-j;/* from the remaining, after bath they becomes double
       & j flowers for second god*/
p=2*l-j;/* from the remaining, after bath they becomes double
       & j flowers for third god*/
if(p==0)/* when there is no flowers left there is a solution*/
   {
   t=1;
   printf("total flowers = %d and number of flowers to each
          god = %d \n", i, j);
   }
}
i++;
}
getch();
}
```

Output
Numbers of flowers picked first time are
total flowers = 7 number of flowers to each god = 8

Now we are changing the above program so that it has to give all possible solutions of the problem within the range 1 to 'n' flowers.

```
/* Program name: spl42.c */
/* Program to print all possible solutions of flower problem
       from 1 to n  */
/* This program uses nested loop*/
#include<stdio.h>
#include<conio.h>
#include<math.h>
void main()
{
int n, i, j, k, l, m, p;
clrscr();
printf("\n Enter upper limit n \n");
scanf("%d", &n);
printf("\n Number of flower picked first time are\n", n);
for(i=1;i<=n; ++i)
{
    m=2*i; /* after first bath it becomes double */
    for(j=1;j<=m; ++j)
```

```
        {
            k=2*i-j; /* suppose j flowers for first god */
            l=2*k-j;/* from the remaining, after bath they becomes
                          double & j flowers for second
                          god*/
            p=2*l-j;/* from the remaining, after bath they becomes
                          double & j flowers for third
                          god*/
            if(p==0)/* when there is no flowers left there is a
                          solution*/
            printf("total flowers = %d and number of flowers to each
                          god = %d \n", i, j);
        }
    }
    getch();
    }
```

Output
Enter upper limit n
50
number of flowers picked first time are
total flowers = 7 and number of flowers to each god = 8
total flowers = 14 and number of flowers to each god = 16
total flowers = 21 and number of flowers to each god = 24
total flowers = 28 and number of flowers to each god = 32
total flowers = 35 and number of flowers to each god = 40
total flowers = 42 and number of flowers to each god = 48
total flowers = 49 and number of flowers to each god = 56

Here is a general problem. The problem is to print magic square. A non prime integer is given, we have to find two factors which are close to each other. Then print the numbers from given number down to 1 in such a way that, the helical traversing of the matrix formed will give all the numbers in descending order. For example, for the number 20 we can take the factors as 1,2,4,5,10 and 20. The close factors that make the matrix closer to the square are 4 and 5. So we should get the following output.

20	19	18	17
7	6	5	16
8	1	4	15
9	2	3	14
10	11	12	13

This program makes use of functions to check whether the given number is prime or not and to print the magic square.

```
/* Program name: spl43.c */
/* Magic square */
#include<stdio.h>
#include<conio.h>
int prime(int);
void magic(int,int,int);
void main()
{
int n1,n,i,a,b,t;
clrscr();

printf("\n enter n\n ");
scanf("%d",&n);
t=prime(n);
if(t==0)
printf("\n prime number\n");
else
{
a=1;
b=1;
for(i=2;i<=n/2;++i)
{
if(n%i==0)
{
   if(b>1)
   {
   a=b;
   b=i;
   }
   else
   {
   b=i;
   }
}
if(a*b==n) /* finding the two consecutive factors */
break;
else
if(b*b==n)
{
a=b;
break;
}
}printf("%d\n%d\n",a,b);
getch();
clrscr();
```

```
magic(a,b,n);
}
getch();
}

int prime(int n)
{
int t=0,i;
for(i=2;i<=n/2;++i)
if(n%i==0)
{
t=1;
break;
}
return(t);
}

void magic(int a,int b,int n)
{
int i,j,k;
int p1,p2,p3,p4;
k=n;
p1=4;
p2=1;
p3=a*4;
p4=b;
while(k>=1)
{
for(i=p1;i<=p3;i+=4)
{
gotoxy(i,p2);
printf("%3d",k);
k--;
}
p2++;
for(i=p2;i<=p4;i++)
{
gotoxy(p3,i);
printf("%3d",k);
k--;
}

p3-=4;
for(i=p3;i>=p1;i-=4)
{
```

```
gotoxy(i,p4);
printf("%3d",k);
k--;
}
p4-=1;
for(i=p4;i>=p2;i-=1)
{
gotoxy(p1,i);
printf("%3d",k);
k--;
}
p1+=4;
}
}
```

Output

enter n
100

100	99	98	97	96	95	94	93	92	91
65	64	63	62	61	60	59	58	57	90
66	37	36	35	34	33	32	31	56	89
67	38	17	16	15	14	13	30	55	88
68	39	18	5	4	3	12	29	54	87
69	40	19	6	1	2	11	28	53	86
70	41	20	7	8	9	10	27	52	85
71	42	21	22	23	24	25	26	51	84
72	43	44	45	46	47	48	49	50	83
73	74	75	76	77	78	79	80	81	82

This is more general program. It switches between upward and downward counting. The up counter starts from zero and down counter start from 100. Whenever we are switching between the counters, they will start with their previous values. Functions are used for both upcounter and down counters. The functions make use of global variables.

```
/* program name: spl44.c */
/* program to generate up counter and down counter */
#include<stdio.h>
#include<conio.h>
#include<dos.h>
void upcounter();
void downcounter();
int u,d;
#define maxup 100
void main()
{
char ch='u';
clrscr();
```

```
printf("Press U for upcounter\n D for down counter\n Any key
      to exit \n");
while(1)
{

fflush(stdin);
ch=getche();

if(ch=='u' || ch=='U')
upcounter();
else
if(ch=='d' || ch=='D')
downcounter();
else
break; /* takes the control out of loop */
}
}
void upcounter()
{
clrscr();
gotoxy(20,20);
printf(" press d key to switch any key to stop \n");
while(!kbhit())
{
gotoxy(40,12);
printf(" upcounter");
gotoxy(35,12);
printf("%d",u);
u++;
if(u>maxup)
{
u=0;
clrscr();
gotoxy(40,12);
printf(" upcounter");

gotoxy(20,20);
printf(" press d key to switch any key to stop \n");
}
delay(300);
}
}
void downcounter()
{
```

```
clrscr();
gotoxy(20,20);
printf(" press u key to switch any key to stop \n");
while(!kbhit())
{
gotoxy(40,12);
printf(" Down counter");
if((d+1) %10==0)
{
clrscr();
gotoxy(40,12);
printf(" Down counter");
gotoxy(20,20);
printf(" press u key to switch any key to stop \n");
}
gotoxy(35,12);
printf("%d",d);
d--;
if(d<0)
{
d=100;
}
delay(300);
}
}
```

Appendix A

Glossary of Terms

Algorithm: A step by step procedure to solve a given problem, written in simple and general English.

Array: Data structure used to store values of the same data type.

Arguments: List of values provided when a function is called. The arguments required by the function, are specified a parenthesized parameter list following function name.

Automatic Variable: Variable that is allocated storage upon entry to a segment of code and the storage is deallocated upon exit from this segment of code.

Break: Statement that interrupts the execution of the loop body or compound statement and transfers the program control to the exit point of the loop or compound statement.

Case: used to provide labels in a switch statement.

Continue: Loop interruption statement that interrupts a particular iteration, but does not teminate a loop.

Call by Value. the method of passing a argument or parameters to the function in which a copy of the value of actual argument of the calling function is made and given to the formal argument of the called function.

Call by Reference: the method of passing an argument in which the address of the actual parameter or argument of the calling function is given to the formal parameter or argument of the called function.

Conditional Expression: The expression that results in the logical value i.e., either true or false.

Conditional Operator: Ternary operator that takes three arguments.

Control Flow: Refers to the order in which the statements in a program are executed.

Default: It is the default label in a switch statement. The control is transferred to this statement when none of the case labels match with the expression in the switch.

Do: control statement that creates a loop of operations. It is used with while keyword.

Else: Used to specify an alternative path in it two-way branch control of execution. It is used with if statement.

Flowchart: Diagrammatic representation of the solution to the given problem.

For: control statement used to create a loop of iterative operations,

Global variable: variable defined outside any function at the same level as function definitions and which is both alive and active throughout the entire program

Goto: Transfer statement that skips a group of statements unconditionally. It is preferable to use this statement very rarely.

High-level language: A computer programming language, which follows most of the general English like words but specific computer language syntax.

Language: The media of communication between the two entities or parties, Computer language is the media of communication between the computer and user of the computer.

Low-level language: The language that makes use of only binary digits 0's and 1's. It Is also called as binary or machine levell language.

Middle-level language: The computer language that makes use of certain mnemonic codes for generating the program. It is also called as Assembly level language.

Program: A set of instructions to perform a specific task written in a specific computer language.

Return value:	Values sent by the called function to the calling function.
Static variable:	The local variable whose value persists until, the and of the program execution.
Strings:	Array of characters ended by the null character "\0".
Variable:	The name of the memory location where values are stored and they are subjected to change.
While.:	control statement used to execute a set of statements repeatedly depending on the outcome Of test'.

Appendix B

Keywords

C language has 32 keywords, which are given below.

auto	break	case	char	const
continue	default	do	double	else
enum	extern	float	for	goto
if	int	long	register	return
short	signed	sizeof	static	struct
switch	typedef	union	unsigned	void
volatile	while			

Character constants/escape characters

C language has certain characters that are used with printf statement for output formatting. They use two characters (first character must be \ and second character specifies the purpose) but they will be treated as single character by the compiler.

\n	for new line
\t	horizontal tab
\v	vertical tab
\b	backspace
\r	carriage return
\f	form feed
\a	audible alert (beep sound)
\\	back slash
\?	Question mark
\'	single quote
\"	double quote
\0	null

Appendix C

Operators

C language provides number of operators that can be grouped into different categories as given below.

1) Arithimetic

+	for addition
-	subtraction
*	multiplication
/	division
%	modulo division

2) Assignment

=	simple assign	e.g.	a=b;
+=	add and assign	e.g.	a+=b;
-=	subtract and assign	e.g.	a-=b,
*=	multiply and assign	e.g.	a*=b;
/=	divide and assign	e.g.	a/=b;
%=	take remainder and assign	e.g.	a%=b;

3) Relational

>	greater than
<	less than
>=	greater than or equal to
<=	less than or equal to equal to
==	equal to
!=	not equal to

4) Logical

&&	Logical AND
| |	Logical OR
!	Logical NOT

5) Bitwise

&	Bitewise AND
| |	Bitwise OR
^	Bitwise XOR
~	One's complement

6) Shift

>>	Right shift
<<	Left shift

7) Increment/Decrement

++	pre or post increment	e.g.	a++;	post increment
			++a;	pre increment
--	pre or post decrement	e.g.	a--;	post decrement
			--a;	pre decrement

8) Conditional

?: conditional operator
e.g. (a%2==1)?printf("odd number"):printf("even number");
where a is an integer variable

9) sizeof

gives size of variable in bytes
e.g. int a;
sizeof(a); gives 2

10) Address

& used with simple variable to get its address
* used to declare pointers, which represents address.

11) Membership

used to access structure members, for non-pointer structure variables.
-> used to access structure members, for pointer variables of type structure.

12) Special

used to separate statements
e.g. 1 for(I=1,j=l0;I<=j;++I,--j)
printf("%d\t%d\n".Ij);
where I and j are integers.
e.g.2 a=(b=10,c=5,b+c); This is equivalent to
b=10;
c=5;
a=b+c;
Used with case values and/or labels

Appendix D

Header Files

1)stdio.h contains standard input and output library functions.

Examples:

printf(); : for formatted output on the screen.
scanf(); : for formatted input from the keyboard
getchar(); : inputs a single character from the keyboard
putchar(); : prints a single character on the screen
gets(); : inputs a string (upto the end of line)
puts(); : prints a string on the screen
fopen(); : opens a file
fclose(); : closes a file
fprintf(); : sends formatted output to the file
fscanf(); : reads formatted input from the file
etc.

2) string.h Contains standard library functions for handling strings.

Examples:

strlen(); : returns length of string (total number of characters in the string excluding null).
strrev(); : reverses the string
strupr(); : converts the string to upper case if it is in lower crew
strlwr(); : converts the string to lower case if it is in upper case
strcmp(); : compares two strings lexicographically, and gives 0 when both the strings are equal,
>0 when first string is greater than second string,
<0 otherwise
strcmpi(), : similar to strcmp() but it ignore the case of the letters.
strncmp(); : similar to strcmp() but it compares only first 'n' characters of both the strings

strncmpi(); : similar to strncmp() but it ignores the case of the letters.

3) math.h : contains commonly used mathematical functions

Examples:

sin(); : returns sine value of the given angle, takes angle in radians
cos(); : returns cosine value of the given angle, takes angle in radians
tan(); : returns tangent value of the given angle, takes angle in radians
log(); : returns natural logarithmic value
log 10(); : returns logarithmic value to the base 10
pow(); : gives the power of first argument to the second argument etc.,

4) conio.b contains standard library functions related to console input and output

Examples-.

clrscr(); : clear the screen.
getch(); : inputs a character from input buffer without echoing it on the screen
getche(); : inputs a character from input buffer with echoing it on the screen
gotoxy(); : takes the cursor to the specified row and column in the text mode
kbhit(); : responds to the keyboard press
etc.,

5) ctype.h contains standard library functions for handling characters.

Examples:

isdigit(c) : gives true if the character variable 'c' contains a digit
isalpha(c) : gives true if the character variable 'c' contains an alphabet.
isupper(c) : gives true if the character variable 'c' contains an uppercase alphabet.
islower(c) : gives true if the character variable 'c' contains a lowercase alphabet.
isxdigit(c) : gives true if the character variable 'c' contains an hexadecimal digit.
iscntl(c) : gives true if the character variable 'c' contains a control character.
isspace(c) : gives true if the character variable 'c' contains a space.
etc.

So many other header files are there in C language, and they vary from version to version and compiler to compiler. Reader can check them by taking the help present in respective C compilers.

Appendix E

Common Errors in Programming

There are mainly 3 types of errors, which may appear while entering and executing the programs, they are:

1. Syntax errors
2. Logical errors
3. Run time errors

1. Syntax errors

These are the errors that are detected by the C language compiler, during compilation. These errors are related to the language constructs. When the program statements are not following the syntax rules of the language, then the compiler generates these errors. They include missing of ';', ',', '(', ')', '[', ']', or mispelling of any reserved words or built-in function names etc. While compiling the program, the machine will list all the syntax errors with line numbers if there exists.

2. Logical error

These types of errors will give wrong results when program is executed but compiler does not give error list. The output of the program is not according to the programmer's expectations. For e.g., if you pressed / instead of pressing '*' in the program statement ' a=b*c;' the computer will treat operator as / and gives the result according to the operators, but you are not satisfied with the result. It is difficult to find out logical errors, so for finding these errors, scanning the whole program line by line is necessary.

3. Run time error

This type of errors may come across while running the program. The program will be fully correct syntactically so during compilation, compiler won't generate errors. During the dynamic inputs to the program, when the inputs are entered carelessly and proper input validation is not done in the program then these errors may appear.

For example if we want to do division operation and while entering input numbers if we have entered 0 for denominator and while actually executing that calculation statenment, if we have not checked the *demonstrator apprehend*, then automatically run time error appears.